Reluctant Sleuths, True Detectives

RECENT TITLES

Lucy J. Miller, *Distancing Representations in Transgender Film*

Tomoyuki Sasaki, *Cinema of Discontent*

Mary Ann McDonald Carolan, *Orienting Italy*

Matthew Rukgaber, *Nietzsche in Hollywood*

David Venditto, *Whiteness at the End of the World*

Fareed Ben-Youssef, *No Jurisdiction*

Tony Tracy, *White Cottage, White House*

Tom Conley, *Action, Action, Action*

Lindsay Coleman and Roberto Schaefer, editors, *The Cinematographer's Voice*

Nolwenn Mingant, *Hollywood Films in North Africa and the Middle East*

†Charles Warren, edited by William Rothman and Joshua Schulze, *Writ on Water*

Jason Sperb, *The Hard Sell of Paradise*

William Rothman, *The Holiday in His Eye*

Brendan Hennessey, *Luchino Visconti and the Alchemy of Adaptation*

Alexander Sergeant, *Encountering the Impossible*

Erica Stein, *Seeing Symphonically*

George Toles, *Curtains of Light*

Neil Badmington, *Perpetual Movement*

Merrill Schleier, editor, *Race and the Suburbs in American Film*

Matthew Leggatt, editor, *Was It Yesterday?*

A complete listing of books in this series can be found online at www.sunypress.edu

Reluctant Sleuths, True Detectives

Jason Jacobs

SUNY **PRESS**

Cover image: Jimmy Stewart in *Vertigo* (Alfred Hitchcock, Paramount, 1958). Courtesy Photofest New York.

Published by State University of New York Press, Albany

© 2023 State University of New York

All rights reserved

Printed in the United States of America

No part of this book may be used or reproduced in any manner whatsoever without written permission. No part of this book may be stored in a retrieval system or transmitted in any form or by any means including electronic, electrostatic, magnetic tape, mechanical, photocopying, recording, or otherwise without the prior permission in writing of the publisher.

For information, contact State University of New York Press, Albany, NY
www.sunypress.edu

Library of Congress Cataloging-in-Publication Data

Name: Jacobs, Jason, author.
Title: Reluctant sleuths, true detectives / Jason Jacobs.
Description: Albany : State University of New York Press, 2023. | Series: SUNY series, horizons of cinema | Includes bibliographical references and index.
Identifiers: LCCN 2022026160 | ISBN 9781438492230 (hardcover : alk. paper) | ISBN 9781438492254 (ebook) | ISBN 9781438492247 (pbk. : alk. paper)
Subjects: LCSH: Detective and mystery films—United States—History and criticism. | Film noir—United States—History and criticism. | Knowledge, Theory of, in motion pictures. | Motion pictures—Philosophy. | Out of the past (Motion picture : 1947) | Notorious (Motion picture : 1946) | Vertigo (Motion picture : 1958) | Chinatown (Motion picture)
Classification: LCC PN1995.9.D4 J33 2023 | DDC 791.43/6556—dc23/eng/20220922
LC record available at https://lccn.loc.gov/2022026160

10 9 8 7 6 5 4 3 2 1

To Laura

But he was made as a *detective*, not as a gangster. He is an ordinary guy; that is his chief attraction, his ordinariness; tough, going his own way, as sick of the pretenses of the world as is Hemingway but he has to intervene. That he has to intervene is not merely the necessity of official law and order. It is the necessity of the mass which looks on.

—C. L. R. James, *American Civilization*

Contents

Acknowledgments	xi
Introduction: *The Long Goodbye*	1
1 *Out of the Past*	23
2 *Notorious*	81
3 *Vertigo*	115
4 *Chinatown*	171
Conclusion: True Detectives	213
Notes	233
Bibliography	243
Index	247

Acknowledgments

Thanks to Murray Pomerance for his encouragement and friendship; to my son Henry Jacobs for his research; to Richard Brown for alerting me to the achievement of *Blade Runner 2049*; to Elliott Logan for his insightful reading of an early version of this book; and to Emily Mahnken for her impeccable attention. I am grateful to Renee Courtney for raising my aspirations so that I could see a better place.

Introduction

The Long Goodbye

THE LONG GOODBYE begins with a beautiful picture of a man asleep: Elliott Gould playing the detective Philip Marlowe is shown stretched out and fully dressed on a bed, his deep breath a purr fueled by dreams, the lights still on, magazines and cigarettes hard by.[1] He has dozed off while reading and smoking. How fragile and vulnerable he could seem. Except that the camera's silent creep toward this bedroom scene, accompanied by soft jazzy music, conspires not to disturb a brief look at our protagonist, who remains safe and still, hugged in the oceanic comfort of slumber. All ideal movie detectives begin this way, passively but charismatically *there*, hard to get moving at first, but often dogged and even obsessive by the end; finally hard to stop. What gets Marlowe up and away from the calm shore of sleep is a cat leaping onto the bed, wanting his feed, and the detective wakes to find the day's first demand on his time. Before it introduced us to Gould's Marlowe on the bed, director Robert Altman's camera glided past a decorative plaque on the adjoining wall which is adorned with icons of Los Angeles including the famous HOLLYWOOD letters that beam their claim to artistic and industrial authority across the valleys etched below. This is a showbiz world of languor and late nights and lonely but comfortable apartments. We are already in a dream world looking at a dreamer.

It is also a world that announces itself as a world that is made, that is shown. It is a commonplace thought to see the activity of cinema as akin to that of the detective with its scrutinizing of things and people and sights and sounds; but movies are not metonyms for detection, they *are* a form of detection. The camera and microphone are primarily instruments of selection after all, and what they select they detect, pull out of the world for special attention, point to. Marlowe may be at rest before his cat wakes him, but the camera is already on the move, already searching; it notices the plaque on the wall, the way that Gould is lit like an actor backstage waiting for his cue, and the way that the white wall behind his head, blank and broad and white like a cinema screen, is streaked with black lines, the signs of matches lazily struck by a lengthened arm behind and above one's head. Cinema is a detective too: what moves it to these recursive spectacles, this self-absorbed self-involvement?

What is it that moves us? What keeps us still? Is the desire for and pursuit of knowledge an exclusively animating force or can it paralyze the knower, erode their determination to know in some strange way? How does cinema connect to our desire to know, to hunt down knowledge and meaning? How does it show it to us? How does it calibrate and pattern the force and magnitude of our commitment? These are questions that I find most urgently addressed in the detective movies examined in this book. Is what we do only purposeful to us on the stage of the social, and does cinema, in its detective hunt for meaning, socialize what it selects? The solitude of our movie detective avatars seems to articulate their and our embeddedness in and separation from society. Their solitude is the ledge from which they see emerging enigmas more completely, but it isolates and distances them from the world that they must know intimately in order to apprehend its mysteries. Hence, perhaps, their reluctance to get started. We see movie detectives moved by their job as knowledge seekers, but this often gets all messed around as they find out more about what they purportedly wanted to know in the first place. Messed around by the world, by their own hesitation, as their picture of it enlarges and congeals into the frightening thing that they should have left alone. But then they seem to already have known that before they started their pursuit. How strange.

Again: what moves us, gets us going, prompts us to shift from rest to action? Why would we leave the pretty realm of sleep and stillness to do anything at all? Where does the pressure come from? What conscripts us from the recusant privacy of sleep? Sure, there are external demands—pets, job, loved ones; and internal demands—

appetites, a yearning for autonomy and freedom, the thirst for meaning. But internal and external are mixed up together too, as in the case of the search for love or for dignity or honor. Detectives search for the truth behind the mystery, for the inner that expresses and is expressed by the outer, trying to get at the way things work, at the secret of the world, its name. But they have their privacy too, their dreams. They don't come to that search all ready to go, eager and keen to tear back the curtain and set wrong to right. They are in various ways, *reluctant*. And then, after a time, they are, in various ways, determined, committed, obsessed: *true detectives*.

At the start of *The Long Goodbye* all this important stuff seems muted, otherworldly: we see only an easy dozing interrupted by feline need—not too bad, given all else that will come to pass. (What is delicious about the cat's role as a prime mover is how inconsequential it appears to be to the plot of the rest of the film.) Falling asleep smoking and reading in dreamy Los Angeles, home to the movies, to cool cats and their pets. At the end of the movie when he's solved the enigma and something like justice has been done, Marlowe is seen walking away from us in the distance, humming, lively, happy, half-dancing, all movement and far away as if this was the dream he was dreaming at the start of the film, as if the stillness of the dreamer enabled a dream of dance and song at its end. As noted before, behind Marlowe's sleeping form his white wall is marked by the curved lines made by matches being struck on it: it resembles the dirty white of a movie screen waiting for its thirst to be slaked with dream images.

This is a book about detectives and their eventual emergence as wholehearted pursuers of meaning in five *noirish* films: *The Long Goodbye* (Robert Altman, 1973), *Out of the Past* (Jacques Tourneur, 1947), *Notorious* (Alfred Hitchcock, 1946), *Vertigo* (also Hitchcock, 1958), and *Chinatown* (Roman Polanski, 1974). Each of them explores the issue of what it takes to move a human being from a kind of reluctant, everyday passivity (a reluctant sleuth) to a mode of passionate engagement with the world (true detectives). It tracks our experience of these films in relation to that question of motivation and movement. For me these films more than most capture the compelling strangeness of thinking about and trying to discover why human beings are driven or moved to do anything at all. They concentrate this issue within dramatic patterns where murder, deceit, betrayal, and the threat of knowing (and not knowing) why people do what they do are critically important, just as they also raise the issue (sometimes obliquely, sometimes directly) of whether it would have been better for their protagonists to stay in bed after all. But being a detective (or more broadly, a sleuth) is a job, and one can pursue one's job with vigor and enthusiasm or passive tolerance (or hatred and resentment). In movies we also can observe the work of observation, both of sleuthing as a job, and of cinema-making as the aesthetic force of the work of selecting views, sounds, and movements that give us (and hide from us) an angle on what is going on and why.

The films are also notable for the way in which they evoke peculiarly cinematic tropes, figures, and gestures in their representation of the detective's growing involvement. As the detective begins the work of finding out, of knowing, quite often the manifold apparatus of the cinema itself, including its fundamental relations of seer-seen/camera-object/spectator-screen (not an exhaustive list, but indicative), is *evoked*, especially in the framing and composition of shot, and especially in relation to whether characters are facing (looking at, observing something) the camera or turned away from it. This is not quite the same thing as a self-conscious or self-reflexive *assertion* of cinema and its relevance (as in the case of the Modernist artwork internalizing the processes of its own making); but it rather seems to emerge in these films when the process of finding out what is happening as a detective is aligned with the cinema's forms of knowledge which are, naturally, in the showing and seeing of objects and faces and settings. Baked into these evocations we might feel a tension between the materiality and automatism of the cinematic apparatus as it is ambiently conjured and the fact or presence of intentional authorship or creativity. These moments of cinematic evocation offer a weak kind of self-consciousness (if such a thing is possible), a vague self-awareness not necessarily critical to meaning-making, not often there to be noticed at all, but something that registers on whatever we call the mentation associated with viewing movies, whatever it is that happens to us when we do that. One (admittedly paradoxical) way to frame it is as a kind of demotic or populist modernism, one that is so obvious we hardly notice it as seasoned viewers of audiovisual entertainment. (Perhaps we do not credit either the makers or the audience with the capacity to acknowledge or register such things.) The detective's growing involvement in the film's plot, and the emerging crystallization of what it is he/she wants, is somehow tangled up in such repeated and surprisingly insistent evocative gestures.[2] The detective hunt of the camera/microphone apparatus can end up capturing itself, its own forms of being in its medium-specific locutions.

"Look, this isn't my line. I'm supposed to be retired. I don't want to get mixed up in this darn thing." Scottie Ferguson's (James Stewart) initial reluctance to tail Gavin Elster's (Tom Hellmore) wife in *Vertigo* demonstrates the intuitive suspicion of the experienced sleuth. Scottie is a former cop, not a private detective, and Elster is an acquaintance he hasn't seen since college; the latter's spooky story about his wife's mysterious behavior does not have the urgency of a murder or missing person's case. But their discussion takes place in a room that is framed as a blend of a stage and a cinema, with Scottie himself as a kind of helpless spectator, vulnerable to the manipulations of a master storyteller.[3] It is only when Scottie later sees Madeleine (Kim Novak)—and notably sees her from a seated position, sneaking a look at her as she is "lit" for him artificially)—that he begins on a journey that will leave him wholeheartedly obsessed. It is as if the evocation of cinema here is a solvent of reluctance. According to Robert Pippin, film noir "heroes are endlessly reluctant to act, and when they do, they are mostly responsive and often halfhearted."[4] They do not stay that way, and what follows will explore the transition these heroes undergo from passivity, inertia, and caution to committed pursuit of the truth, justice, and love. Film noirs are fascinated by the transformation of reluctance and its spectrum of shadings (hesitation, caution, lethargy) into obsession and its often destructive consequences. I am treating the figure of the detective in an idiosyncratic way in the analyses that follow. What they share is a process whereby the arc of their commitment gradually evolves such that their separateness from the world becomes a kind of uneasy and dangerous inhabitation of that world. The job they have agreed to do, however reluctantly, becomes an obsession they must pursue, a quest to complete their picture of the world. And at the same time the films also create a picture of their picturing for the audience who follow them and are synchronized emotionally with this curve of rising interest and dedication.

Reluctance is the internal realization of unwillingness, the bringing to the front of the mind the desire not to act. It may be immediate and sharp—as in the response to a difficult command with which one does not agree; or ambient and dispersed, such as the reluctance to do or continue to do a task that one knows one ought to be doing. Indeed, the pressure of "ought" carries precisely with it an internalized prompt to resist, with varying degrees of force. Reluctance is a form of behavior that can be observed but can also be invisible even to the person experiencing it. Why where you reluctant to do X? someone may ask, when X was not even a factor on the horizon of possibilities. And yet on reflection we may agree that, unknown to ourselves at the time, we were indeed reluctant for reasons we did not know but now do. Furthermore, one can be reluctant to do one thing while being strongly committed to doing another. Reluctance can shadow many of our actions, but as a category it is so diffuse, so applicable to such a spectrum of human (and nonhuman) instances that it acquires clear definition only by contrast with the activity which is its negation.

An aspect of the film noir is the way that reluctance of this kind is not only overcome, but often magically transformed by the leading detective into a fully embraced desire to uncover the truth. The private eye is approached to do a job and is immediately wary about accepting it. An index of his experience is his scenting that something is awry, doesn't sit right. But the money, or the girl, or some element piques his interest, and he goes ahead. At some point during the investigation there is a switch. No longer is he reluctant to take the case, but instead he has found the real reason behind the initial approach which is far more compelling than the case itself. The shift between the two is most emblematically pictured in the way a detective pursuing the case as just another job is suddenly transformed from a mere journeyman going through the motions to a human being propelled by a commitment to finding the truth at any cost. It is often said that this happens when the male protagonist catches first sight of the femme fatale, and as we shall see it is a moment so baked into the genre that other members of it can knowingly deny it to us. So, in *Out of the Past* Jeff Markham (Robert Mitchum) seeing Kathie Moffat (Jane Greer) walk into the bar in Mexico, or in *Vertigo* Scottie seeing Madeleine walking past him in the restaurant are often pointed to as moments of epiphany, a picture of "falling for the dame" in an instant (although as we shall see this is not quite true). Whereas *Notorious* starts by making a point of showing us that we *cannot see* the reaction of T. R. Devlin (Cary Grant) to Alicia

Huberman (Ingrid Bergman) since to begin with we see him only from behind in silhouette; *Chinatown* contrives the moment when the detective, J. J. Gittes (Jack Nicholson), eyes the woman (Evelyn Mulwray/Faye Dunaway) as one of embarrassment and humiliation. In each of those films, in complicated ways, the detective has up to this moment taken the job in his stride as just another piece of work. From thereon, it is something more.

Hence, a reluctant sleuth finds himself a true detective by virtue of being held captive by an appetite in himself he did not formerly have or know he had. And by becoming committed to one thing, a person will ipso facto be reluctant to do whatever gets in the way of that commitment. What it means, then, to be a true detective in these films is not merely a matter of having of a strong work ethic or commitment to justice or truth: it is something more like philosopher Harry Frankfurt's sense of "making up one's mind" and becoming wholehearted:

> Wholeheartedness . . . does not consist in a feeling of enthusiasm, or of certainty, concerning a commitment. Nor is it likely to be readily apparent whether a decision which a person intends to be wholehearted is actually so. We do not know our hearts well enough to be confident whether our intention that nothing should interfere with a decision we make is one we ourselves will want carried out when—perhaps recognizing that the point of no return has been reached—we come to understand more completely what carrying it out would require us to do or to sacrifice doing.[5]

And whatever internal authority, stable or not, we might impute to the fictional detectives we follow in these movies, they, too, are in the business of tracking the reasons why people do the things they do. Choosing detectives as a focus allows a concentration on a central aspect of Hollywood movies: their interest in and staging of characters in the midst of an enigma or puzzle about the *reasons* they are doing or wanting to do what they are doing or want to do. Rather than following legible chains of cause and effect, our experience of movies is far more an involvement in the drama of characters discovering, rejecting, deciding, ignoring, or obsessing over the things they want or don't want, things that they believe or do not believe, desires that they follow purposively or without knowing what it is they have as a purpose, and yet acting anyway. As Frankfurt notes:

> We are particularly concerned with our own motives. It matters greatly to us whether the desires by which we are moved to act as we do motivate us because we want them to be effective in moving us, or whether they move us regardless of ourselves or even despite ourselves. In the latter cases we are moved to act as we do without it being the case that we want wholeheartedly to be motivated as we are. Our hearts are at best divided, and they may not be in what we are doing at all.[6]

This is a familiar enough aspect of our own inner lives that it can be credibly deployed in movie fiction. Frankfurt goes on to discuss the matter of duration of a commitment, particularly when it comes to a time (or the repetition of the time) when that commitment is cashed out in action or inaction. For me, the matter of wholeheartedness, and its mysterious obscurity both as a secure, durable sense of having made up one's mind, and as a feeling or appetite for one action in preference to another, is an important aspect in general of these films. More than this, it is of course part of the modus operandi of the detective that he or she is skilled in figuring out what it is that motivates others to do what they do, especially given that many other characters are either deceivers or self-deceivers or likely both. And if the picture of commitment that Frankfurt outlines has any purchase on our experience of fictional characters, such motivation is likely to be obscure, provisional, or precarious at best. More than that, the detective protagonists even when wholehearted in their own made-up minds frequently encounter a further moment of transformation when the true nature of the world and its evil is made fully apparent to them. Any commitment stands to be drastically revised in the face of the now revealed truth. This is certainly pictured in *Out of the Past*, *Vertigo*, and *Chinatown* where late in their narratives the scale and depth of the evil ranged against the detective is shown to be deeper and more intransigent than previously assumed.

If any of this is descriptively accurate—if not to the noir genre as a whole, then at least to the films I am considering—an important question is why these works engage with the issue of, say, the duration of a made-up mind (*Out of the Past*), or of a commitment that undermines the fulfillment of romantic desire (*Notorious*), or a wholehearted commitment that seems perverse or pathological (*Vertigo*), or naïve (*Chinatown*). One answer from Robert Pippin is that the films are attempting to make "some feature of human life more intelligible that it otherwise would have been."[7] He argues that "some films can be said to attempt to illuminate something about human conduct that would otherwise remain poorly understood. The point or purpose of such narrating seems to be such an illumination," for example, "that a film noir's credibility and illuminating power might throw into doubt that we ever really know our own minds."[8] In doing so these films connect with and evoke their own powers of knowledge, modeling our shared sense of the desire to search for meaning. Domesticated, such a search may seem harmless, but once we associate it with the ultimate stakes of our shared evolutionary past, the tracking and hunting of prey, or of foe, we can see the danger. Perhaps our detectives apprehend all too well the consequences of involvement in in tracking dangerous prey.

In *Out of the Past* Jeff Markham is notably cool about taking on Whit's (Kirk Douglas) job to find the lover (Kathie) who shot him and stole his $40,000; Jeff senses that something bad could happen to her if he finds her; only the money is good, plus expenses, so what could he say, especially in front of his partner Jack Fisher, who will also come to regret his eagerness to take on this case? And it is only when he sees Kathie framed in the arch of a bar in Acapulco that he becomes committed—but not to the job. *Notorious* is a symphony of reluctance: government agent Devlin has to drag daughter of Nazi spy Alicia Huberman into a realization that her patriotism demands practical allegiance to the national interest. And after they fall in love their shared discovery about what they both have to do in order to honor that allegiance produces a deadly dance between their commitment to each other, to their flag, and the Nazi organization Alicia has to infiltrate by marrying its leader. And despite Scottie saying that he does not want to "get mixed up" with the case of Gavin Elster's disturbed wife and her unexplained wandering around the city in *Vertigo*, he, too, is swiftly absorbed into a world of obsession and death and repetition, like the others becoming self-propelled by his appetite to know the name of the world, its secret. And, on finding it out, he is left paralyzed, suspended above it. Jack Nicholson's J. J. Gittes in *Chinatown* moves through the film with too much finesse, too much faith in his ability to compass the political corruption he imagines; what impedes him is a failure to realize the extent political and familial corruption are in the service of something transcendentally evil. This way of figuring detectives continues into more recent period of noir on television. In *True Detective*'s first season (2014), as in *Notorious*, the detective role is split between two central characters, cops Marty Hart (Woody Harrelson) and Rust Cohle (Matthew McConaughey), the former reluctant to pursue a serial killer case to its end, the latter obsessive to the neglect of all else. That season paints a picture of detectives finding their "truth" in their capacity to work together, properly, outside the police system. Later seasons of the show circle around the theme of what it takes for human beings in great difficulty to find their true commitment in an apparently irredeemably corrupt world. In each instance, we see variations on the theme of commitment and hesitation, obsession and paralysis, often not as linear alternatives, but intermeshed and interacting as characters and their performers seek ways to demonstrate determination and its discontents.

Since things like reasons, obsession, reluctance are aspects of interior processes, we experience them as film viewers only externally, as surface movement of events and characters. Part of the great mystery of film is how we experience these outer aspects of character and plot as having an inner life—indeed, that most of the time such outer things—talk, movement, action—make little sense unless we ascribe an inner life to them. Why is it that the characters we are so close to do the things they do? Detective narratives tend to make such inner drama prominent since it is the job of the detective to find out what happened, and a large portion of doing that involves them speculating on the inner motives, often well hidden, of those involved in the mystery to be solved. In *Chinatown* this culminates in the scene where Gittes, having finally uncovered the villain behind the murderous events in Los Angeles, the elderly Noah Cross (John Huston), and confronts him asking the *reason why* he did them: "Why are you doing it? How much better can you eat? What can you buy that you can't already afford?" When he hears the answer, Nicholson holds his face perfectly still (he is shot in profile), expressionless, as if now with the enigma "solved" he has entered into an entirely new universe of mystery, and he has no ready-made or spontaneous way to express the fact. For the first time Gittes is speechless.

Caught up in these films' depiction of obsession, determination, and pursuit of truth are the contrary forces of avoidance, evasion, and other kinds of turning away from what must be done. There is the peculiar but common aspect of human experience where we avoid or delay doing precisely those things we most want to do. And some of our detectives appear suspended and motionless before they are moved. What is Scottie actually doing during his retirement up to the point when he takes on Elster's mission? In *The Long Goodbye* Marlowe appears to have nothing to do before he is woken by the hungry cat and then by his friend Terry Lennox (Jim Bouton) demanding a lift to the Mexican border; Alicia seems committed to the life of a wanton before Devlin recruits her; and Gittes is building a reputable business with "finesse," doing mostly "marital" work (his "métier"), hardly the white knight driven to bust political and industrial corruption in Southern California. In *True Detective* Cohle's obsessive detailing of crime scenes in his large black notebook is seen by his colleagues as peculiar, earning him the nickname "The Taxman"; his partner Hart enjoys an easy, if immoral, life as a career detective in a local force. None of them start off wanting to do what they end up wanting to do. And this brings us back to Elliott Gould's Marlowe about to be woken by his cat at 3 a.m. in his Los Angeles apartment; for *The Long Goodbye* is a film that tutors us to see the way in which wholehearted commitment is less the product of a sudden Damascene moment or decision, but something that emerges gradually, born of adhesive dogged habit: a kind of steady and consistent being in a world which cannot help but shed its signs and clues.

The Long Goodbye: Floating above the Genre

In a remarkable essay on the film Murray Pomerance rightly claims that its characters are "all self-promoters, except Marlowe, who seems to float among them like an alien" and notes that he "is a kind of phantom detective"[9]:

> His soft voice, his kinky locks, his sheepdog bearing, his tranquil but also weary (but intensely observant) eyes, his ease of manner, his proclivity toward rational and verbal, rather than physical, response, are all post-Beat, vaguely poetic, intoxicating . . . He moves like a dancer,

yet without the anxious impulse, without "drive"; he even drives without drive . . . Marlowe's repartee is snide, sarcastic, self-defeating, self-deprecating, mushy, modest, mumbling. He's a charmer, a tender heart. In the opening sequence (a tour-de-force of acting, animal wrangling and cinematography) he demonstrates that he and his cat are brothers under the skin. The cat . . . is also a Beat hero; Marlowe is a cool cat.[10]

As we have seen the movie begins with Marlowe being woken by his hungry cat, just after we have been ostentatiously shown a plaque on his apartment wall with "Hollywood" prominent. So what we are going to see is already "in a frame," the frame of the movies, of showbiz, acting, performance. By the end of the film we might reflect that this plaque is an early declaration that this is an end-of-genre movie, one that declares that the genre it inhabits is no longer workable, no longer intelligible as dramatic art (another instance would be Arthur Penn's *Night Moves*, 1975). It sets out to show us why this is so and starts by crosscutting the de-dramatized business with Marlowe and his cat with the fast-paced shots of Terry Lennox speeding in his sports car toward the Malibu home of his lover. Only later do we find out that as Marlowe was sleeping Lennox was killing his wife, and this car journey is a rendezvous with his lover, the blonde femme fatale Eileen Wade (Nina van Pallandt). But this is all plot to be cashed out. Altman overtly blends Hollywood action and European art cinema nonaction as he cuts between Marlowe/cat and Lennox/car. That heady generic mixture that characterizes much of New Hollywood in the early 1970s is worked up eloquently in this dream born out of a dream.

Marlowe wakes to be confronted by an emblem of reluctance, his fussy cat (is there another kind?) who won't be fed except what it wants. Its owner first makes what he mumbles is a "concoction" out of cottage cheese, an egg, and some salt, a feeble substitute for cat food which the animal sensibly rejects by knocking it to the floor with its paw; "Don't believe it, huh?" With the cat still mewling for food, Marlowe leaves the apartment; strikes a louche, lovely figure, greeting his hippie female neighbors with bemusement but no erotic interest, and drives to a twenty-four-hour store, where he discovers that they are out of stock of his pet's favorite brand, Coury cat food.

He returns home with a different cat food, locks the cat out of the kitchen, and spoons the new non-Coury-brand food into an old Coury-brand empty tin. The cat, however, is not fooled for a moment and exits through his improvised cardboard flap.

Raymond Chandler's love of cats was turned in Robert Altman's mind to the notion that the scene was, as he told Gould, about the fact that you can't lie to a cat. Its reluctance to take the meal is the obverse of its wholehearted liking of Coury brand. If the cat is a mirror of Marlowe and he is the detective in the film, what picture of the detective is this? It must mean that being a detective and doing "detection" is, like appetite, both driven and fickle. It floats above the world seemingly uncaring ("It's OK with me" is Marlowe's response to the world around him for most of the film), and yet it is single-minded in its pursuit of what ends up driving it. You can't lie, or fake, that kind of commitment. Marlowe gets it later in the film, but for a long while it seems that he will not get it at all.

Shortly afterward Terry Lennox (Jim Bouton) arrives at Marlowe's apartment. They are clearly long-standing friends: they banter a bit, play a game of liar's poker, which Marlowe loses before he notices scratches on Lennox's face. Lennox admits he's had a fight with his wife, Sylvia (the one he has just beaten to death), then asks Marlowe to drive him to Tijuana. And Marlowe couldn't be further from suspicion; he acts the patsy, the good friend. We see them arrive at the Mexico border just before dawn, and when he returns to his apartment Marlowe is confronted by two plainclothes detectives, Dayton (John Davies) and Green (Jerry Jones). They arrest him, and he is booked and interviewed by Detective Farmer (Steve Coit) who tells him Sylvia Lennox has been found brutally murdered. It looks to the cops like Marlowe aided the chief suspect's escape over the border. He did. Everything is in a frame, everything a kind of performance, a spectacle of a film spectacle: as Marlowe is interviewed under pressure from the cops he rubs the ink from his fingerprinted hands on his face, offering a desultory Al Jolson "mammie"; they assume he's making a performance to protect his friend. He's just a performer.

Three days later Marlowe is released—the case is now closed, because Lennox has been found dead with a suicide note that confesses to killing Sylvia. Marlowe then goes to a bar which stands in for his office, where he accepts a phoned-in job from a literary publicist to locate a missing alcoholic writer, Roger Wade (Sterling Hayden).

The floating dancer's mission is to find a Hemingwayesque novelist played by one of the greats of the Hollywood Golden Age. He drives to Wade's house on the beach in a gated Malibu Colony where he meets Wade's wife Eileen. The Malibu complex was where Robert Altman was living at the time, so its scenes have a further dimension hidden from the audience. She tells Marlowe her husband may have checked himself into a private rehab clinic. We seem at once to be in a regular detective movie. There is some nice sleuthing as Marlowe infiltrates the clinic and locates Wade's room. Watching from outside the window (another frame: the film is like a fertile womb blossoming with its own self-consciousness), Marlowe sees the clinic's chief, Dr. Verringer (Henry Gibson), asking a reluctant Wade to pay his bills. Marlowe collects Wade and takes him home, job done. As he does these things Marlowe seems to be behaving as he was at the beginning of the film: waiting for events and appetites to emerge from the world into his view.

Once home Wade is drunk and belligerent and goes to bed. Eileen asks Marlowe about Terry Lennox who, it transpires, lived nearby. Not much is made of this until later, but when Marlowe gets back to his apartment he is confronted by a gangster, Marty Augustine (Mark Rydell), accompanied by a motley crew of hoods and his mistress Jo Ann (Jo Ann Eggenweiler). We discover that Lennox was carrying money in a bag (which we see at the beginning of the film), some $335,000, that he was due to deliver to Mexico City, but didn't. With Lennox dead, Marlowe is the final link to it. Before they leave Augustine performs his capacity for violence by breaking a Coke bottle across Jo Ann's face, disfiguring her. Such performances punctuate a film where all the characters seem to know they live in the City of Movies and tend toward large performative gestures as if they are auditioning for an unseen employer. Marlowe follows the hoods to the Malibu Colony—in fact to Wade's house where he watches Augustine intimidate Eileen, and the next day the sleuth returns to ask the couple how they know him. Eileen is evasive and asks Marlowe to step outside on the beach.

We are already some way into the film and it has presented a thickened plot that always feels less important than the performers and the settings in which it slowly unfolds. At the Malibu beach house Marlowe witnesses another scene, one of marital disintegration, as Wade, clearly made impotent by his age and alcoholic condition, expresses violent contempt, prompted by sexual jealousy, toward Eileen. Back at his apartment Marlowe finds a five-thousand-dollar bill (a "Madison") in his mail with a note from Lennox thanking him. Prompted by this unexpected delivery, Marlowe travels to the Mexican village, Otatoclan, where Lennox was found dead. There he meets the chief of police and coroner and sees the documentation associated with Lennox's death and burial. Again, Marlowe's investigation, if that is what it is, seems inconclusive. He's caught between whatever is going on in the Wade household and the strange mix of criminal activities that Lennox was clearly involved with. At the heart of all this we might wonder what it is that Marlowe wants: he is floating above all this, and it is hard to see that anything has involved him beyond that sad fact of losing his friend. And yet he has continued in his pursuit of things, albeit in a louche seemingly disconnected fashion. It is as if he is awaiting the moment of commitment to occur.

Returning to the Malibu Colony, Marlowe finds the Wades having a party on the beach. This is promptly interrupted by Dr. Verringer demanding payment for Wade's rehab bill. When the drunken Wade refuses and insults the diminutive doctor ("Minnie Mouse! Peter Pan!"), Verringer strikes him hard across the face, and the party collapses. A strangely humiliated Wade writes Verringer a check and seemingly falls asleep. Eileen invites Marlowe to stay for dinner. Their dinner conversation is pleasant, but Marlowe gently presses some questions, with Gould gently revealing Marlowe's expert sleuthing instincts. There is a flavor of flirtation in the air, but nothing is said. Eileen tells him Wade also owed Augustine money, but her husband hates repaying his debts. For the first time we hear that Marlowe suspects Wade may have had an affair with Sylvia Lennox, although we do not hear his line of reasoning since while they are talking we see that Wade is awake and walking into the ocean in the dark. And once again, this is shown to us via cinematic shapes and tropes, this time the wide rectangular windows looking out onto the beach at night, such that both reflect the interior scene with Marlowe and Eileen but also show Wade "wading in" to the Pacific ocean where he drowns himself.

In a lengthy rescue attempt, both Marlowe and Eileen are drenched (and nearly drown) but fail to save the old man. When the police arrive the beach is lit up as a crime scene, becoming a stage where Marlowe, agitated and angry at Eileen, for the first time expresses his theory about the Lennox deaths. It is that Roger Wade, an abusive "looney tunes" drunk, beat Sylvia Lennox to death. Marlowe thinks this is connected to whoever killed Terry Lennox. Eileen says that perhaps Wade did kill Sylvia. And she admits her husband was having an affair with her: Terry found out about the affair, and when it stopped Roger killed her out of jealousy. Marlowe then says to her, "I know what to do and I know what to think." But when he tells Detective Farmer, the cop says he knows Wade saw Sylvia the day of her murder but that he has an alibi—he was at Verringer's clinic sedated at the time of death. But for Marlowe this just confirms corruption—Wade promised to pay Verringer to supply this alibi to the police (which explains—almost—the business over the check), who in turn have no further interest in finding out the truth. Marlowe is incensed: "You don't deserve to be alive you fucking pig!" he bellows at Farmer as leaves the beach scene. This moment of heightened emotion, perhaps the closest Marlowe comes to rage, ought to be the generic moment of commitment, but it falls short of that.

As viewers we may not be at all sure where the movie is going to take us next, but it has at least two more surprises. Marlowe is taken to Augustine's office, where Marty once again threatens him in a bizarre performance where he demands they all remove their clothes. Unexpectedly (as if cued by the director) the money just turns up, and Marlowe is free to go, but as he leaves he notices Eileen leaving Augustine's office in her car. In a remarkable action scene, he chases it through the streets on foot, calling her name, but another car hits him and he wakes up, unhurt, in hospital. (Next to his hospital bed is a patient almost entirely wrapped in bandages, a clear reference to the Universal *Mummy* movie series of the 1930s and 40s.)

After looking for his cat one more time, we see Marlowe travel again to Otatoclan. There, he bribes the officials with the "Madison" note, and they reveal the true circumstances of Lennox's death. Appropriately enough for this film, it transpires that the whole thing was a bit of theater, a fake death. Finally, we see Marlowe walking down an avenue, eventually arriving at Lennox's hideout. Lennox, reclining in a hammock, is pleasantly surprised to see him: he admits he killed Sylvia because, after Wade told her about Eileen and him, Sylvia was going to tell the cops about the cash Lennox was moving for Augustine. So Lennox killed her and used Marlowe to take him to the border, knowing he would be interrogated. "You're a born loser," Lennox tells him. "Yeah, I even lost my cat," says Marlowe and, quite unexpectedly, shoots him dead. The film ends with Marlowe walking into the distance back along the tree-lined avenue, seemingly jovial as Eileen passes him in her jeep; instead of yet another rendition of the Johnny Mercer number, "The Long Goodbye"—versions of which have been ubiquitous throughout the movie—his exit is accompanied by "Hooray for Hollywood" on the soundtrack.

This is a strange ending to a peculiar film, but at least we can see it depicts its protagonist as enthusiastically satisfied with the outcome of events, even if we don't know quite why. For *The Long Goodbye* offers us neither a satisfying picture of reluctance nor of wholehearted detection: Marlowe instead has, until the ending, appeared passive, noncommittal, and largely low-energy. That he even owns a gun, let alone shoots dead his unarmed friend Terry Lennox, is a surprise to viewers who have followed his languid and louche journey through its blurred plotting. For although the movie has a central noir aspect—its dogged insistence on narrative confusion, on deceit and betrayal—it feels as if there is something more, another lining of meaning.

Certainly audiences and reviewers experiencing it on first release were confused: the poster for the film has Marlowe/Gould in profile (and somewhat handsomer) pointing a Colt Detective Special .38 (not in fact the gun he uses in the film), with the tagline "Nothing says goodbye like a bullet." But while the poster, possibly an allusion—equally misleading if so—to the poster for *Dirty Harry* (1971), suggests action and confrontation, apart from the disfiguring of Jo Ann and the killing of Lennox, there is little physical violence at all in the film and no threat of it emanating from Marlowe whose typical response to encounters and events in the movie is, "It's OK with me." Only when the film was released in New York in October 1973, with a different *Mad Magazine*-styled poster that emphasized its zany "fun," as well as referencing the previous Altman-Gould collaboration *M*A*S*H*, was it a critical and commercial success. Subsequent posters, including the cover of the tie-in release of Chandler's novel, have Marlowe/Gould with the cat on his shoulder. By the end of 1973 it had been rereleased at the Beverly Canon where Kevin Thomas for the *Los Angeles Times* tried to account for its uneven reception: "Altman's far-out updating of Chandler had been both praised and damned as a desecration of its source. Needless to say, the casting of a shaggy, sloppy, hangdog Gould in a part made mythical by Humphrey Bogart has also been considered a sacrilege."[11] He goes on to praise the film for placing Marlowe in a contemporary setting (Altman described the script as about "Rip van Marlowe"), which allows it to be: "Alternately and sometimes simultaneously outrageous, hilarious and chilling [he] has given us a moral perspective that is profoundly disquieting and challenging in its subtle and complex ambiguities." Part of the "sacrilege," as Jeremy Kaye points out, is in the casting of Gould (born Goldstein): his Jewish appearance, as well as his youth and the colorful contemporary setting, replete with the markers of adult cinema (nudity and cursing), are in friction with the Anglo-Saxon tarnished knight depicted by Dick Powell (*Murder, My Sweet*, 1944), Humphrey Bogart (*The Big Sleep*, 1946), or even twenty years later Robert Mitchum (*Farewell, My Lovely*, 1975—set in 1941) that had been absorbed into the cultural imagination. And yet there is something about the privacy embodied in Gould's performance that connects him in particular to Bogart's version of Marlowe. As David Thomson says of Gould's performance:

> If you lifted off the music in *The Long Goodbye*, the endless attempts at the title tune, you might not realize that Elliot Gould's performance is like a brilliant, very cool, stoned musician—Art Pepper, say—doing "I Can't Get Started" in a Bogart mood. He's hunched over his instrument, very sad, very alone, yet chronically musical. It's a great performance with a lovely, secret beat that everyone else in the movie feels but cannot quite get. Who knows if even Altman got it?[12]

That Bogart mood is, in Stanley Cavell's words, one of "private heroism," the heroism of privacy: there is a secret, banked resource that propels Gould's Marlowe, but it seems lighter, more democratic, than Bogart's tense, focused version. Cavell designates Bogart as the greatest instance of the cinematic dandy, a figure defined by his capacity for self-knowledge whose depth of private passion establishes confidence and resolve in the face of betrayal and evil.[13] We need to keep this Cavellian sense of the Bogart mood in mind if we are to make sense of why Gould's Marlowe acts as he does in the film.

In one sense Gould plays Marlowe as a cat in the sense of languid, cool, aloof, and distant, and he carries some of that Bogart mood in terms of the intense privateness communicated to us through his odd, often incoherent mumbling. But Thomson is wrong to suggest that Altman may not have "got it." Altman's interest in Leigh Bracket's script was prompted by the ending—indeed he insisted in his contract that he would only complete the film if the ending where Marlowe kills Lennox was left intact. One reason for this is that, while the film has all the plot confusions associated with noir, its engagement with those traditions is bracketed by an interest in Los Angeles as a place where Hollywood, and therefore the spectacle of performance, is the dominant reference for the rest of the world. Hence we get a series of frames—achieved through mise-en-scène, imagery, and soundtrack—around the plot that consistently irritate our attempts to define the meaning of what the characters say and do.

It does so most of all by framing the entire film between two apparently unconnected scenes, one of reluctance—the cat's refusal to eat—and one of wholeheartedness, Marlowe's execution of Lennox. The opening business with the cat and its food is one of several sleeper moments where events seemingly tangential to the plot are banked and then cashed out later. (This structural design echoes the "banked" resources of the Bogart/dandy that Cavell writes about that are "cashed out" when the hero applies his inner code to the corrupted world around him, as a kind of shield as much as a revelation.) Nor is this the only frame in a movie that revels in its visual and thematic composition around literal and figurative frames.

One of these frames begins before we see the first shot and ends way after the final one. This is the usage of Johnny Mercer's "Hooray for Hollywood" number lifted from the 1937 Busby Berkeley musical *Hollywood Hotel*. The film begins with the sound of a band playing the song as we fade up on a plaque mounted above a bookshelf in Marlowe's apartment, an object just slightly more substantial than something a tourist might pick up from a gift shop near the Walk of Fame. It is silver metal mounted in a thick rectangular wooden frame (part of it is in shadow but its dimensions are close to the film's aspect ratio of 2.35:1), and shapes are cut into the metal to represent iconic emblems of the region: Los Angeles City Hall, swooping searchlights, some palm trees, the hills with the HOLLYWOOD sign, the ocean. The iconography and soundtrack of the dream factory are shown as literally a frame within a frame. The same musical number carries us out of the final moments of the movie, beginning just before the credits are supered over a continuing shot of Marlowe celebrating in the distance on the avenue (as we shall see this is not music that we are led to believe Marlowe can hear or the tune he is dancing to). In the latter case we hear the extended version with vocals sung by Johnnie Davis and Frances Langford from the sequence at the beginning of Berkeley's film. Why bookend a movie that uses familiar sleazy noir touch points like murder, betrayal, adultery, deceit, and sudden violence with reference to this song, which gently mocks the desire to make it big in the industry even as it celebrates that desire at every Academy Awards show?

One answer to this is that it is a comment on the false, even deceitful, nature of that Hollywood fantasy that the film intends to undermine or counter with its own content. This would be in keeping with auteurist accounts of Robert Altman's work, which tend to emphasize his anti-Hollywood, maverick, or at least whimsical approach in his films, and the way he uses satire, irony, and black humor to disturb genre convention. But that only gets us so far into the "why?" For there must be something further, something relevant to the first and final times we see Marlowe being so proximate to this music that we need to consider. Marlowe is not presented as a dogged incorruptible detective from the 1930s and 40s, but a young man living in LA in the 1970s; he does not deal with corrupt aristocratic disputes from the past but contemporary gangsters and crooks living on Malibu beach. Which is to say he lives in a world where the stories, performances, genres, and tropes of Hollywood cinema, including film noir, are already part of the cultural imagination. One of the problems with using irony and satire as evaluative positives is that they tend to fetishize distance (and in Brechtian terms, distanciation) as positive aesthetic values. *The Long Goodbye* can be confusing and even irritating on occasion, but it is not difficult to watch and nor do its gestures toward the attractions of a confected Hollywood fantasy necessarily sneer at those who are attracted by them.

In framing Marlowe as a construction, a Hollywood *figure* who also delivers a new, fresh kind of inhabitation of the detective, *The Long Goodbye* offers us not reasons for why people do what they do, but more a collection of stances toward reality that are pictured in offbeat, often lightweight, and funny ways. That Marlowe can shoot Terry Lennox dead, a former friend, relaxed and unarmed, and moments later dance down an avenue without so much as a care in the world suggests that the stakes of successful sleuthing have reached a generic end point, where nothing matters but the tune in one's head and the lightness of one's feet on the ground. But we can also take Marlowe's hurt and sense of betrayal as real—the film allows us to take up that stance, too: but we need, then, to remember the very start of the film, the wonderful easy way the two men played liar's poker in Marlowe's apartment, the beautiful dawn as they reached the Mexican border in the car, and Marlowe's love for his loveless, fussy cat. Losing a cat is maybe an odd reason—there are others—to enact revenge, but just before he shoots, it is the last thing Marlowe mentions. In killing Lennox Marlowe seems to have found a way to be in the world of people again or, at least, the world of Hollywood people: a cinematic utopia where he can be among us, effortlessly dancing along the avenue, humming a tune, no longer an isolated dreamer but part of things, part of the nonsecret, free, and open world that is our ideal reality.

1

Out of the Past

"All I can see is the frame."

*O*UT OF THE *P*AST BEGINS in the small town of Bridgeport, a name that evokes connection between locations, indeed one that itself connects a thing that connects ("bridge") with a word associated with coming home, although *port* also carries the frisson of a border and the associated lawful and unlawful activities that might happen there.[1] The central character, a former private detective, Jeff Markham (Robert Mitchum), is indeed attempting to gain entry to this quiet settlement having changed his name to Jeff Bailey, a name he then displays above his car repair/gas station business. The images that background the title credits suggest that this little town is nestled in a wooded valley surrounded by high mountains, and one of these title images drops the credits briefly to show a long shot of fenced grazing farmland near a road sign that indicates Bridgeport's comfortable distance from urban dangers (349 miles to Los Angeles, 98 to Reno).

The signpost is clear enough on-screen for the film audience to read these distances (especially its considerable distance from that shining city of noir and movie making), but to the location of the sign is less legible. Indeed the mystery of the film inheres in more than its congested plot, which is rightly often remarked upon. It has something to do with its uneven alternation between clarity and opacity—as here, in the clarity of the signpost and the unfamiliarity of Bridgeport, a place that seems itself to be an uneven assemblage of locations (shop-lined main road, dark forests, bright lakes, high cliffs, a lonesome homestead). The duality of legibility/opacity is a feature that runs throughout the movie and makes it very challenging to read. Like the signpost, the film's characters often present as dyads—Jeff (Robert Mitchum)/Ann (Virginia Huston), Jeff/Kathie (Jane Greer), Whit (Kirk Douglas)/Kathie, Whit/Jeff—and yet how they fit together overall is often not clear. There are lots of pairs in the film, but what makes them pair up seems hidden, secret. The same effect haunts the locations of the film: they are all clear enough when we are "in" them, and yet they don't seem to fit together as coming from the same film, designed by the same hand. They belong together as part of the overall genre of film noir in a way that they do not seem to as part of this single film. The morning scenes at Lake Tahoe seem from a different movie to those that take place in San Francisco or Mexico; Bridgeport-by-the-lake is a very different world from Bridgeport-outside-the-town-café. Secrecy is embedded all the way through the film, and however hard one looks at it, it refuses to disclose. Director Jacques Tourneur, an intelligent director of considerable finesse, cannot have failed to notice this, and yet he appears not to have wanted to tidy up or clarify matters, as if keeping the mystery intact was more important than telling the story or even making an effectively legible movie. As I watch *Out of the Past* my sense of it is a film in which noir-like events take place (a degenerate relationship, a deception, a frame, a fated doomed ending), and yet by its end it feels like an incoherent, mysterious experience. The mystery of this remarkable film is something I will track in this chapter, moment by moment: to some extent this means that my writing will take on some of the "problems" (which in the film may well be aesthetic patterns) that the film has. This is to say the film is the opposite of Jeff's sense of things when midway through the film he says, "All I can see is the frame." The film is a picture without a frame: an assemblage of coherent elements without a coherent border. In tracking each moment of the film I am attempting to map out how this framelessness feels and what it may mean to us as we hunt through it. Associated with this sense of framelessness I should also note how strange it is that there seems to be no gradation to the instruments that present the immediacy of the film to us, such as music or editing: the lighting, for example, while it changes from night to day appropriately, is always the same throughout. The only thing that seems to change—and this is a startling claim given the reputation of the actor for gestural and expressive minimalism—is Robert Mitchum's performance. Michael Eaton points to some prosaic reasons why the film feels this way: "*Out of the Past*'s already complicated flashback plotting was not made any more comprehensible when several expository scenes got lost *en route* from the mimeo machine and aesthetician Jacques Tourneur's complex visual symbolism was stymied by the exigencies of RKO's legendary stinginess."[2] Most importantly, in terms of the movement from reluctance to commitment, it forces the viewer to adopt the role of detective, *a detective committed to solving the enigma of what it is that the film is doing to us as it is doing it*. It may be that the film's incoherence, its mysteriousness, is the reason that it has been taken up as emblematic of what a film noir version of a detective looks like. To go one step further, the film feels like a confirmation that sleuthing—the tracking of signs and signals emanating from the world of people and things—is not merely metonymic with cinema but is the same kind of thing as cinema. Detection in this way—the directed tracking of things in order to follow the (sometimes guided) disclosure of significant information or meaning—is the same as our experience of cinema's recording mechanisms that attend to a world already pointed (because it is artistically shaped) toward their discriminating capacities. Unlike the commitment of the detective which we see in formation, these capacities are always already wholehearted even as the story they disclose seems indifferent to being shown.

As we register the information on the signposts, we see a car pass heading into town. It is driven by Joe Stephanos (Paul Valentine), a gangster who works for Whit Sterling who, as we find out shortly, lives in Lake Tahoe (78 miles away according to the sign). We find out that Joe has been here before and had noticed Jeff working outside his garage. Very quickly the movie establishes what might be called the imaginative coordinates of contemporary forms of movement and settlement: that this town is "protected" (at least in a scenic imagination) by the ancient forms of geology and nature, and yet is accessible fairly easily (and with helpful signage) by car. It comes to mean—again very quickly—that Jeff's dream of changing his life by changing his name and taking up another profession is at best rather optimistic, especially given his commercial decision to name his business so curiously and so prominently. Surely he was bound to be found out eventually. It is almost as if he wanted to be found, just as road signage cannot be coy about the information it beams to the world. It is as if Jeff in his new incarnation eschews all mystery in a world that thrives only on secrets and mystery—a world where everyone is on the make except Jeff who simply pumps gas. *He insists to the world that this is his identity even when he must know that this is not the kind of world that will allow that identity to continue unmolested.* Jeff's declaration of settlement seems to declare then that this is his desired world, a world beyond the need to hustle, beyond the necessity to figure things out, to read the mystery behind the signs. A world where there is no need to interpret, where we can just see things directly as they are, and a thing is what it looks like—a full correspondence between the appearance of something and its truth.

The central character of *Ghosts* (the second part of Paul Auster's mysterious "New York Trilogy"), a detective enigmatically called "Blue," after watching *Out of the Past* on its first release reflects on Jeff's curious choice of name for his new identity:

> His ambition was simple enough: to become a normal citizen in a normal American town, to marry the girl next door, to live a quiet life. It's strange, Blue thinks, that the new name Mitchum chooses for himself is Jeff Bailey. This is remarkably close to the name of another character in a movie he saw the previous year with the future Mrs. Blue—George Bailey, played by James Stewart in *It's a Wonderful Life*. That story was about small town America, but from the opposite point of view: the frustrations of a man who spends his whole life trying to escape. But in the end he comes to understand that his life has been a good one, that he has done the right thing all along. Mitchum's Bailey would no doubt like to be the same man as Stewart's Bailey. But in his case the name is false, a product of wishful thinking. His real name is Markham—or, as Blue sounds it out to himself, mark him—and that is the whole point. He has been marked by the past, and once that happens, nothing can be done about it. Something happens, Blue

thinks, and then it goes on happening forever. It can never be changed, can never be otherwise.[3]

Blue becomes haunted by this notion which, broadly, is that of fate, of one's fatedness to be what one cannot escape being. But George Bailey's desire to leave Bedford Falls makes no sense dramatically if it were not in theory possible for him to do it; in the context of World War II it would have been obvious to those either working in a militarized society on the domestic front, or as combatants, that once the conflict was over, one's lives would have to change from one thing to another. Hidden deeper in the comparison between the Baileys is the question of whether one's origins—past, parents, background—are determining factors in what one wants to do now and in the future. This is the matter of *social class*. For George Bailey, the realization that the satisfactions of petit-bourgeois life in a small town where one has considerable connection and adoration from the community is sufficient in order to live a good life requires merely that he give up the adolescent dream of being a world adventurer (although it takes an enormous confluence of devastating events to bring him to this decision). For Jeff Bailey, the stakes are considerably different. His past as a private eye meant he had his own business, and business partner Jack Fisher (Steve Brodie), but also that he was vulnerable to getting mixed up in the kind of temptations and criminality we see later in the film. Even Fisher is untrustworthy, suspicious, and eventually threatens his former partner with ratting him out to Whit; in Bridgeport by contrast, Jeff's "partner" (insofar as he is Jeff's only assistant) is the deaf and dumb young man (the credits call him The Kid and he is played by Dickie Moore, who was already a child star and known for his role in Hawks's *Sergeant York*, 1941) who demonstrates immense loyalty to Jeff at considerable danger to himself. That The Kid communicates by signing is a further attempt by the film to clarify through opacity that Jeff's desire for settlement is almost impossible to articulate, is somehow beyond legible communication. There is some irony in that this form of communication is visual, direct, and seemingly fluent in delivery and reception although it remains obscure to everyone except the Jeff/Kid dyad; the entire meaning of the film's ending rests on our interpretation of a gesture made by The Kid. The gas station business continues to connect Jeff to the wider world since its customers are car owners; fatefully that is the reason he is discovered by Joe who was presumably passing through on the way to see his boss at Lake Tahoe.

In reinventing himself Jeff chose a job that demands straightforward business transactions (repair, service, gas, etc.) in contrast to the forms of disguise and deception required of the private eye. As a detective one's job is to know the world, and to know the world is to know it too much, to allow it to tell you how it changes. Jeff in Bridgeport eschews change for settlement and stability but, as noted above, the film has a problem seeing how this could possibly work for him. Even though he is still self-employed in a private business, Jeff has chosen something like honest work (when they meet later Joe somewhat derisively calls it "respectable"), and it is wrong to characterize him as "hiding out" (unless we assume he is very bad at it; in fact he has two signs above his shop that name him Jeff Bailey as if to underline his commitment to it).[4] To complete the picture, he has been courting a local girl, Ann, and our first sight of him is as part of a couple, our first dyad.

They are beneath a tree near a lake in a setting that reminds us of the scenery shown during the titles: mountains and woods, almost Walden Pond. Bailey is dressed in warm outdoor clothes, and we see him in a long shot, dwarfed by the landscape carrying a fishing rod and line but no catch. "They're just not feeding today," he tells Ann. "They will later, it's clouding up," she tells him. And then, looking up dreamily at the sky, she continues as he puts his bait away:

ANN: They say the day you die your name is written on a cloud.

JEFF: Who says?

ANN: They.

JEFF: Never heard of them.

It is quite easy to dismiss Ann as a fairly simple small-town girl and her cloud-writing comment an emblem of unworldliness. As she speaks she is positioned frontally so that the camera captures her looking up and off-screen left, while Jeff's face is mostly hidden in profile (as we shall see partially hiding Jeff's face is a central aesthetic trope across the film). And five minutes into a film where names have already accrued a prominence makes Ann's odd remark an evocative assertion. The day anyone dies one at least expects planning for some kind of memorial, a headstone, plaque, or entry in the records: "written on a cloud" is no less ephemeral than "on the wind." But Jeff's response is playful rather than ridiculing; and Ann's comment indicates a preference for prominence over permanence, a clue—perhaps—as to her attraction to the "stranger with a past" compared to her other romantic option Jim (Richard Webb) who we find out has known her since they were children. Jeff's interest in Ann is exactly the opposite to her interest in him: she is grounded, presumably born and bred in Bridgeport, a regular wholesome woman with whom he imagines he can settle and grow in Bridgeport. For Ann it is precisely Jeff's otherness, his mystery, that is attractive and she asks him about the best place he's seen; his response ("this one right here") is hardly likely to be what she was fishing for, but then her reply, "I bet you say that to all the places" once again enjoys the playful frisson of thinking of Jeff as a kind of man of experience who is used to quipping smart things. Jeff signals toward a cove and tells her, "I'd like to build a house right there, marry you, live in it and never go anywhere else"; this is what Jeff, now, *wants*. It is plain, visible, goal-centered, and orientates action in the present that can be directed toward achievement in the future. But Ann continues to probe his past: she asks if he was "married before." For all her apparent lack of sophistication, Ann is quite right to check if Jeff remains vulnerable to some romantic entanglement (the film later seems to imply that he may be), right to be alert to the possible threats as well as attractions of "the mysterious Jeff Bailey."

With impressive economy Tourneur delivers a snapshot of the difficulty in moving between identities, in particular when one's former identity is shrouded or hidden either as a matter of shame, or because in order to thrive in the new role and the new place, one must shed off all references to a past that would precisely disable that aim. And it is easy to see, following Ann, the attractions of finding out about that past. For the bourgeois settled world, a more difficult and threatening world of survival, deception, struggle, and violence can seem dramatic and exciting. A film in which this fishing scene was not interrupted by The Kid bringing Jeff news about Joe's arrival, one that tracked the gradual settlement of Ann and Jeff in Bridgeport, would no doubt be far less engaging than the one we have. But Ann and Jeff and their future, just like George Bailey's desire to travel the world, have to remain theoretical possibilities in order for that drama to offer a plausible, however difficult, outcome—a prize—at its end. But in order to do that we have to believe that Jeff could credibly exist in both roles, both as a man with a past and one who has—however hackneyed—a dream for his future.

Class is strangely embedded in the film at almost the point it begins to vanish as a force for change. A knowledge of social, economic, and cultural spectra across both working and bourgeois worlds and the ability to detect reasons, motivations, and desires in either is an advantage for the private eye. In Jeff's case he has demonstrated particularly good judgment in his choice of loyal friend and workmate, The Kid, and potential romantic partner in Ann. What he lacks is the ability to imprint himself productively, in a bourgeois sense, on the wider town, both in its gossipy (Marny) and respected quarters (the latter represented by Ann's parents), a legitimate stake as a member of that community. But this not just a question of competence, that Jeff is simply bad at mixing with people, for example. It seems much more a product of the peculiar direction that postwar US society is portrayed in the film as having chosen, one where justice and fairness no longer have a right to win the day in a happy ending.

Our apprehension of such matters comes from two sources, the historical context and the casting of Mitchum as Jeff. The context is one of the immediate postwar world, particularly in the US where returning from combat allowed access to the G.I. Bill providing low-interest loans and college education, a significant advantage for the largely working-class military combatants. The world conflict had also shaken up human experience for vast numbers of people across the globe. As James Heartfield points out:

> The lives of women and men were changed greatly by the war, which brought many more women into the workforce, and many men into the services. Family life was turned upside down as the division of domestic labor was changed. There was a strong move towards socialized childcare. People were moved around all over the world, breaking up traditional domestic life, and bringing the young especially, into contact with people and experiences that they would never have seen. Despite the conservative motives of the

war leaders, sexual relations were revolutionized, with a great acceleration of sex outside marriage, marriage for love, divorce and, pointedly, towards a much greater prevalence of homosexuality . . . War time had turned sexual relations on their heads, pushing men and women into all kinds of relations that defied tradition. When the war was over, the authorities struggled to put the Genie back in the Bottle. One of the greatest challenges they faced was to recreate the patriarchal family after the war.[5]

Out of the Past itself follows this pattern, looking back to Jeff's past of sexual passion and betrayal, hiding and deceit, from an idealized present only to find that those energies continue to disrupt the here and now. The shake-up of human experience, in particular the world's exposure to extended violence and conflict, no doubt sharpened the appeal of noir worlds depicted in Hollywood cinema. However, that experience also established the plausibility that new places carried new and disruptive potential.

One of the ways in which class figures in this mix is the paradoxical way that the progressive working-class movements of the prewar years were gradually defeated by the emergent geopolitical structures after the end of World War II. In the context of the Cold War, Stalinist communist parties and separatist national movements tended to dominate progressive thinking and activities. What remained was the promise, captured by the title of Michael Young's 1958 satirical essay "The Rise of the Meritocracy," of transcending one's class origins, and moving up the social, educational, and economic ladder toward a better life by using one's talent, hard work, and dedication rather than relying on or suffering under the advantages and disadvantages of one's class position at birth. However phantasmal this notion was in practice, it gained traction in popular forms of mass entertainment. Living honestly and respectably, working hard, and so on were the magic ingredients that allowed an internationalized version of the American Dream to gain purchase in the cultural imagination of the world. There are traces of this in Jeff's desire to build his home in the protected natural setting of a cove, in his friendship with The Kid, and his honesty with Ann.

Mitchum is particularly good at representing working-class figures disconnected from collective forms of solidarity; he often depicts a rugged individuality which carries a vague air of being in mourning for something ineffable and ephemeral that has been lost. Born in Bridgeport (in Connecticut, not California), he grew up during the Great Depression in an impoverished family, at first on a farm in Delaware, and then in the slums of Hell's Kitchen in New York. He left home at fourteen, becoming a vagrant for several years before washing up at Long Beach, California, and getting mixed up in local theater. His physical stature—tall, bulky, yet long-boned and graceful—and his deep-eyed almost impassive face connotes a solidity and privacy that make his reactions appear almost subliminal, slowed-down without being slow. David Thompson captures him well, noting the "intriguing ambiguity in Mitchum's work, the idea of a man thinking and feeling beneath a calm exterior" such that "there is no need to put 'acting' on the surface. And for a big man, he is immensely agile, capable of unsmiling humor, menace, stoicism, and above all, of watching other people as though he were waiting to make up his mind."[6] That is another way to say he does not exude a sense of anxiety about being judged by others. However, the dream of class mobility is already one that appears disconnected from actual social forces: class loosens itself around Mitchum as Bailey, and the potential for class mobility gets compressed into the Markham-Bailey transformation, confused or muddled with matters of plot and other storied elements. Combine the peculiar version of working-class fortitude embodied by Mitchum with a cultural imagination responsive to the idea of class mobility, and we have a clearer sense of why a figure like Jeff Bailey might be both mysterious and compelling for someone like Ann; but at the same time *Out of the Past* is skeptical about whether this model of class has any future. Part of its darkness seems to be that it acknowledged the ascendency of a kind of gangsterism, or a racket society of the kind posited by Max Horkheimer earlier in the 1940s.[7] *Out of the Past* seems haunted by an earlier sense of what detective and gangster films offered the mass audience ideologically and aesthetically.

In his book *American Civilization* (written in 1950), C. L. R. James argues that the dynamism of mass cultural forms ought to be embraced as an epistemology of the national imagination:

> The modern popular film, the modern newspaper (the *Daily News*, *not* the *Times*), the comic strip, the evolution

of jazz, a popular periodical like *Life*, these mirror from year to year the deep social responses and evolution of the American people in relation to the fate which has overtaken the original concepts of freedom, free individuality, free association, etc. To put it more harshly still, it is in the serious study of, above all, Charles Chaplin, Dick Tracy, Gasoline Alley, James Cagney, Edward G. Robinson, Rita Hayworth, Humphrey Bogart, genuinely popular novels like those of Frank Yerby . . . men like David Selznick, Cecil B. deMille, and Henry Luce, that you find the clearest ideological expression of the sentiments and deepest feelings of the American people and a great window into the future of America and the modern world. This insight is *not* to be found in the works of T. S. Eliot, of Hemingway, or Joyce, of famous directors like John Ford or Rene Clair.[8]

For James, the importance of Dick Tracy is that he is not a cop but an ordinary guy joining the police only after his girlfriend's father is killed by criminals. After the success of gangster movies in the 1930s, James points to the emergence of figures such as Dashiell Hammett's Sam Spade and Raymond Chandler's Philip Marlowe as an amalgam of detective-gangsters, exemplified by Humphrey Bogart's role in *High Sierra* (John Huston, 1941). In that film, James argues, Bogart plays:

> a gangster hurt by society who fought back and, trapped in the end, went up and up among the sierras, going to his death, but defying the police below. Ida Lupino, his girlfriend, was led off at the end, asking: Why should this be? From this moment Bogart was made. But he was made as a *detective*, not as a gangster. He is an ordinary guy, that is his chief attraction, his ordinariness; tough, going his own way, as sick of the pretenses of the world as is Hemingway but he has to intervene. That he has to intervene is not merely the necessity of official law and order. It is a necessity of the mass which looks on. Society would fall entirely to pieces if the gangster were to triumph. But gangster and private detective are one character, each being absolutely necessary to the other.[9]

James reasons that this is so because the gangster is:

> a persistent symbol of the national past which now has no meaning—the past in which energy, determination, bravery were certain to get a man somewhere in the line of opportunity. Now the man on the assembly line, the farmer, know that they are there for life; and the gangster who displays all the old heroic qualities in the only way he can display them, is the derisive symbol of the contrast between ideals and reality.[10]

More recent discussions of the role of class in detective movies tend to elide this dimension, focusing on matters of representation, masculinity, or global industries.[11] However, James's insight is to locate the appeal of the detective in the fusion of volatile and violent gangsterism with the necessity to intervene as an aspect of readily felt ordinary aspirations to be sovereign over our destiny as individuals:

> The film, strip, radio-drama are a form of art which must satisfy the mass, the individual seeking individuality in a mechanized, socialized society, where his life is ordered and restricted at every turn, where there is no certainty of employment, far less of being able to rise by energy and ability or going West as in the old days. In such a society, the individual demands an esthetic compensation in the contemplation of free individuals who go out into the world and settle their problems by free activity and individualistic methods. In these perpetual isolated wars free individuals are pitted against free individuals, live grandly and boldly. What they want, they go for. Gangsters get what they want, trying it for a while, then are killed. In the end "crime does not pay" but for an hour and a half highly skilled actors and a huge organization of production and distribution have given to many millions a sense of active living, and in the bloodshed, the violence, the freedom from restraint to allow pent-up feelings free play, they have released the bitterness, hate, fear and sadism which simmer just below the surface.[12]

James is particularly contemptuous of intellectual commentary that seeks to fix American crime drama as only associated with horror, boredom, and despair ("The boredom is not the boredom of freedom at all. Intellectuals are bored. The masses are not. They have no freedom and they resent it"[13]); with, in other words, an acceptance of fate. For James the mass response that he posits is entirely positive ("a consuming anger and rage"); it is precisely the "passionate individualistic American temperament" that a Trotskyite Marxist like him finds so refreshing, since it indicates a stance that is ultimately a refusal of traditional ethics, ideas, and "formal concepts of social living" and hence a society "ripe for drastic social transformations."[14] James is careful to temper this positivity by noting the utility of the gangster-detective amalgam to totalitarian regimes (although he does not see this as a threat in the US), but he counters this by returning to his beloved Greek theater (particularly Aeschylus) as a model for how the new forms of mass art might better engage with the lived experiences of the masses they serve. James has an admirable confidence that "when modern popular art is free" and given the same democratic environment of Athens "great masterpieces would appear as in Greece and shake the nation to its soul."[15] And yet, *Out of the Past* seems to indicate that the forces ranged against individual temperaments are now decisive, that however cunning and agile avatars like Jeff are shown to be, they cannot escape the gangsterist logic that corrupts all forces such that it feels like fate itself is ranged against them.

James's embrace of the dynamism of mass culture reminds us that there was a time when movies and television could be treated as vibrant emblems of popular consciousness, rather than illusionistic, trivial traps designed to distract us from more important social, cultural, and political issues.[16] It allows us to consider the appeal of Jeff's meritocratic impulse to settle down as dramatically sprung against the iron-clad realities of the world which has come back from his past to recruit him again. Without that understanding, Jeff is merely in hiding and distracting himself with Ann and the gas station business; Jeff has something he wants that the film wants to tell us is impossible for him to have: but the want has to be real, it is the thing that haunts Jeff and our understanding of why he is ultimately doomed. It is the remnant of James's sense of the masses and their wish for freedom, the spark that lights the film, drives it, and unsettles it dynamically and stylistically.

In expressing his desire to settle down with Ann, Jeff aligns himself with a conventional desire for domestic settlement, but before we even hear about it the film has framed that wish as under threat. After Joe arrives at the gas station, he questions The Kid who immediately notices Joe's unease when a police cruiser passes behind him. Getting little out of The Kid, Joe goes across the street to Marny's Café where we see Jim, who turns out to be another current love interest of Ann. While Joe turns on the jukebox, we watch Marny (Mary Field) tease Jim as she serves him a sandwich ("First she's got you, now she's got you and Bailey"), and when Jim leaves, no doubt irritated by her questioning (which implies he should be doing more about the situation), it is Joe who takes up the story with Marny. After she asks if he knows Bailey ("I knew him. Once."), Marny says, "If he keeps mooning around Jim's girl, nobody will know him and that'll be too bad." It's easy to miss this comment since the stress of the scene is on the charm that Joe exudes that has just enough lining of menace that even before we have encountered Jeff we might feel concerned that a fellow such as this is looking for him. What Marny appears to be saying is that Jeff risks being ostracized by the town if he continues to pursue Ann who is "Jim's"; perhaps the creation of such drama is Marny's aim in her not very subtle reminder to Jim that, while he eats his ham sandwich, Jeff is fishing with Ann. What Jeff wants is already causing drama in Bridgeport, and in another of the film's many gestures of doubling we are soon to find out that this is not the first time he has pursued another man's girl or had a dream of settlement: he is repeating his past in Bridgeport even before it catches up with him.

Ann and Jeff are interrupted by The Kid just at the point Ann is on the brink of revealing something about her family ("My father. . ."). She says her mother has told her (as if she didn't know) that she's only known Jeff for a short time, and after we see Jeff reading The Kid's signing, she lights his cigarette (two matches), commenting, "You sure are a secret man." The cut-short conversation has the air of one that has been developing for some time, and later, as Jeff drives with Ann to Lake Tahoe, we find out that he has already promised to tell her the truth at some point, meaning they both acknowledge there *is* a secret to him that needs to be shared. What secrets do we have that might inhibit our entry into "respectable" society, in this case by preventing the sort of trust necessary for a romance to flourish? Of course, it is possible to imagine a setting where one's earlier privations, difficulties, even criminality might be sources of boastfulness now that one is successful. But that is not *Jeff's preferred world*, and what is at issue seems to be something shameful for him. As he later tells Ann, "I should have told you before, I meant to but I kept putting it off because I didn't like any part of it."

The next scene has Jeff and Joe meet at the gas station. It is a remarkably good-natured conversation given the story we are about to be told. We find out that Joe's boss, Whit, wants to see Jeff again, the next morning at his Lake Tahoe place. For most of the conversation Jeff leans passively against some work shelves, but when he agrees to meet Whit I don't think we are meant to take him as passively indifferent to the invitation. Clearly it is an opportunity, a kind of prompting, to tell Ann about his past now that an element of it has caught up with him. But when we see him in the next scene he is standing outside Ann's parents' garden gate, strikingly dressed in the costume of the private eye, belted trench coat and fedora; Tourneur shoots him from two angles, one behind and high to his left, the other low from the same side; both angles emphasize the dappling of light and shadow that bring out the textures of his face (smooth), the coat (coarse), and the almost abstract white lines of the wire fence and its gate his hands rest on. It is as if in these shots, the film presents us with the iconic figure of the noir detective that Jeff wants Ann to see in all its angular oddity. But what he hears during these shots direct us off-screen: it is Ann's mother and her voice is lined with the anxiety of social disgrace: "Ann? John? Are you letting her out like this? Are you gonna stand for it, with a man who won't even come to the front door?" When Ann meets him at the gate and tells him not to worry about it, Jeff says, "It's no good," but a moment later he says he is not worried about it at all. This is a small moment, but the film takes the time to include it (and a shot of Ann's house as they drive away) that makes the scene an incoherent picture of Jeff's courtship. Jeff *won't* come to their front door—why? Is he ashamed of his past, of taking another man's girl, or something else? It is as if he has only a partial sense of what it means to commit to settling down in a community, which involves, minimally, an appetite to get to know one's neighbors and the parents of the woman one wishes to marry. Two other things are called to mind when watching Jeff at this border listening to parental anxiety: that fact that town gossip Marny appears to know little about Jeff beyond seeing him every day across the road, in contrast to Jim who is clearly a regular, and that Jeff's dream of settlement is not a place in town, or even a house slightly outside it like this one, but in a cove markedly outside of town in what we might call a lakeside kind of fantasy of separateness (one that mirrors Whit's far more substantial lakeside mansion that we shall shortly encounter in all its vulgar majesty). Jeff may not be hiding, but he is not integrating very well either: his chosen ally, The Kid, seems like a ready-made emblem of his desire for companionship and settlement, yet radically restricted socially by his impairment such that only Jeff can communicate with him fluently. Jeff/Mitchum wants to be *near* this community, but apart from it too.

During the car journey Jeff tells Ann that it's time for him to tell the truth, as she once told him he would have to; they drive to Lake Tahoe, and we get a flashback of the events that led to Jeff's arrival in Bridgeport. That this is the only flashback in the entire film is quite surprising, since the film *feels* as if much more of its content is a retelling of already past events. As usual with flashbacks narrated by film characters, we should always be alert to the ways in which their telling may be subjectively distorted, even though the sequences we see here take on much the same style as the rest of the film. Jeff tells her his real name and that he worked as a private detective in New York with his partner, "a sort of stupid, oily gent by the name of Jack Fisher"; they get a call to visit a high-powered gambler, Whit Sterling, who has been shot by his girl, Kathie Moffat. As we transition to the flashback, Jeff notes that "he [Whit] was taking it in his stride, but he had friend who was a ball of fire," and we dissolve to a shot of Joe, sweating and angry, ranting about the newspaper reports of Whit's shooting in a way that seems quite hysterical in his condemnation of the press hysteria, and in marked contrast to the way we've seen him act in Bridgeport. Whit brilliantly spots that Joe's overreaction matches that of the media hysteria and tells him to smoke a cigarette. It is our first look at Kirk Douglas, who Lee Server describes as giving a "brilliantly controlled and charismatic performance" in the film; however, it is a performance propelled by a kind of mutual feeding on time and space whenever he and Mitchum share a shot.[17] Server notes a competitive edge between the actors during shooting, but whatever the truth, we see them as characters suited to one another in a homosocial pact of mutual understanding.

Their first shot together evolves out of a pan right as Joe leaves the frame and Jeff is revealed slouching in the shadows across the desk from a brightly lit Whit; the conceit of the shot is made clear by the inclusion of a statuette behind Whit's right shoulder (the far left of shot) the shadow of which is cast next to it. It means something like: we have two identical but different things in front of us (in front of the statue). Douglas, centered and toward the rear of the shot, is brightly lit so that his angular face has an icy unsculpted shape, whilst Mitchum, low in the far right of shot, looks as if he has been poured out of a bottle of shadows into the chair; he stares at a forty-five degree angle across and above Whit's eyeline at the ceiling as if utterly indifferent not only to his prospective employer, but to anything in the room at all. The composition suggests a tension that might form a balance, and this is matched by the dialogue between them. So, for example, their intelligent wit:

> WHIT: You just sit and stay inside yourself. You wait for me to talk. I like that.
>
> JEFF: I never found out much listening to myself.[18]

Lines seem to cancel each other out; being "inside yourself" means "not listening to myself," another kind of passivity or disposition that is also an occupational advantage. It is the kind of wit that Jeff's partner lacks since his dialogue seems to come from a feeble effort to mimic the lingo of hard-boiled detective fiction; when Whit expresses surprise that "she [Kathie] missed so often," Jack Fisher comments that "a dame with a rod is like a guy with a knitting needle." Whit is immediately annoyed and asks Jeff why Fisher is there: "my partner." Cut to a shot of both partners, Joe and Jack, the former standing above the seated Fisher; behind them is the same statue, but the lighting is arranged such as to disturb the perfectly cast shadow from the previous framing, so what we have is an indistinct, unbalanced assembly of shapes, faces, and objects. Both "unbalanced" partners will cause significant trouble for each other, Fisher by attempting to blackmail Jeff, and Joe by working with Kathie behind Whit's back in order to betray him *and* Jeff.

Whit explains that Kathie ran out on him, and Joe adds that she took $40,000 of his money with her. But Whit makes it clear the cash means nothing to him (he has an odd story about losing a $40,000 bet on a horse and buying the horse and looking after it "in a nice green pasture"), that he just wants the girl back. Reluctant, Jeff says he can "let it all go" until Whit offers him a healthy fee plus expenses. "Why me?" Jeff asks. "Because I know a lot of smart guys and a few honest ones and you're both"; but, again the issue between them seems to be what Whit is prepared to do once Jeff finds the girl. "I won't touch her," he claims and we cut back to a shot of Jeff, now standing, face strongly illuminated by the nearby lamp, weighing this up. It is an exemplary scene of recruitment, where the detective probes for motivation, reasons, hidden traps, and the recruiter responds with just enough cagey truthfulness that we can be both intrigued by the job and suspicious of the motives. Jeff and his partner leave, but as they wait by the elevator Fisher complains that since he won't be on the job (Whit doesn't like him, a fact that has been absorbed by both without comment so far), he still needs fifty percent of the fee as a partner. Jeff agrees. "Don't get any cute ideas," Fisher says as the elevator doors close; cut to an extreme close up of a trumpet blasting out a jazz intro with verve, an unsubtle transition that underlines, like an alarm going off, the fatefulness of Jack's words.

The trumpet takes us to a club, exclusively frequented by African Americans, and we see another reason that Jeff is the preferred man for the job. It is hard to imagine Fisher having the persistence or charm to enter and question Kathie's maid Eunice Leonard (Theresa Harris) who is drinking there with her partner. Jeff is at ease here, as he appears to be in all the "exotic" places we are taken during the flashback. He flies to Mexico City, takes a bus south to Taxco following Eunice's lead. As we hear Jeff's narration we see an aerial shot of the city, and when he mentions the Reforma Hotel we have an exterior shot of a large building—pictures that illustrate his words. (Moments of extreme legibility like this only contrast strongly with the more cognitively obstinate scenes that come later.) Our entrance to Taxco is provided by the camera anchored to the side of the bus, low down, so that we get an impressive shot of an old building against a mountain backdrop as the vehicle angles itself around a corner. Then we get a high long shot of Acapulco Beach beneath a bright mess of white clouds, fading to some street-level shots where we eventually see Jeff walking toward the La Mar Azul Café which, as he tells us, was "next to a movie house," Cine Pico. He sits in the bar opposite the cinema and drinks beer, and finally Kathie walks into his life.

All of those places, exotic and beautiful and hot and lazy: this is precisely the kind of story that Ann was angling for by the fishing lake. Ann listens to Jeff as he drives; the camera frames them from the driver's side, with Jeff nearest to us, and Ann sitting next to him, looking toward him (as we are, but from the opposite side in the passenger seat). She is, then, a kind of surrogate for the film viewer, and Jeff the holder of the imaginative authority that tells her and us the story of his past three years ago. We know that flashbacks of this kind in noir are vulnerable to claims of unreliable narration: perhaps we should take Jeff's narrative as his opportunity to organize and make sense of what happened. The images we see are available to be taken as both Ann's visualization of what he says, as well as his own (perhaps necessarily biased and partial) recollection. While driving, Jeff adopts even more intensely the persona of the hard-boiled private eye, tersely explaining that Whit was an "op—an operator: gambler." And Ann's desire to find out the sources of Jeff's secret, his mystery, is finally being satisfied even though, as he warns her, "some of it's gonna hurt you." She was, we now find, quite right to assume Jeff's past involved "all the places I've never been." It is important to keep Ann in view even in light of Kathie's first appearance, one famous as the epitome of the staggering entrance and appeal of the femme fatale in noir. Robert Pippin describes the moment eloquently:

> Femme fatale entrances in noirs often suggest the extreme view of a magical spell or mysterious erotic power that can render the male forever afterward a mere dupe, a passive victim of such power, a nonagent. The femme fatale theme is far and away the most written-about issue in film noir criticism, and there is much more to say about it, but at least these entrances do demonstrate how utterly a life can be altered in a single moment. Even doing nothing about what one feels still alters everything, because doing nothing now becomes a fateful decision, an event that then shadows everything else one does. One *cannot* now act in complete indifference to how one's fate has been altered, where "cannot" in this one of its many fatalistic

senses means that such indifference would make no sense in one's life. The depth of feeling is such that one could not recognize oneself in any picture of indifference and so cannot act indifferently.[19]

The power of such moments depends quite a bit on how willing we are to accept that "a single moment" can have quite that effect. It is not entirely clear, even in Jeff's telling (or Ann's imagining) that Kathie's entrance *is* that single moment. It is true that such moments can take on, in the light of subsequent events, a special kind of force as *the beginning* of an infatuation, or deep love. But as *Out of the Past* reminds us in these scenes, this is not done outside of self-awareness. Jeff says (tells Ann) that he *knew* what was happening to him after he met Kathie but that he was unwilling (unable) to stop it happening, and this is repeatedly echoed later in the film by the most conniving character of all, Kathie herself. He even frames his mood *as a frame* in his narration by describing the dreamlike nature of his mood before he sees Kathie walk into the bar: "I used to sit there half-asleep with a beer and the darkness, only that music from the movie next door kept jarring me awake. And then I saw her coming out of the sun." As he narrates these lines we see Jeff himself "framed" as he sits alone at a table with his beer by an arch structure that is part of the ceiling above him and two walls either side of the shot. His waiting, half-drunk, alone in a bar where any company might be welcome—certainly we see in the background other patrons with companions—is the stage or portal through which Kathie is then born "out of the sun" (from the direction of the movie house and its music), almost as if he magicked her into reality. He is jarred awake by movie music (we see him look up and notice something) and then we cut to Jane Greer walking through another frame—the brightly lit doorway.[20] The composition tells us that Jeff's imagination of himself is precisely that of a character in a genre film for whom and to whom something must and will happen eventually. And at the same time he is framed as an audience for Kathie's entrance, a spectator: not for the last time the film will recruit in its staging and handling of space and performers a "cinematic" flourish: an arrangement of figures and objects to evoke cinema, often some combination of beings or devices that see (spectator, audience, camera) and entities that are placed to be seen (objects, faces, bodies). And these cinematic visual tropes are often also pointed to by things such as frames, doorways, or most striking in this film, a rear view of characters (often their back and/or back of their head), as if we are not only being aligned with the forward direction of their seeing but at the same time necessarily denied a clear view of their facial reaction to what it is they are seeing. What is remarkable about Mitchum as a performer is that even when we are given a frontal view of his face, its expressionless nature feels often as if something is being withheld and when, as happens in several key moments, we are located behind or to the extreme side of that face, this feeling is significantly amplified. Again, this kind of camera-performer alignment often feels like a kind of cinematic ostension quite beyond the ordinary "classical" handling of mise-en-scène and cinematographic style.

As we see Kathie, he says, "Then I knew why Whit didn't care about that forty grand." Perhaps that is the first element in the tale that will "hurt" Ann, but by this point it is increasingly difficult to keep the latter even imaginatively in view. Jeff goes to pay for his beer but drops the coin, which rolls near to the table where Kathie has just sat down. As he goes to retrieve it, the Mexican tour guide, Jose Rodriguez (Tony Roux), walks in and takes their proximity to indicate a couple, asking Jeff to be seated at Kathie's table. This "meet cute" (the cinema is just outside the arched door next to them) evolves into Jeff playing the role of a lonely tourist, unwilling to see the sights because "nothing in the world is any good unless you can share it." And as he says this we have a shot of Kathie, smoking, weighing Jeff up. Given subsequent events it is plausible to assume Kathie knows exactly who Jeff is and who sent him. She is then assessing his skills as an actor and, seemingly satisfied with his performance and her capacity to match and overcome its guile, she invites him to join her at a cantina, Pablo's, that reminds her of a bar in New York. Jeff has been picked up. (The gender reversal is part of their cute banter: Jeff has bought earrings from Rodriguez for Kathie who refuses them; the joke is that he'll wear them at Pablo's.)

Up to this point it is entirely clear that Jeff has done his job for Whit very effectively: he has rapidly tracked Kathie down and, by chance, found her in a bar, and struck up a conversation (by chance again—the coin and Rodriguez's mistaking them for a couple). And while he did not have to talk or even meet her, all that remains is for him to contact Whit with her whereabouts. In the next part of the narration, he says he went to send a message to Whit saying that he'd found Kathie but that the telegram office was closed for siesta: "I was glad it was and I suddenly knew why." That is the extent of his effort to complete the job. He goes to Pablo's every night to wait for Kathie: "I drank bourbon and I shut my eyes . . . I knew where I was and what I was doing. I just thought what a sucker I was." Whatever radical change has come over Jeff, it is associated with drinking and waiting. At Pablo's he is once again alone, isolated from the other patrons, drinking steadily ("grinding it out") until, once again, Kathie emerges from the door this time born not of the sun but "out of the moonlight, smiling."

This time he needs no Rodriguez to come over to her table and sit with Kathie. A violinist is playing the kind of tune ("American music," notes Kathie) that one would expect of a film soundtrack. Their conversation is an odd echo of the first meeting: Jeff's voice-over narration (what he is saying to Ann) tells us he knew full well Kathie would come and he had to wait it out (a bit like the audience for a genre film); but their conversation is a pretend game of hiding what they both know:

JEFF: You know I've been here for two nights.

KATHIE: Thinking?

JEFF: No just waiting.

KATHIE: I haven't been lonely.

What does Jeff want? He's had two days at least to send the telegram, and we must know that the smart private eye has figured out when the siesta is. What does he mean that he sees himself as a "sucker"? We are supposed to assume that he is not only attracted to Kathie, but willing to betray his employer in order to deepen his involvement with her. And Kathie's motives are also obscure. She echoes Whit (and to some extent Ann) in her assessment of Jeff's passivity:

KATHIE: You know you're a curious man.

JEFF: You're gonna make every guy you meet a little bit curious.

KATHIE: That's not what I mean. You don't ask questions. You don't even ask me what my name is.

Kathie takes him to a gambling joint and continues to be enigmatic, suggestive, and imprecise. Jeff warns her about her gambling technique, as if she appears to be reckless or "impulsive" as he has already suggested to Whit that she may be. But this sits uneasily with Jeff's already stated opinion that Kathie was manipulative in making him wait several nights for her at Pablo's, and there is a muted sense that he is a willing participant in her plan to sucker him. It is quite explicit in the culmination of "framing" compositions after she leads him to the Acapulco beach among the fishing nets; that they kiss for the first time here, near the ocean but among the means to catch its bounty, is almost vulgar in its bold assertion that it is Jeff who has been "landed" by Kathie. Shortly after the kiss they sit near the stern of a fishing boat, and Kathie reveals she knew Whit had sent Jeff to get her, confirming our sense (and no doubt Jeff's) that she has been playing him all along. This has to be one of the more unusual parts of the story that Jeff narrates to Ann. The scene mirrors, in moonlight, the earlier scene with Jeff and Ann fishing at the Bridgeport lake; but here what Jeff wants has become opaque even to him:

KATHIE: I could have run away last night.

JEFF: I'd find you.

KATHIE: Yes I believe you would. Are you glad you did?

JEFF: I don't know.

In the light of this uncertainty Kathie continues to play the impulsive girl ("I didn't know what I was doing. I didn't know anything except how much I hated him"), but Jeff appears to mirror her. Nothing seems to fit: Why did Kathie hate Whit? Has Jeff just set aside the revelation that Kathie knew that Whit had sent him all along? The issue is whether he will turn her in to Whit, and for Kathie that means persuading Jeff that she didn't steal the money. Note that she does not deny she shot Whit in hatred. Jeff's response, "Baby, I don't care," before they kiss, is a radical abandonment of responsibility for anything—especially his own well-being—except his immediate attraction to her. He doesn't care if she stole the money, if she is playing him, if he is a sucker. The sheer relief of abdicating one's moral and professional orientation in the face of exotic and impulsive romantic and sexual promise utterly vaporizes his judgment. Everything up to the past ten minutes of the film confirms Whit's description of him as the rare detective who is both smart and honest. Why, we should ask, is Jeff so willing to let go of that? A lot depends not so much on how attractive we find Jane Greer and her performance as Kathie but how we take Jeff's credibility: his honest and hardworking commitment to his job and his sense of the way the world works. After he admits to her "I don't care," he carries on as if he has abandoned not only his mission, but any ordinary idea of what a detective should do. He is not a true detective but a slavish lover. As he narrates again we see him outside the bar opposite the cinema: he says he only saw her at night, that he didn't know where she lived, and never followed her: "I don't know what we were waiting for. Maybe we thought the world would end." In this part of his tale it seems unclear to Jeff what either of them were doing or what they wanted. He can't explain why Kathie didn't take a boat to escape and continues to describe himself as a kind of fool for love ("How big a chump can you get to be? I was finding out"). What he is actually describing is something like the seductive convulsions and entanglement of holiday romance: when they run to get out of the rain into the ersatz domestic comfort of Kathie's cottage, Jeff's narration is filled with a kind of childish longing for the moment of that cozy space: "It was a nice little joint with bamboo furniture and Mexican gimcracks. One little lamp burned. It was all right. And the rain hammering like that on the window made it good to be in there." The scene is lit so that the little lamp appears to illuminate the room from below, throwing shadows up on the low ceiling and partially lighting the rain outside the window on the trees; Kathie fetches a towel and roughly dries Jeff's hair before putting music on the record player. When Jeff takes the towel to do Kathie's hair ("now yours") she says, "No, Joe, it's all right," and as he rubs her dry she warns him to be careful: "No! My earring." Both things can be easy to miss given that the scene rapidly moves to suggest they have sex next (a shot of the wind blowing the door open and knocking the lamp over accompanied by overt swelling music evoke this, again, in a seemingly exaggerated fashion). The only Joe we know is of course Whit's partner, Joe Stephano. We have already seen how the calm and deliberate Joe who tracks Jeff down in Bridgeport is quite different from the fiery type we see complaining in the flashback about the press coverage of Whit's injury. Kathie's slip, if that is what it is, implies she and Joe may well have shared some similarly intimate moments. Later we find out that Joe is indeed another lover that Kathie uses. In fact, there is no reason to have this scene *at all* except to embed this moment and the odd detail of the earring: overtly the rainstorm providing the excuse to get the couple back to her place for sex, but also to get to the business of playful hair-drying with a towel that allows us to register, even if we do not notice, the word *Joe* and the rather large earrings worn by Kathie. It was Kathie who refused the earrings Jeff bought from Jose Rodriguez when they first met ("I never wear them"), shortly before Jeff pretend-complains to her that, "I haven't talked to anybody who hasn't tried to sell me something for ten days." The implication of the embedding of both these clues is that Jeff has missed the very thing that is being sold to him, Kathie's version of a "Kathie" that is indeed seductive and manipulative as Jeff no doubt already appreciates, but also one that in being *just this* manipulative actually masks the true depth of her criminality and betrayal. The manipulation is just a mask for a deeper form of deception. Jeff only works that out once she has left another cottage setting (also with low-key lighting) once she has murdered his former partner.

After an interim shot of pouring rain, there is a cut inside the darkened cottage where the mood has changed; it is shadowy and postcoital, and the couple talk of plans for them to get away. Jeff tells her Whit knows where they are, that they should "make a life for ourselves," and we get a shot of Kathie with her back to us. It becomes clear that Kathie is far more afraid of Whit than Jeff is; the bargain seems to be that his love for her and his wits will protect them from Whit's vengeance as Kathie warns he will be unable to forget about them.

When Whit and Joe turn up at Jeff's hotel the next day, as he is preparing to leave with Kathie, Jeff is particularly dexterous in spinning a tale that Kathie has eluded him, somehow detecting his "squeaking shoes" and implying that Whit himself misled him about Kathie's cunning nature. Somehow Kathie's earrings have appeared on a table near Jeff's cigarettes, and he deftly hides them and just as skillfully persuades the pair to join him at the bar. Once again, Douglas is adept at depicting Whit as both charming, threatening, and suspicious, as if he recognizes in Jeff the behavior of a man who has indeed met and been manipulated by Kathie. And this raises a further question—not one apparently probed by Jeff himself—of why it was that Kathie shot Whit at all. Jeff uses all his guile to throw Joe and Whit off the scent, pretending that he is professionally insulted by Whit for not doing a thorough enough job and distracting them so they don't notice Kathie's entrance for their rendezvous. But it is Whit who is the most surprising: he refuses to let Jeff quit the task ("Joe couldn't find a prayer in a bible"), despite what we now know about Kathie and her evident capacity for seductive manipulation. Is there some way in which Whit—who never forgets—*knows* about Jeff and Kathie and despite all that, lets it go? Why? Does Whit *want* Jeff to go through the same thing in order to be *more like him*: a victim of Kathie's murderous rage, a lonely gangster who craves the company and approval of a man he admires?

At this point Jeff's narration brings us back to his car journey to Lake Tahoe with Ann. "I set up an office in San Francisco," he tells her, "cheap little rat hole that suited the work I did. Shabby jobs for who'd ever hire me. It was the bottom of the barrel and I scraped it, but I didn't care. I had her." Not caring about status or respectability is the price Jeff is willing to pay for Kathie. Ann is suitably muted on this line, and Jeff seems willing to revel almost in his debasement, describing their mutual fun at living on the run, eventually enjoying themselves at the racetrack, the point where the "one chance in a million" happens and Jack Fisher sees Jeff collecting his winnings. Jeff and Kathie separate, with Jeff leading Fisher away to Los Angeles. There is considerable ellipsis here: we must assume Fisher was hired by Whit to track Kathie and Jeff down, but we also do not see the fact that Fisher had been following Kathie all along which is how he tracks them down to another ersatz domestic hideaway, another place in the woods. As Jeff arrives at the rendezvous he sees Kathie for the first time in the light—this time not sunlight or moonlight, but the headlights of his car as she walks toward the cabin. Their meeting here is another kind of role play, with Jeff offering her a lift and Kathie coquettishly hesitant, before becoming more direct:

> JEFF: You're a kind of cute little package to be walking alone at night.

KATHIE: You're kinda cute yourself to be walking alone any night.

"It was meeting her somewhere like in the first times. There was still that something about her that got me. A kind of magic or whatever it was." She is the thrill of the strange, the new, a woman who can reproduce the freshness and excitement of a first touch however familiar one is with her. A capacity, by Jeff's lights, to replenish the first flush of a sexual romance without diminishing its novelty or excitement. A fantasy.

The confrontation with Fisher in the cabin is brief and cruel. Kathie immediately suggests violence: "Why don't you break his head, Jeff?" Fisher's sense of the story is immediately contrastive with what we've heard so far: Whit, he argues, might forgive the shooting, the stolen money, even Jeff's betrayal, but not the fact of Jeff and Kathie as a couple. Being Kathie's lover on top of everything is rubbing Whit's face in it. Jeff and Fisher fight, but just as Jeff gets the upper hand and appears ready to subdue his smaller opponent, Kathie shoots and kills him. Her defense is simply that Jeff would not have done so, and that would have left them vulnerable to Whit's revenge. But that excuse is negated almost immediately when she takes Jeff's car and vanishes from the scene. If she cared about their coupledom why run from it? She leaves Jeff a gift, an emblem of herself, and Jeff finds it instantly as soon as he sees her drive away. It is a bank book in her purse with a single deposit entry for forty thousand dollars; the flashback ends and we return to the cabin of the car. It is dawn.

It is worth thinking about what Jeff did between burying Fisher's body and coming to Bridgeport. Perhaps we are meant to assume that he was done with the life of the detective, preferring a world that consisted of more straightforward transactions (which is the gist of what he will soon tell Whit); that coming to Bridgeport, somehow having the means to set up a gas station and car repair store, befriending The Kid, and wooing Ann add up to something like the life he now wants. "I buried him up there. I wasn't sorry for him or sore at her. I wasn't anything," he tells Ann, which suggests a clean conscience, ripe for a fresh start. But it also has a lining of nihilism to it ("I wasn't anything"), another way that the film's components, even in dialogue that recollects unseen events, fail to mesh. "I told you once that whatever happened was done," Ann tells him; and he replies in a way that suggests a certain recklessness in involving Ann in his life at all (certainly the way her parents and Jim will later see the matter): "I'm tired of running. I gotta clean this up some way," he says, kissing her and watching her drive away in his car (mirroring Kathie's drive away shortly before).

In his mansion Whit seems excessively pleased to see Jeff again and is further delighted by Jeff's discomfort when Kathie joins them for breakfast on the balcony overlooking the lake. It is important to appreciate that Whit and Jeff are fundamentally the same class: the former has made enough to buy the luxurious setting of the Lake Tahoe house and its "nice view," but the cost is a precarious one because he has hidden his tax liability from the government. Jeff by contrast describes the incremental, undramatic nature of his business to Whit:

WHIT: I understand you're operating a little gasoline station?

JEFF: You say it like it was hard to understand.

WHIT: Well, it is.

JEFF: It's very simple. I sell gasoline, I make a small profit. With that I buy groceries, the grocer makes a profit. They call it earning a living. You may have heard of it somewhere.

WHIT: I may have, but it wasn't from you.

In the postwar Los Angeles, in Reno, in San Francisco—all over the world—everyone is on the make except Jeff: he pumps gas, he doesn't hustle. Jeff wants to believe he lives in a capitalist world of straightforward transaction. This film is a way of pointing out to us (and to Jeff) that that world has vanished, that this is a new world of advertising and neon and deceit and where everyone is on the make, where everything is vulnerable to the hustle (rather like the Pottersville of *It's a Wonderful Life*).

Despite the differences in their material success, what Jeff and Whit share is Kathie, and it is her actions—shooting Whit, killing Fisher, and then running out on Jeff—that unite both men in a negative relation to her. Whit wants Jeff to get his income tax records from an accountant, Leonard Eels (Ken Niles), who is attempting to extort him. Jeff refuses; then he sees Kathie.

With Kathie "back in the fold now," as Whit puts it, that means Jeff is too. He has to assume that Kathie has told Whit everything about their romance, and Whit himself appeals to Jeff's sense of inner orientation: "You see Jeff, you owe me something. You'll never be happy until you square yourself." "Squaring" means something like alignment, a neatness of transaction every bit as pure as paying the grocer for groceries so that one profit generates another. There is a twinkle in Whit's eye as he presses the advantage of his putative lack of sentimentality, knowing that Jeff's commitment to his sense of right-standing is a disadvantage that advantages Whit's plans. Again, we have a moment of reluctance ("I'll pass," says Jeff to Whit a few seconds before Kathie appears at the breakfast table) that rapidly switches almost faster than the viewer can absorb it. To return to C. L. R. James's analysis, the fusion of the gangster-detective is here split apart between Whit—the unscrupulous gambler, avoiding the authority of the government's imposition of taxation and able to recruit nefarious means to do so—and Jeff, now honest, seeking a respectable life, and yet seemingly trapped in debt to a gangster by his inclination toward duty and rectitude. We see how easily Jeff starts to settle into what is clearly a trap, as he holds the chair at the breakfast table for Kathie and dutifully passes her a coffee cup and saucer as Whit chatters on about his plan. The sense of being trapped by circumstance, despite one's best efforts, is further compounded by the bare-faced dishonesty of those around him.

Resigned to comply with Whit's plan to steal the tax records, Jeff goes to his room (he's quickly agreed to stay at the Lake Tahoe mansion) and begins to write a letter: "Ann Darling" we see in close up as he writes, "I'm going to San Francisco. . ." Another jagged piece of the film that belongs nowhere in film noir. The bright morning sun casts a shadow from the nib of his fountain pen to the edge and beyond of the paper. These scenes at Whit's place have been conducted in the full light of day, and Jeff now takes the opportunity of isolation to reengage in dialogue with Ann, who he has recently kissed goodbye (for good measure he kisses her hand afterward and tells her to "keep that in your pocket"). As he writes we cut away to a medium shot of Jeff at a neat desk bedecked with higher quality "gimcracks": a vintage lamp, cigarette box, telephone, ashtray, and, just in front of his writing paper, two inkwells on a plinth between which is the small metal form of a dog, rearing back slightly on its hind legs, head turned toward Jeff as if to ask, "What's next?"

We watch movies mainly in order to observe and become involved with the imaginative entities called characters that are shown to us through a patterned, controlled selection of views. Prominent in our experience of these characters is the matter of choice, of how we get to see them do and say what they do and say. Choice is not merely a prominent dimension of the medium, but an aspect of its interest in these characters who also are shown to make choices, juggle and struggle with reasons and hesitation about doing and saying what they do and say. While it is a mistake to see them as real people, it is equally a mistake to pretend that we do not, in some odd imaginative way, take them as if they were real people, since we must do this in order to enjoy the aesthetic experience of movies at all. To be sure, some of the best movies handle this aesthetic balancing, or oddity, with skill and intelligence. But whatever we think of Jeff and Ann and Kathie and Whit, to get some grip on what they do and why they do it, we must grant them (at least temporarily and with a graded and evolving kind of commitment) a life not wholly so distant from our own. More than this, the "life" we grant those characters, and the way we are given access to them, seems to cast a light back on us, a glow that can—if we are willing to let it—illuminate our own orientation as if we were in their shoes. We see the little metal dog for a few seconds only; but like us viewers it seems instinctively rapt with anticipation, frozen in expectation. It is a tiny instance of the "cinematic evocation" mentioned earlier: it points out our relation to things put before us like movie characters. What will Jeff do next?

As if in answer, Kathie knocks and comes in and attempts to justify the fact that after killing Fisher and running out on the man she up to that point seemed to be in love with, she has gone back to live with the man she claimed to hate, whom she has previously stolen money from and shot four times. It is quite hard, both here and in the rest of the film, to figure out what it is that Kathie wants or wanted, beyond a simple recognition that she is just (eloquently, marvelously) "bad." Jeff treats her coldly, and we sense his wound from her betrayal still has a vitality to its sting, that it has not healed, despite what he told Ann moments before during their car journey to Lake Tahoe. We might recall Jeff's initial assessment before meeting Kathie that she was "an impulsive girl." "You can never help anything can you?" he tells her, "You're like a leaf that the wind blows from one gutter to another." (This latter sentiment coincides with the insult that provoked the fight between Jeff and Fisher in the cabin; it better describes Jeff's seemingly feeble willpower in returning also to the fold.) Greer and Mitchum in this scene give extraordinary performances: as Kathie, Greer exudes convincing, earnest sincerity: "I was always afraid of him and afraid of what I've done. I couldn't live that way anymore. I couldn't stand it." As he sits against desk before her, these lines seem to travel into Jeff's consciousness more than the rest, his eyes break from hers, move downward, and track slowly right; perhaps he too wants to lose the discomfort of "running" to "clean this up someway." The echo of his own desire that he hears in Kathie's pleading is only halted when she overplays the scene, claiming she'd "prayed [he'd] understand"; that sounds a wrong note. Unlike Ann, Kathie is hardly the Christian praying type. "Let's just leave it where it all is," he tells her. "Get out." Kathie leaves and he goes back to his writing, but everything has subtly shifted. For Jeff has indeed agreed to collude with Whit in stealing (somehow) the tax records, in defrauding the state, to work with the "op" again and in the knowledge that Kathie is in some unspecified way part of the same fold.[21] So, "where it all is" is something of an enigma for him and us (and no doubt Ann too if she ever receives the letter—we don't find out if she does). Jeff's commitment—what he wants—is at its most obscure here: hence we need to place as much faith in Kathie's claim that she "couldn't live that way anymore" as we do in Jeff's to make things "square" since, apart from that, there is little to go on.

Out of the Past now shifts fully into noir: it is quite striking for a film often described as an exemplar of the genre that so little of its first half really occupies that mode. Jeff's "detecting" was a straightforward following of Kathie's trail to Mexico and then literally waiting in a bar for her to walk through the door. Apart from the meeting with Whit and Joe in New York, the settings are bright and mostly in daylight except for the melodramatic scenes of romance between Kathie and Jeff among the fishing nets on the Acapulco beach and the murder of Fisher in the cabin. The next part of the film is, however, emphatically noir in making prominent the double cross and the detective struggling to understand forces beyond his control. Deborah Thomas in her book *Beyond Genre* makes the useful distinction between the melodramatic and comedic modes that film genres inhabit (the comedic or melodramatic western for example); the critical distinction is that in the former events seem under the control of some malign force, much like fate, that the characters caught up in them have little understanding of (in the comedic mode, by contrast, that authority or force is benign, benevolent). *Out of the Past* like most noirs is clearly in the melodramatic mode, but it would be wrong to say that Jeff is totally powerless in the way that, say, Ed Avery (James Mason) is in *Bigger Than Life* (Nicholas Ray, 1956). In fact, it is precisely his problem of choice that dominates the thickened plotting that Jeff is about to walk into.

The next sequence shows Jeff's arrival in San Francisco and his meeting with Leonard Eels's secretary, Meta Carson (Rhonda Fleming), at her apartment. Jeff introduces himself as "Bailey" instead of "Markham," but the flirtatious banter between them as she pours him a whiskey is obviously false until Jeff puts an end to what he calls "this Junior League patter." (So their meeting mirrors, in a compressed form, Jeff and Kathie's courtship that begins with playful deception.) Carson tells him to come to Eels's house that night to "look around" and then "in a day or so" come back there to steal the tax records; Eels will be out with her because "I'm his secretary." Even hearing this a few times, it is difficult to understand: Why would Jeff need to visit that night and then return later to steal the papers? Why not just call him when Eels is gone? "Sounds simple enough . . . like two and two make four," says Jeff, and it is only later we realize why. For it is at this moment, surely, that he realizes he is being set up: the first visit is designed such that his fingerprints are left at Eels's place, the second visit so that he can be framed for Eels's murder and presumably be apprehended at the scene after a tip-off to the police from Carson. We don't know for sure how much of this Jeff gets during this scene, but it is safe to assume he has most of it: before he leaves he grabs Carson's shoulder and warns her that he intends to come "out of this in one piece." And Carson—who resembles Kathie—fumbles her attempt at flirtation (this is a quite brilliant performance from Fleming, just falling short of the assurance and authenticity Greer brought to Kathie's approach to Jeff), for example, by speaking a little too quickly, looking at him a little too directly, ever so slightly overplaying the part.

We see Jeff waiting at night in the rain outside a bar where he meets an old friend (presumably met during the time he lived with Kathie in the city; he tells Meta Carson he knew the city "intimately"), a cab driver called Petey. Daniel Mainwaring (credited as Geoffrey Homes), the pulp fiction novelist who wrote the book *Build My Gallows High* on which the film is based (and adapted it as screenwriter), had worked as a private eye and a journalist and knew well the value of friends like Petey who would naturally encounter a broad spectrum of people as part of his job, a natural intelligence gatherer.[22] As he drives Jeff to Eels's apartment, Petey immediately remarks to Jeff that he looks "like you're in trouble":

JEFF: Why?

PETEY: Because you don't act like it.

JEFF: I think I'm in a frame.

PETEY: Don't sound like you.

JEFF: I don't know. All I can see is the frame. I'm going in there now to look at the picture.

The detective plot is now centered on how the detective is being set up. Jeff walks right into it: 114 Fulton Street is the address the camera points out for us, and inside he walks past and pauses outside a room that looks as if it is still in the process of construction, as if everything is being fabricated, like a film set. Eels's apartment (408) is lit such that its decorative objects throw shadows upward, as they did in Whit's rooms in New York. Eels himself looks like an afterthought of a character, pale, thin, ineffectual, already a kind of ghost (Meta Carson later describes him as "an underweight ghost," as if she's never met him before). Carson is sitting on the balcony outside and invites them both to join her; the whole scene is a piece of theater, an improvised exchange of calculated lies. Carson calls Jeff, "Jeffrey," her cousin, and Eels apparently impressed by their fake familial closeness invites them to stay for dinner with him. When Carson objects that they have to meet "the Bigelows," Jeff demurs, saying, "We can meet them any time." (Fleming stumbles on the B of Bigelow, giving the improvisation a miniscule lining of anxiety at Jeff's failure to play along.) Here and elsewhere in this sequence, Jeff seems determined to undermine the plan to rob Eels, to force events in order to see "the picture" in the frame. When Carson leaves the balcony he comes clean with Eels: he says he's from Tahoe "where we worry about the income tax as much as anybody else":

EELS: Frankly you don't make sense.

JEFF: Neither does my being her cousin. Or my being brought up here to leave my fingerprints around. On the other hand maybe it does.

It's hard not to think at this point that Eels is simply an accomplice pretending to be Eels; as they leave together Carson tells Jeff he's "acting like an idiot" to which he replies, "That's one way to be clever: act like an idiot." But we can't be sure. What is striking is how Jeff sees his own ill-fated entanglement with Kathie reflected in the relationship between Eels and Carson. "He's in love with you," he tells her, "doesn't your conscience bother you crossing a nice guy like that?" to which she points out that maybe he is not a nice guy, maybe he crosses people too—a kind of perverse scale where immoral transactions cancel each other out.

Petey drops Carson off at her place (The "Mason Building"— again Tourneur's composition overemphasizes the solidity of places, locations, buildings in direct contrast to their ephemeral function as sites of deception, fantasy); but Jeff goes inside where he discovers this is Eels's workplace, his offices. Carson has simply gone there to steal the tax records, rendering Jeff's role merely as a "patsy," the mark who takes the fall either for the theft or worse. Each of these discoveries seems not to come as a surprise to Jeff but rather as the expected unfolding of a preordained script. He is "seeing the frame." It's as easy as "1234," the number of the taxi company that Carson uses as she leaves the Mason Building. Jeff then tells Petey to follow Carson and then pick him up at Eels's apartment.

Once again there's no surprise to Jeff's discovery of Eels's corpse which, as he did with Fisher's body, he hides away, this time unceremoniously locking it in the closet of the apartment next door (the "unfinished" film-set space we saw him pause in earlier). Here the plot of the film becomes thickened and congested, and difficult to follow: unlike Fisher, we don't know why Jeff would conceal the body, especially in a place where it was bound to be found eventually. Bizarrely, we see him taking extra care not to use the "Call Elevator" button even though we know his fingerprints must already be all over Eels's apartment. When Petey picks him up, he asks to go to Telegraph Hill, another location we know nothing about (beyond being an iconic city landmark): "You have some bad luck?" "Yeah my timing was a few minutes off." What Jeff wanted to do was presumably forestall or prevent Eel's murder, but Carson's diversion (the trip to the Mason Building) proved enough time for whoever it was (Joe Stephano) to do the deed. At Telegraph Hill Jeff breaks into the lower level of a house where a party is going on upstairs; he begins searching the room, finds some keys, but is disturbed when a phone rings and he hides. Once again Mitchum's performance gives Jeff an air of expectancy, as if the world is running to a preordained clock or script: he smiles as the phone rings, as if its sound confirms the picture of the plot, the trap, the frame in his mind.

What happens next is even more confusing, but we are aligned so strongly with Jeff's confidence (confirmed by that smile, as if he was expecting the call to happen) that events are unfolding as expected that there is little else to do as a viewer but try to process what we cannot yet understand. The information disclosed by the guiding movement of the film is just ahead of us as viewers but at a pace with Jeff's understanding; so we stick to him closely. The phone stops ringing, and Kathie enters the room and dials. Unlike when we saw her at Whit's place in Lake Tahoe dressed in penitent white, here she wears a luxurious fur, a tight black dress with a jeweled brooch at the décolletage. The phone ring was a signal. Kathie calls Mr. Tillotson (Oliver Blake) whilst pretending to be Meta Carson; Tillotson is the apartment manager at Eels's place, and the call is a prompt for him to discover Eels's body since Kathie-as-Meta tells Tillotson she's "worried about him." But when Tillotson calls back he tells her what we already know: that Eels's corpse isn't there (he's not far away, though). Immediately Kathie calls Joe Stephanos, although the man who answers the call says he "isn't there" either. We might realize (although most first-time viewers do not) that Jeff has set a countertrap to flush out Kathie and Whit's trap, and this phone exchange confirms it. Jeff has to be the audience to it happening, and the plot we have been watching is his attempt to reveal theirs. What should he do now?

The subsequent confrontation between Jeff and Kathie not only attempts to clarify the circumstances of the "frame" but makes prominent, more than anywhere else in the film, the uncertainty of what, exactly, it is that Jeff *wants*. First of all, he lies to Kathie telling her Eels is alive because he tipped him off in time. She claims to be glad because "if he dies they'll say you did it," and Jeff now explains to Kathie his understanding of their plan as he circles her watching him (spectating) from a chair. It is another cinematic evocation, but one that echoes another medium too. As he comes to his reasoned conclusion, he's framed by two curtains on either side of a large window; as in the theater, here is the supreme moment of exegesis for his seated audience: "Whit wants to get Eels out of the picture, he wants to square an old account with me. Two birds together . . . A redhead takes me up to the chump who has to go. I have a drink, leave my prints around. I leave and somebody gets him. Eels dies and the tax papers—they were in the briefcase that Meta took weren't they?" But as he moves toward her away from this frame, he asks the central question missing from the picture: What motive on earth would Jeff have for killing Eels? The answer is as slippery as his name. Kathie makes another strange claim, that she signed an affidavit attesting that Jeff murdered Fisher. So, their "framing" story is that Jeff killed Eels because as Whit's attorney he held the affidavit incriminating Jeff. How Jeff found out about it, along with the fact that even after killing Eels he never recovered it, are matters avoided in the dialogue. Jeff leans over Kathie seated on a sofa as she pleads that "they made me" sign the affidavit: we see her face clearly, and Jeff only from the side. Instead, the issue is about memory and hatred, and the longevity of each: Jeff remarks that Whit can "really hate" and "can remember." For Jeff it is the longevity, the duration of vengeance, that has surprised him, caught him out. Kathie, meanwhile, insists on her helplessness: twice in a few seconds she claims that she could not "help" betraying him as she felt "caught." She gets up from the sofa to stand in front of Jeff as he is (apparently) staring out of the window in contemplation at this bitter turn of events. Again, we see her face clearly and Jeff from the side as she pleads her case that, she too "never stopped" hating Whit. Kathie's lie about being helpless and her admission that she can sustain long-term hatred constitute significant warning for those, like Jeff, now alert to their implications. He has just realized the depth of depravity possible when long-term resentments are cultivated; now the issue is Kathie's truthfulness about her claim that she was trapped in a situation where she was forced to help Whit and betray Jeff.

Framed from behind and to the side in close-up, Mitchum is turned away from us, so that his upper back and shoulders are in shadow; only the right side of his face is exquisitely lit by a thin line of bright light that draws the shape of his profile such that we cannot read his reaction straight on in response to Kathie's pleading. By contrast, in the same shot, Greer's performance is vivid and visible: "I couldn't help myself," she says, "I was caught too." Standing opposite to him, her eyes scan his face as she tries to convince him that "we can make them do anything" as long as they have the briefcase containing the tax records. She moves slightly closer as she says, "I never stopped loving you," the bright light sculpting the right side of his face (so bright, in fact, it highlights individual hairs of his right eyelash and occasionally strikes her right pupil creating a bright circular disk of light); "I was afraid and no good but I never stopped."

KATHIE: Even if you hated me. Did you?

JEFF: Yes.

KATHIE: But you don't now?

JEFF: No.

KATHIE: We can be together again. In a way we never were. We can go back to Acapulco and start all over as though nothing had happened.

JEFF: (*very quietly*) Yes. (*They kiss.*) How do we get the briefcase?

There is a beat before Jeff answers Kathie's question about hating, and he tilts his head further to the right, further restricting our access to his expression, almost as if what is under erasure is the thought that her desperate pleading-performance has once again made him a "sucker." His final "yes" is as croakily throated as a half-decent line delivery could get before dissolving into pure camp. By showing us her face clearly, the framing makes us a spectator literally over Jeff's shoulder; but we also see her seeing his performance too. We are ultimately sutured between two deceivers, each carefully reading the other. Our estimation of who is doing what depends in part on how much we feel and remember about Jeff's previous meeting with Kathie when she interrupted him writing the letter to Ann. As Robert Pippin points out, that scene too contained a similar composition, a "kind of half profile from behind, and so withholding of vital information about his reaction and attitudes."[23] He was utterly unconvinced at that point, even mocking her claims of praying for him. So, what has changed? Why is he seemingly convinced by her suggestion that they would return to Acapulco and "start all over as though nothing had happened"; why does he kiss her? Again, all of this is further complicated by the framing of Jeff turned away as if it is being pointed out to us that Kathie can see clearly something we cannot. But, like us, Kathie is so caught up in her performance (the framing seems to say) that she is *missing* what it is about Jeff that is deceptive. So the framing teaches us about what Kathie is missing about Jeff. The directionality of the framing means the camera's position drives us through Jeff's back toward Kathie's face, and that alignment is of course in keeping with the way the entire film up to now has aligned us with Jeff.

Additionally, the tone of the sequence so far implies strongly that it is Jeff as much as Kathie who is doing the manipulation. He needs the briefcase and the affidavit to get out of the past and its present consequences. That is, it is a key sequence indicating that he has learned to "be on the make," to "hustle," and it looks as if he will be skillful at it. Allowing Kathie to imagine she's manipulated him with a fantasy of returning to *their past* in Acapulco would be the rational strategy of a man who knows (as Kathie does not) that Eels is dead and he is in much deeper trouble than she realizes. Pippin, by contrast, contends that if we are "charitable" we might say that "Jeff is confused about his feelings, is mystified by his continuing involvement with Kathie, and just doesn't know who he loves and to what degree"[24]; however, it seems clear, given the way the film has led us along with Jeff to uncover the plot against him, that he is taking the only rational action available, whatever it looks like. That means pretending to fall for Kathie again and going along with her plan to get the briefcase. It's true that he changes sides "smoothly" as he accuses Kathie of doing, but at least we have a fairly good sense of the reasons why he does so.

She immediately tells him the briefcase is located at one of Whit's clubs in the city, the Sterling Club in North Beach, and that Meta took it there to a man called Baylord (John Kellogg). A door buzzer sounds (like a theatrical cue), and Kathie takes charge, hurrying Jeff out of the window where he came in. Whatever we think of Jeff's intentions, the next scene with Kathie and Joe Stephanos leaves us in no doubt about hers. The desperate, pleading face used during the make-up kiss shot vanishes instantly; and, like an actress backstage prepping for the next scene, she efficiently puts her fur back on and answers the door. It opens to frame Stephanos. Joe reports that he's been drinking at a bar: "I must be slipping," he tells her. Kathie is angry: "I guess you must be." "He just stood there shaking so hard he couldn't even pray. I never saw anyone so afraid to die. I didn't like it." As in the scene in Marny's Café, Paul Valentine plays the gangster type with reluctant menace. His appearance so soon after Kathie's performance for Jeff and, now, her cold disappointment in his failure to kill Eels (so she initially thinks) ought to remind us of our initial encounter with Joe in Bridgeport, especially the scene in Marny's Café.

This small sequence at the beginning of the movie alerts us to two ways in which our perception of the world can be distorted. The first human the film depicts is Joe himself driving into Bridgeport, the camera anchored to the rear of his convertible, so that we see him driving from behind, only the shape of his upper body and hat visible at first, in a compositional tendency that, as we have already seen, becomes a motif in this film. Far from hiding a sense of his expression and face, the framing paradoxically allows us to project the force and vitality of the composition itself *onto* our imaginative sense of his interiority: in this case the force has strong directionality and purpose, a kind of direct bullet-like trajectory, one not to be put off course. (In stark contrast to the deflated nature of Joe's entrance to the room in Meta's apartment where he meets Kathie.) In Marny's Café he overhears the conversation between her and Jim, where the former is clearly drumming up some local melodrama by stoking

Jim's jealousy about Jeff and Ann's regular dalliance, namely their daily "fishing" trips.

"Bailey don't miss nothing," Marney says, "Neither do you," retorts Jim. "I just see what I see," she responds, and Jim comes straight back with, "You sure you don't see what you hear?" But Marny straightforwardly avoids the implication she is distorting reality by pointing out to Jim that nothing *can* happen in the town that she doesn't hear about, and once again she insists, "I'm just saying what I see." And the fact is, at least in this case, *she is right*. Bailey and Ann are clearly in love, and if Jim has any claim to be a rival it is indeed odd that he seems so little bothered by the fact this is public knowledge apparently discussed freely at the local café. The "cost"—if that is how one feels about it—of having a romantic life in Bridgeport is being seen to have one.

After Jim leaves abruptly, Joe offers the laconic comment that "you've talked enough" and, undeterred by this, Marny warms to her theme, this time giving it the strength of a universal maxim: "Seems like everything people ought to know they just don't want to hear. I guess that's the big trouble with the world." What is it that we "ought to know" such that the world would be less troublesome? That the object of our love loves another? That she is impulsive, murderous? What if we see something—know it—yet don't want to hear—think it? One of the oddities in reading criticism about the femme fatale in film noir is how easy a time they get in any moral evaluation of their actions. Kathie Moffat, Phyllis Dietrichson (Barbara Stanwyck) in *Double Indemnity* (Wilder, 1944), Kitty March (Joan Bennett) in *Scarlet Street* (Lang, 1944), and even Judy Barton (Kim Novak) in *Vertigo* (Hitchcock, 1958), as well as many others, all carry these qualities of what Jeff quips to Whit as the "impulsive girl," or the wanton, an ultimately destructive inability to hew to the codes of decent morality.[25] But none of these women are "wantons" in the way Jeff means (if he actually means that); they are a match and more for the men that get entangled with them. Kathie is a clever, skillful, and manipulative murderer, who not only killed the unarmed Fisher in cold blood, but sets up Jeff to take the blame for the murder of Eels in order to facilitate Whit's security and revenge on Jeff. She also seems to take great pleasure in doing these things. That is morally repugnant behavior. And at the same time we may wonder why, as viewers of the film, we can find such behavior (as I do, not only here but also with Phyllis, Kitty, and Judy) aesthetically thrilling and somehow more morally courageous (if ultimately obnoxious) than the worlds in which they find themselves forced to operate. Noir's doubleness ploughs all the way down to the rudiments of shared moral life.

Given what we observed at Marny's Café, when we hear Kathie's pleading to Jeff it is hard not to be extremely skeptical about "seeing what we hear" and to grant Jeff at least the same powers of skepticism. For, like Joe on his arrival in Bridgeport, it is framed in such a way that the force of our imaginative assessment of her pleading is funnelled like a beam of light through the shadow of Jeff's profile and the lit side of his face as her big eyes switch from side to side to assess the impact of her performance, her lies. We certainly "ought" to know, as Marny tells us, what we may not want to hear: that Jeff is caught up with a very dangerous group of people. Indeed, if we do not, then the force of the film, its sheer drama, starts to ebb away. And we fail to grant Jeff as having learned the lesson of *his* past, that he must now, not as an honest gas station owner but as a modern hustler in a world of operators, bring to the table in this contest all his powers of performance such that his acquiescence to her plan and the kiss that seals it is as convincing as it has to be.

There is a delicious moment, perhaps the acme of Greer's performance, when it dawns on her that after questioning Joe, Jeff has moved Eels's body and effectively cheated her into telling him the location of the briefcase, possession of which allows him, as she told him (in fact truthfully), "to get them to do anything." She stands against the door, her eyes tracking down and left following the thought as it evolves, as Joe asks, "What's going on?" and she answers, "I don't know." And before the shot dissolves to the exterior of the Sterling Club, we see her eyes frozen and bright as if caught between fear and rage.

Jeff's private eye costume acts as a kind of magic cloak as he enters the club and effortlessly penetrates the manager's office, socking Baylord in the act of lighting a fat cigar, calling off his security, and immediately rifling through his desk for the briefcase. Baylord is out of shot, but once Jeff has the briefcase he stores it in a fluid motion within his great trench coat and, in a triumphant gesture, uses the fancy lighter on the desk to spark up a cigarette. The next shot is emblematic of that triumph, once again from behind as Jeff in silhouette walks down the shadows of the corridor, bullshits the inept guards, and vanishes in a cab. Next we see him arranging his escape by aircraft from the city and mailing the briefcase for safety; he quips to his postman helper, "You know sometimes a bad memory is like an ill wind, it can blow somebody luck," and we know that memory is Kathie. He's won. Instead of being captured by the memory of betrayal (like Whit) he has, in a stylish, clever, and effective way, overcome his past. Imagine vanquishing one's enemies through cunning, courage, and playing them at their own manipulative game—it might make one lyrical.

As he leaves the building Jeff is immediately apprehended by Joe and bundled into Petey's cab. Joe takes the briefcase we thought we saw Jeff mailing a few seconds ago, and his next journey down the corridor in the Sterling Club is as a prisoner. Kathie sits in the manager's office, and Baylord opens the briefcase to find the San Francisco telephone directory inside. One step ahead? Jeff tells them he could send the files to the Treasury Department. What comes next is another bid by Jeff to maintain the performance he sold to Kathie. When asked how he knew about their location, Jeff claims he had Meta Carson tailed, hence he covers for Kathie. But now he must know that Kathie knows he manipulated her in order to find out the location of the briefcase. What is he selling her now? Why is he covering for her? The deal is he gives Baylord, Joe, and Whit the files in return for telling them where Eels's body is located, and they give him the affidavit framing him for Fisher's murder which is still in Eels's safe. As Baylord points out, only four of them knew about the affidavit so somebody talked: "Did Meta tell you?" Kathie asks as she moves toward the door. Kathie effectively is asking Jeff to continue the performance of covering for her, just as Meta asked him to follow her to dinner with "the Bigelows," but in another mirroring moment Jeff inexplicably refuses to bite: "No. Sorry." This moment can be confusing for the audience unless we are keyed into Jeff's emergent identity as a knowledge hustler. It's as if he's testing her powers of improvisation, her security as part of this team, the depth of her involvement. But that goes for the rest of them too: he leaves them to figure out how to get the files and avoid revealing to Whit the depth of their mess-up of the plot to frame him.

The final half hour of the film progresses rapidly, and the legitimate forces of law and order are now far more prominent, making clear the stakes to all participants. Tillotson, Eels's apartment manager, has called the police, making it impossible for Carson and the others to get the affidavit; Jeff watches from a distance as their cab avoids the squad car outside the Mason Building. Kathie calls Whit at the Blue Sky Club in Reno and tells him (in code) that their plan has gone badly awry, warning him not to go home to Tahoe. All that is left for Joe and Kathie to do now is find Jeff and force him to give them the papers.

We now cut back for the first time in over an hour to Bridgeport and it is morning, a worn white picket fence in the foreground, the cozy lights of the town in the distance. A boy on a bike throws newspapers into gardens because even here news travels, as it does to Ann's parents' house. For the first time we see her father as he opens their front door and collects the paper, and Ann comes down the stairs fixing her hair as he reads the headline: "Bridgeport service station operator sought in San Francisco slaying." (Note the usage of "operator" as a call-back to Jeff's explanation to Ann of what it is Whit does for a living.) Kathie and Joe have framed Jeff for the Eels and Fisher murders. "I knew he was no good," says Ann's mother, an "I told you so" moment for these parents who seem little concerned with the impact on Ann. They are lightly sketched as forgettable types, so thin in fact that it is little wonder that Ann might seek a romantic partner of more substance and mystery. More sketched types cluster around the police station as we hear over the radio a voice announcing that Bridgeport has been blocked off; if Jeff is now there, he is trapped in the place he once again escaped to.

And for the first time since the beginning of the film, Jim appears. In some ways he is the younger version of Ann's parents, genuinely concerned about Jeff's criminality as a threat to Ann, but knowing full well that if Jeff does return to the town he'll reach out to her. Where Jeff is, what he wants, what he can do—all of these things are in suspension; all we can know is that The Kid has locked up his gas station and has vanished too. As one of the cops puts it, "I'd want a partner." We are now in a world where Jeff's guile and courage confront vast impersonal forces whose perception of the world is as partial as it is dominant: the media and the armed forces of the state. Whit can play poker in his club in Reno with impunity, but he is surrounded by those for whom trust is transactional. By contrast, Jeff is hiding in the very landscape of wooded mountains we saw during the titles of the film and his fishing trip with Ann.

These natural elements supply the iconic backdrop for the Western frontiersman dreaming of domesticity; but it is the loyalty of Ann and The Kid that are precisely the things the state forces will weaponize in order to capture him. This turns us once again to the sheer excitement of C. L. R. James's fascination with the fusion of the gangster and detective, for it captures the ways in which the masses' own communal bonds and desires can be turned against them. We have witnessed Jeff's brilliant attempts to turn an ill wind into good fortune, and now he is trapped in the town that was the receptacle for his dreams of a better, ordinary life. So, there are two kinds of "suckers": the ones who fall for creatures like Kathie Moffat, for the spell that allows one to abdicate responsibility for building a good life; and those who want to live that life by wit, cunning, and hard work but are blocked by the very forces intended to protect it.

The cruelty of such a trap is given expression in the next scene in which Jim discovers Ann near the mountains, waiting next to a brook. She defends Jeff's reputation and expresses her loyalty to him. "You expect me to help him get away?" says Jim, petulantly turning away from her. It's a small moment, but it indicates that however hurt Jim is by Ann's love for Jeff it stops just short of being vicious. And the next scene, at Whit's place in Lake Tahoe, is equally revealing. Remember that Kathie has warned Whit to stay away. Now we see Joe and Kathie with The Kid, sent on Jeff's behalf to negotiate with Whit. As Joe tells Kathie, The Kid can read lips: he literally has to "see" to "hear." But what Kathie tells him is a trap: that they are sending for Whit and need to know where to find Jeff once Whit arrives back at Tahoe. The Kid writes something down and leaves. As they watch him go, Kathie makes a gesture to Joe with her eyes (we see what she means—follow him and kill Jeff).

During these scenes the mountains are prominent as part of the setting, and the next shot is the most emphatic of all, placing The Kid's car against the backdrop of a vast craggy mountain that dwarfs its surroundings, as if the indifferent crust of the planet is crouching toward the mortal events unfolding upon it. As Joe follows him we get a spectacular long shot of his black noirish profile negotiating the slanted rocky side of the mountain, high long wisps of cloud above and dark evergreens thickening the foreground, with seemingly endless ranges in the distance. The gangster killer of noir is out of his element in an elemental world. Joe tracks The Kid below him in a ravine, fishing in a fast-running stream, and as he does so, he notices Jeff also wearing the noir trench coat, standing beside a pathetic tent (his poor hideout) drinking coffee from a tin cup, smoking a cigarette. When Joe first set eyes on The Kid he got his attention by callously flicking a spent match at his back; now the gesture is returned, mirrored. As Joe pulls a gun and fires at Jeff, The Kid hooks the back of his jacket with the fishing line and pulls him off balance into the ravine below. In a beautiful gesture, The Kid begins winding the line in. There's something equally powerful about the exchange between Jeff and the boy afterward, when the latter gives Jeff his signed appraisal of Kathie and Joe (unintelligible to us nonsigners): "Cute kids aren't they?" says Jeff in response.

It is difficult to see what move is now left for Jeff or why he would want to see Whit short of fully betraying Kathie, giving him the tax records in return for the affidavit. Even if that happens Jeff is a wanted man, and neither Kathie nor Whit are likely to make convincing witnesses for the defense even if they were willing to play ball. The film avoids giving us a chance to wonder too much about this by immediately playing a confrontation between Kathie and Jeff.

Sleeping in the shadows at Lake Tahoe, Kathie is woken by Jeff once again breaking in through the window. (This is a man who can't avoid walking into frames.) Also, the symbolic accumulation of the film is cashed out in these final scenes—all that talk about fishing (which Whit was supposed to be doing) and "Fisher" opens our imaginative ears to matters of hook, line, and bait.) They go down to meet Whit, and once again Kathie tries to align Jeff with her alleged vulnerability ("Don't let him trick you"). The setting is a heavily furnished library, but we see Whit burning papers as Kathie and Jeff come in. The deal Jeff proposes is that Whit pins the Eels murder on Joe, gives him fifty thousand "to spend my waning years in Mazatlán," and sends Kathie to the "woman's prison in Tehachapi" for the murder of Fisher. At this point Jeff is under maximum pressure, although he carries himself with the assured calm and focused cunning that has characterized his behavior since his reunion with the both of them. As becomes clear, his plan is to make plain to Whit Kathie's true nature by showing him that not only did she lie to him about Fisher's murder but that she has continued to work behind his back by recruiting Joe to murder Jeff (there are further implications there about her possible relationship with Joe, but the film leaves this unexplored). But Whit greets Jeff with a line that is repeated often in the film and once more after this: "Let's get down to business. Start all over again, right?" Starting again is not merely the mythic foundational bedrock of the nation's cultural imagination but an insistent promise that whatever the past and its traumas, we have the agency, the capacity, the resilience, confidence, and fortitude to begin again. Kathie came crawling back to Whit, begging for forgiveness because Jeff had murdered Fisher; panicked, lost, helpless (her best acting role) she had no choice. But Whit is about to find out that the past can certainly be altered by the present, and everything that he had assumed up to that point was based on her betrayal of him. We actually can see how this cuts into him like a wound and the chilling response it prompts.

Performance is critical here, in particular who gets to occupy the frame at any one time. After hearing Jeff's plan to lift the frame from him, Kathie moves to get up—presumably to make her countercase to Whit—but Jeff roughly grabs her arm and slings her back onto the sofa saying, "You make me nervous." We then cut to a two-shot, Whit and Jeff, as Jeff points out to him that his only choice is to send Kathie to the cops, to prison for Fisher's murder. He *knows* of course that Whit thinks *he* killed Fisher, that Kathie has lied to Whit, and this is the moment where he captures her (off-screen) in a fine pincer movement. "I'm not framing any woman," says Whit; it's worth remembering at this point why it was that Jeff was hired in the first place—to find Kathie, not the money, because "you'll know when you see her." It means, perhaps, that Whit has never recovered from his infatuation with her, has, as we have seen, even been prepared to forgive her shooting and years-long romance living with Jeff in San Francisco (a lot rests on the ambiguity of his claim to Jeff that if she is brought back, "I won't touch her"; the menace with which Douglas delivers the line leaves enough ambiguity open to make it credible Jeff would betray his job not only because of his own infatuation but because he wanted to protect Kathie from Whit's vengeance). But here Douglas delivers the line with absolute sincerity and is even affronted when Jeff mocks it ("When did you reform?"). Jeff sits down next to Kathie so that the next shot isolates Whit standing and has Jeff next to Kathie as she confesses: "I'll say you killed him. They'll believe me." Greer's face evolves during these lines to reveal malicious, vicious confidence in her ability to manipulate anyone and the law itself. But the confidence implicates Whit's credulity as just one more of Kathie's "suckers" (as he puts it a few moments later). Jeff now completes the pincer move: "Go on Kathie, tell him about Joe." Another two-shot, this time frontal of Jeff and Kathie watching incredulous at his exposure of her, explaining the circumstances of Joe's death. Kathie now leaps from the sofa to plead her case at Whit's side, but the damage is done. The point Jeff makes is not so much that Joe is dead, but that he was working for Kathie, trailing Jeff with the intention of killing him; it opens the possibility that Kathie (as we have seen) has been running Whit's operation behind his back. The shot evolves elegantly, the camera moving right to lose Kathie and follow Whit as he turns his back (petulantly throwing the scroll of papers he has been holding into a wooden box), so that the shot mirrors those we have seen before, with the man turned away but the force and direction of his thoughts *intensified* (not defined or clarified or stated, but emphatically *there*) as Jeff's words land on his back in a way that alerts us precisely to how he *looks* even though we don't "see" it in a conventional way: "Don't look so stricken Whit. You'll get over it. I did."[26]

We have seen how. After Kathie kills Fisher, and Jeff discovers that she had indeed stolen the money and was therefore a calculating murderer as well as a liar (her apparent arduous devotion to him implying she found *more* pleasure in having her man in these circumstances than any other), he gives up the life of the urban private eye and starts again in Bridgeport, even allows himself a fantasy of settlement. If he could learn to fish properly (Ann has good advice), he might be able to take advantage of Marny's offer, displayed on the sign outside her café, to freeze his catch. But Jeff had the advantage of Kathie fleeing the scene of the crime, absenting herself from his life, clearing the way for renewal; Whit doesn't get that chance.

In the final move, this time in another shot that cuts ninety degrees to the right of Whit who has not moved from his stony staring ahead near the wooden box, Kathie now in the foreground with her back to camera stands in front of Jeff who questions her in a way that reveals Whit for the sucker he truly is: "One thing, Kathie. Did it take much persuasion to make you say I killed Fisher? Come on. Feed my ego. Tell me he beat you. Tell me he had to drag every word out of you." At the word "drag" Whit turns to look at them both, and we should notice now that Whit's earlier assertion that he "wouldn't touch her" was indeed part of his code *up to now*:

he doesn't frame women or beat them. All that is about to change. It is a breathtaking exposure of Kathie's mendacity, but also deadly: as Jeff leaves the room so that they can talk it out, he has a well-earned grin on his face.

The soundtrack becomes silent as Whit closes the sliding doors behind Jeff (who is merely waiting by the fire in the next room) and walks back toward Kathie, explosively slapping her face as hard as he can.[27] Everything in our experience of this film is colored by how we take the truthfulness of the characters and their actions we see. Kathie reacts like someone who has never been slapped, certainly not by Whit. It is the violence of the infuriated cuckold, the betrayed, fooled lover, the man of strength brought down to his baby, infantile stature. It is as if only violence can break through lies, only the physical shock of the face being stunned, stung in such an atrocious manner that, broken open, a flicker of truth may emerge on it. But this physical violence is overshadowed by the way Whit now proposes to punish Kathie; he conjures a world where the past itself becomes vengeance, a world where she is permanently in fear of its return:

> What a sucker you must think I am. I took you back when you came whimpering and crawling. I should have kicked your teeth in. No, I'm not going to. Not now Kathie. We'll let the law push you around . . . You're gonna take the rap and play along. You're gonna make every exact move I tell you. If you don't I'll kill you. And I'll promise you one thing it won't be quick. I'll break you first. You won't be able to answer a telephone or open a door without thinking, "This is it." And when it comes it still won't be quick. And it won't be pretty. You can take your choice.

Seeing that Whit is implacable, a close shot of Greer reveals the moment where Kathie composes herself and decides what to do next (murder Whit); Greer's performance indicates the breathtaking capacity of her character to shift from pleading victim to calculated operator in a matter of brief eye movements and slight and incremental adjustments of facial expression. (Lasting under a second, these cluster of performative gestures might be written up as: Whit says I can take my choice. So be it. But I have the choice to remove the choice-giver, too, and that is what I now choose to do.) It is possible to argue that none of this is clear until the unfolding of plot events tells us so, but movies have the capacity, as most other works of fiction do, to confect experiences that allow us to register possibilities without giving us the time to reflect upon or even notice that they are such. One of them, fairly obvious given Kathie's consistency in dealing with obstacles, is that she also notices that Whit has failed to kill her, a mistake that she would never make herself in the same circumstances. We only need observe her actions at the end of the movie to see how this expression now is fully cashed out by them. In case there is any doubt, notice the way, as Whit and Kathie enter the room where Jeff has been waiting, Kathie leans against the wall, arms folded, as if impatient at the men's business taking place next to her: she has other plans for both of them.

Their negotiation appears remarkably trusting, a mutuality as joint-holders of the Kathie-is-to-blame cup, that binds them in an odd picture of homosocial dignity. Jeff reassures Whit that he won't cross him again because, "I crossed you once. I know better than to try a second time. I got a reason for wanting to be let alone." Jeff stares into the fire as he says this: it is I believe simply impossible to imagine at this point that he harbors a shred of affection for Kathie, or that he is in any way vulnerable to her pleading. If the thought was possible before that lies with Greer's remarkable power to convey performance-as-performance, and Mitchum's matching skill in rising to the occasion in his depiction of Jeff as a fast learner in the field of emotional deception and fake devotional declaration. Her mistake is to underestimate his capacity for agency, to imagine that his sense of himself was less skilled and less assured than hers. Whit agrees that he will get Jeff's money from Reno and organize a plane to meet him at dawn and Jeff leaves.

The final scenes of the film are painful to watch, particularly if we are minded to heed James's description of the popular arts as one where "the individual demands an esthetic compensation in the contemplation of free individuals who go out into the world and settle their problems by free activity and individualistic methods"[28]; Jeff, Whit, and Kathie represent versions of this, but only Jeff avoids a pathological descent into murder and nihilism in part because his past ("Baby, I don't care") has precisely taught him the consequences of doing so. The pain of the film is that even with the strongest cunning and the greatest courage, Jeff cannot disentangle himself such that his character can stand as a force of "compensation." Jeff is more than a victim of fate, without choices: the final scenes are all about the strangeness of his still having a choice even in the most restricted of circumstances.

Leaving the drama of Lake Tahoe, we watch as Ann sneaks out of her parents' house accompanied by a soundtrack that feels somehow magical and elegiac, almost hopeful. She is being followed by Jim (while, as we later find out, The Kid is leading the cops away from the town). She journeys through autumnal trees, their branches creating congested cradles and spikey spokes of shadow; from these Jeff emerges and Ann's face is bathed in a glow of welcome. It is perhaps too easy to take Ann as a mere cipher, an emblem of small-town virtue, of Christian fortitude and forgiveness, but we should also remember that she is the person who Jeff has invested everything in, risking a great deal even coming here to meet her. And her questions to him are searching and relevant—they destabilize him to the extent that the mystery of his own motivation is put before him to contemplate:

JEFF: You believe everything I say, don't you?

ANN: Everything you say I believe.

JEFF: I don't know why I do this. I don't know why I let you come back into my stinking life. Why I don't slap your face and send you home. I don't know.

We have been warned about seeing what we hear. The dialogue is congested with allusions to the film's own past, even to the extent that Ann mirrors Jeff's question by repeating his words back to him instead of saying yes. What Jeff says is equally a mirror of what Whit may well have been thinking about Kathie when we saw him from behind a few moments before: he did indeed slap her face and threaten to send her, if not home, to jail. But as Jeff talks it is clear why he does all these things: he gradually moves closer to her, the inky shadows sliding and evolving across his trench coat, to tenderly hold her. And it is reasonable for Ann to ask if he's "seen her again"; for the question is the extent to which such a deep love, the kind that Jeff narrated so effectively to Ann in the car, might leave its hooks as well as its scars on anyone. But after his effective—even brutal—betrayal of Kathie we cannot doubt his response to her question about the extent of his feelings for her:

ANN: Was it the same?

JEFF: I saw her and it was nothing.

ANN: She can't be all bad. No one is.

JEFF: Well, she comes the closest.

When Jeff says he will see Kathie one last time (which comes as a surprise I think since we might assume he would simply rendezvous with the plane as arranged with Whit), Ann suggests that he look at her and "look at yourself" in order to gauge if he has any love left for her, but Jeff is adamant:

JEFF: I don't have to find out I know it now. (*He kisses her.*)

ANN: That's all I wanted to hear.

JEFF: You know maybe I was wrong and luck is like love. You have to go all the way to find it.

ANN: You do to keep it.

While not denying a kind of sentimental childlike sense to these lines, there is some truth we should find in them. If love and luck are the same—one has to be enormously lucky to find love, especially reciprocated love, and many lovers in fiction are a lot less than lucky—then the key seems to be a willingness to "go all the way," which I take to mean not merely the effort and work of consistent companionship but also the risk and the danger of giving oneself to the practical realization of a felt ideal. Whatever its apparent simplicity and naiveté, it is not a bad foundation for growth, family, and settlement. It is an emblem of two people willing to face and take on the risks of a new start.

But promises made in the fairytale shadows of a wood need to withstand the historical reality of the wider community, its meanness and prejudice. After his meeting with Ann, Jeff is confronted by Jim who has followed them. Once again framed from behind, Jeff pulls a gun (up to this point we had no idea he owned one), but he quickly puts it away when Jim reveals that he was going to kill him, or call the cops, but didn't. What stopped him was hearing what Jeff said to Ann. He doesn't say what bit of that conversation has moved him, but he does let Jeff know that Ann matters to him too (this is not so much a claim on Ann, but I take it as a reason he doesn't want to hurt Jeff, and hence Ann): "I grew up with her. I've loved her ever since I fixed her roller skates. I don't know whether I'm good enough for her but I know you aren't . . . You told her yourself you didn't know why you let her back into your dirty life. I don't know who you were or what got you where you are or where it's gonna take you. She's not going with it."

This protectiveness, an understandable concern from someone who loves Ann but whom Ann does not love in return, plays upon the very doubts that Jeff and Ann seem to have moments before put behind them. Jim's words echo the way that Kathie tells Jeff he should orient himself to the past: as a template for continuing and future action. These words argue that Jeff *ought* to see himself as irredeemably tarnished by the past, and that it would be reckless of him to pull Ann into a world where she would have to share that moral uncleanliness. But by my lights, Jeff is having none of it: it smacks of the very pious self-righteous adoration of virtuous hygiene that Ann herself (remarkably, in her comments about Kathie) rejects. Little wonder that Jeff ignores him with the stinging retort, "Why don't you tell it to the law? Then all the rest of your life you can tell her how you did it."

When Jeff arrives back at Lake Tahoe he discovers the body of Whit, murdered by Kathie. She has changed costume, wearing an austere almost nun-like set of clothes, undecorated. She straightforwardly asks Jeff to come with her: "You're running the show now?" he asks, clearly ready for another performance. She leads him to the balcony where they had breakfast with Whit, but now it is night and the mountains under cloud in the distance prompt her to conjure memories of Acapulco for Jeff—that time when they were in the midst of her first performance, which she now claims was merely her authentic self there for all to see: "I never told you I was anything but what I am. You just wanted to imagine that I was. That's why I left you. Now we're back to stay." She left him because he imagined things, was fanciful. "We're starting over" back in Mexico she tells him. Her final gamble is, like Jim, to assume that Jeff really believes he is dirty and worthless, to appeal to the authority of his past self, his past feelings as the authentic compass for his present moral actions. Reversing the critical compositional set up earlier in the film, the camera is now behind the hood that Kathie wears so that we can see the impact her words have on Jeff's face: "If you're thinking of anyone else, don't—it wouldn't work. You're no good for anyone but me. You're no good and neither am I. (*Camera cuts to behind Jeff.*) That's why we deserve each other." And *it is Kathie*, clearly, who pulls him in for a kiss, wrapping her right arm forcefully around his neck and holding his left shoulder with her other hand; and *it is Jeff* who stops the kiss by raising his hands underneath her raised arms and pushing her back. When Jeff fishes for information about the plane and the money, she curtly reminds him, "I'm running the show, don't forget." Robert Pippin describes the scene differently and sees this as evidence of Jeff's "lack of clarity about how he finally feels about Kathie":

> No one can be sure about any of this, but it seems to be that *even at that point* the kiss is not completely staged (a lot comes down to how you read the position of his hands), or merely strategic on Jeff's part, and, in another startling reversal, it appears genuine *on Kathie's part*. He appears to visibly wilt or melt yet again, as if he realizes that Kathie is right. Neither of them *is* any good; they belong together. That is, she is encouraging Jeff to realize something about his fate, that neither of them belongs in the square or straight world, content with the limited room for maneuver as agents that fate allows them.[29]

I think Pippin has to squint quite a bit as a reader of this film in order to make that case, and even he concedes that in the next and final scenes, Jeff does indeed take charge of the show and "ends up an agent."[30] In fact, as far as that scene goes, even Kathie realizes that her bid to activate Jeff's self-loathing, his nihilistic "don't care" has not quite stuck—note the way she hesitates as they leave the balcony and she walks through the windowed frame of the door; it is a minute hesitation, a mere beat, but it is enough to signal to us that, once again, she has failed to recapture his devotion even temporarily, and she knows it.

Jeff is now faced with the only moral path left to him: he must contact the police alerting them to Kathie's whereabouts (or his, they amount—now—to the same thing) while protecting himself as much as is feasible. He knows that Kathie has already murdered Whit and has no real use for him, particularly given his less than convincing performance (although how willing should he have been? It is, once again, a carefully graded display of cunning on Jeff's part in the midst of considerable danger). Even though we know he is armed and has talked his way out of tough situations throughout the film, facing down the armed forces of the state with Kathie at his side is a terrible risk. He hasn't in any real sense been "trapped by his past," but by real and malevolent forces directly in his present that, despite his best and often ingenious efforts, he has not been able to avoid. So while Kathie goes upstairs to collect the bags, he calls the police.

Moments before, as they left the balcony he told her to pack a couple of bags: "Put a few things in for me"; "I have," she responded. Now upstairs, we see her take a pistol from a wardrobe and place it in a small briefcase (it is not clear if this is the case containing the money). That is another signal that what Kathie has planned (packed) for Jeff is death. She takes the little case downstairs and joins Jeff who is pouring them a drink in front of the fire. Now it is his turn to recall their past: "Remember La Mar Azul? [the bar where he first saw her] We owe it all to Jose Rodriguez. I wonder if he'll ever know what a bad guide he was." It was Rodriguez who provided the opportunity, by chance, for Jeff to introduce himself to Kathie; but he was never their guide; it was Kathie, in fact, who promised to be Jeff's guide. Kathie doesn't take the implication—"We deserve a break," she says to which Jeff responds, "We deserve each other" and violently throws his glass into the fire. Does he believe that right now? Again, I doubt it. I think that even if this is part of his play, an apparent acquiescence to her claim they are both no good, it can also be taken as a further bid to delay their journey, to allow the police time to arrive. The gesture of throwing the glass can both be a true expression of his frustration that he has ended up with Kathie despite his best efforts, as well as a performative underlining of the "deserve each other" line. He walks slowly behind her as they go outside to the car carrying the larger (unarmed) suitcase, and he even pretends that their car won't start until Kathie reaches down to pull out the choke and they exchange a glance full of mistrust. Jeff is playing for time, but his options are diminishing. As they drive ahead through the wooded mountains, Kathie is framed similarly to Ann when she listened to Jeff's story; but now they reach a police roadblock, Kathie pulls the gun from the little case, and shoots Jeff. She grabs the steering wheel, fires at the police, who kill both of them with submachine gun fire, and their car crashes. The cop's torchlight reveals Kathie's corpse next to the money; they open the driver side door and Jeff's body falls out. Half cloaked in shadow, his right hand flat on the earth.

Sunshine, the shadow of the American flag against a white building, a crowd of people as Jim escorts Ann from what must be an inquest hearing. His miserable lines to her describe a future not of strange places and exotic views, but of confinement, routine, domestic desperation:

> JIM: Too many people. Too much talk. Maybe that's why I like this town. Here three people are really a crowd. Let's get in the car and get away from them. I won't talk to you, Ann. I just wanna be with you.
>
> ANN: Thanks Jim. But I can't.

He's hardly an estimable prospect; Ann walks away over to Jeff's gas station, where The Kid has nothing to do except trace his thoughts in the dirt with a stick. She says to him, "You can tell me. You knew him better than I did. Was he going away with her? I have to know." She asks him again and he nods. For a brief moment as she walks away we see her stricken face; and then in long shot she walks up to Jim's sheriff's car, gets in, and they drive off (not toward the mountainous woods, but a low-lying almost featureless landscape). The Kid looks up at Bailey's name on the gas station sign and salutes it with his finger, as if to say, "I did what you asked, she'll live better not thinking about you as a lost lover, but a lost betrayer of love." The virtue of this moment is underlined by the little chapel prominent in the background as he turns away and the film ends. One can only take this as remotely uplifting if one believes Ann gets what she deserves, because it is hard to imagine a world where one might think

Jeff does. What he wanted, to be in this small town with Ann as a companion is, effectively, what Jim gets, and yet we feel for peculiar reasons that this is another kind of betrayal, that even Jeff's final redemptive gesture empties the town of meaning, deadens it in some odd untranslatable way. For however noble is the secret that only we and The Kid know (and we might wonder how The Kid knows this at all, or whether knowing Jeff well he imagined that Jeff would want this response rather than one that might bind Ann's heart forever to *their past*), it cannot negate the erasure of Jeff's vitality, imagination, wit, and courage from the somewhat shabby world he has left behind. Whereas Gould's Marlowe wanders his world apparently indifferent to its moral degeneracy until the very end ("It's OK with me"), Jeff at least learns to overcome his submission to the nihilism of Kathie's manipulation. Having The Kid articulate an ending seems to mean that this is a world where one cannot trust words, for words are the substance and currency of "being on the make," they are duplicitous, made of lies. The Kid's gesture is a sign, but a lie too, if we believe that Jeff was throughout learning to be on the make in order to survive and return to Ann, rather than to deceive her. If words, gestures, pictures—if everything we see and hear is vulnerable to manipulation, what is there left to trust? To return to James for a final time, the "esthetic compensation" is cruelly withheld in this ending but, if we trust our past recall of the film, it may be that at least Ann's imaginative restlessness will not confine her there forever.

Perhaps: but it might be that Ann's memory of her time with Jeff is sufficiently vital to sustain her through the rest of life with Jim. The modernity of the femme fatales like Kathie has traditionally been associated with sexual freedom and experimentation. But a more lasting aspect of Kathie's modernity is her faith in the past as a manipulative tool: again and again she tries to convince Jeff that he is locked into a future determined by their past together. Jeff, meanwhile, clings to an older sense that whatever mistakes one made in the past can be transcended by reform, discipline, hard work, and self-transformation (a view no doubt shared by thinkers like C. L. R. James whose intellectual foundations drew strength from radical Enlightenment values of the autonomy of human freedom and agency whatever one's origins). Kathie by contrast holds an idea of the past as a weapon that leans over, orders, and shadows our future (in T. S. Eliot's haunting phrase, it has "constable clutches"). Jeff resists this until the end, and The Kid's gesture to Ann unwittingly confirms Kathie's grim faith that our idea of what is past can determine, if we choose to submit to it, our present and future. We are left in a world that does not seem to care any more about what is true or false or honest or good, and only within unspoken cocoons of private understanding can we approach the kind of supportive mutuality of feeling necessary for building a better one.

2

Notorious

THE HUMAN FACE IS A communicative delicacy, projecting its signals of inner to outer in finely or crudely graded expressions across a vast spectrum of interlinked combinations, a kind of lamp whose glow we can bathe in, absorb, respond to instinctively before cognitively. Writing about the character played by Jim Caviezel in Terrence Malick's *The Thin Red Line* (1998), V. F. Perkins notes "the trusting eyes of Private Witt—Malick's understanding of what an extraordinary thing a face can be, his correct judgment of the weight of meaning that can be carried by an expression which is not offered as a specific reaction to an event or a spectacle. These are eyes that have seen, are to some degree continuously seeing, the brightness, the glory: kindly, pained, bemused."[1] The eyes are the most active of the signaling agents of the face, indicating the direction of attention, and of a range of emotional activity: fear, sadness, anger; but Perkins goes further in his description to give Witt's eyes deeper, more complex notions, that they do "see" (not react) and *are* (instead of expressing) "kindly," "pained," "bemused." They mirror and illuminate the world around him. Perkins rightly notes that faces in the film carry the weight of meaning often unanchored to something seen (although the film does have many examples of that more common approach as well). In *Out of the Past* I pointed to the importance of *directionality* of the camera and the performer's body when faces are wholly or partially obscured. In the case of Jeff and Whit turned away from the camera, we saw that far from encouraging a reading of ambiguity or deliberate obfuscation, we follow the force of the direction of their turned bodies, undistracted by what the face—in all its expressive complexity—would tell us. The expressionality of the face ought to assist in our understanding of why it is detectives (or those occupying that actantial role in the movie) shift from reluctant interest to wholehearted commitment: surely the face and its reactions are central to our understanding? A further complicating aspect is that the act of commitment and a facial expression we might associate with that commitment may not be congruent, as we might initially believe, and the face may be hiding that inner decision from any viewer. Perkins notes that Witt's eyes *are* kindly, but that does not always mean expressive of kindliness; we may be skilled at making our faces appear what we are not, a skill that all secret agents need to master. The face is therefore also a tool that can be recruited for deception.

Alfred Hitchcock's *Notorious*[2] opens with a kind of lesson or, to hijack Murray Pomerance's superb insight, a visualization of thought—in his own words: "A Hitchcockian shot must be seen thoughtfully. This means: it must be seen as though it constitutes, in itself, thought. And when we see it we must turn it in our minds, see all there is to see in it, see it again and again–this multiple seeing—this memory of seeing—amounting to a way of thinking about film and a way of thinking in general."[3] After an initial scene setting, unnervingly precise in its written statement of time and place—where John Huberman (Fred Nurney), an atomic scientist and Nazi spy, is convicted and sentenced for treason in a Florida court—Hitchcock takes us outside a house, its location and status by contrast unverified.[4] He has already *pointed* (if we recall any number of production shots with the great director pointing—staged or not, are we surprised?) to the centrality of point of view, and the risks of its dispersal, by beginning the film with a shot of a number of press photographer cameras (five in total). Cameras and objects (one person) to be photographed, a flourish evoking the cinematic. Their story is the beautiful daughter of the traitor, Alicia Huberman (Ingrid Bergman) who, unlike her loquacious father, leaves the courtroom in silence. Before she emerges, we see the father from behind, only glimpsing the side of his face briefly when he turns to his lawyer who wisely tells him to keep his Nazi revival guff to himself; vertical wooden pillars frame the foreground and are mirrored by those astride the sentencing judge. Only shadows disrupt this symmetry (including a diagonal one that slices right across the judge himself), and as the sentence is concluded we cut to a side-view shot of the back of a man's head, presumably a journo poking his nose through the door—what we saw in the previous shot may have been his point of view. Bergman as Alicia walks out of the courtroom into the press pack like an automaton, silent in the face of their questions about her father and her opinions. We only know that the authorities are going to keep tabs on her and, hence, to the shot outside her house where we see one of their agents checking his watch as he paces outside. Then it becomes night and the anonymous cop is gone; we are left with music, something like a celebration is in progress. The cut inside Alicia's house reveals a party of five or so guests, with her as drinks master pushing the booze on the others, wanting some company on her journey to oblivion. All the time in this sequence Bergman's face and her reactions are studied by the camera, in particular her attention to the one guest whose face we cannot see.

Like her father, his back is "facing" us (a visual trope expertly purloined in the conclusion of the title sequence of the television show *Mad Men*: there and here the refusal of the face acts as a paradoxical form of confident facingness). As Alicia repeatedly replenishes his drink, we feel the interest of the camera in this shadow figure as much as she does. "How about you, handsome?" she says, pouring him another drink, and the camera pivots just behind his head as she sits facing him, looking him directly in the eye with all the confidence of a drunken daughter of a Nazi traitor with nothing to lose and nothing to gain. There is a lining of dark, resentful bitterness to her frivolity—the Commodore (Charles Mendl, effortlessly playing some ageing, overweight parasite eager to have her aboard his boat to Havana) warns her not to drink too much, for "we sail tomorrow." "Really?" she asks. "We just sail away!" Again, her attention is magnetically drawn to the man we cannot see but must surely guess—as she does, "Haven't I seen you somewhere before?"—is Cary Grant playing government agent T. R. Devlin. She is recklessly, wantonly direct to him: "You know something? I like you." We can see and hear her reaction to his face, but we also can *feel* his attention to her *because we cannot see his*. His attention is something like a dark spotlight, its scrutinizing beam steady and direct and motionless. Just watching, never speaking. John Gibbs rightly observes that "Cary Grant's darkened silhouette makes it look as though he was sitting in the row in front of us in the cinema. We join Grant in his observation, we are behind him, we share in a similar perspective. Grant is scrutinizing the inebriated and incautious Bergman, as are we, but we cannot scrutinize Grant."[5] Hitchcock has perfectly judged the weight of meaning the *withholding* of a face can carry, doubling down by using one of the most beautiful faces ever to grace the planet to react to it (Grant's withheld face), half suspicious, half taken by the role of nihilistic wanton she wants to play to the full. "Handsome": what it must be to be handsome; its opposite, "hideous": "a perfectly hideous party" as Alicia puts it, as Hitchcock pivots his camera to the closest it can get to the back of handsomeness.

What do these people want and what do they deserve to get? What we have already seen is a key element that is not merely recruited for plot ends later on but sustains itself as an aspect of the film's answer: appetite. We can encourage appetite by eating a lot of what we like, say sweets or cakes or pies, or by drinking a lot of what we like, until we reach a kind of summit where appetite no longer has legs and, perversely, something like willpower has to step up from wherever it had vanished to. *Notorious* wants to visualize what it means to serve the authority of appetite and more importantly, to deny it, hold it at bay, even at its most healthy and dangerous as the yearning for the love of another.

Fade up to a later time in the party, where our two stars are now face to face with Grant/Devlin revealed and in full close-up, remarking that there are only two drinks left and no ice. This is the bit in their relationship before love happens but "before" is also the start of it in some way, like a journey is before an arrival, and it has already started happening before we've seen Grant's face. We have seen Alicia's steadfast attempts to keep despair at bay during the party, but her eyes were magnetically drawn to the face we cannot see (was this manipulation?). And now, they face a final drink at dawn facing each other.

For Alicia, the party is the lowest point of her life, a time to dirty herself with abandon, to embrace her wantonness: but even in this early scene we can see how she can't quite indulge it with maximum abandonment. And that is because it is her luck to have this shadow appear at just the point in her life when all else seemed to be cast forever in the shade of being her father's daughter. She is lucky, too, that Devlin is playful and demonstrates to her the drinking stamina of a man used to hardier tests. "It's a lot of hooey. There's nothing like a love song to give you a good laugh," she tells him bitterly, a comment that reveals more about her disappointment in that region of life than her lack of experience of it. When he drinks, leaving the final atoms of alcohol in her house for her to finish, she watches with a kind of sotted awe, impressed but then in an instant determined to unsettle him: nothing should stand right in her world knocked on its side. She decides it's too stuffy in the house and that they should have a "picnic," driving to it in her car. As they step out into the shadow-flecked Florida dawn, Devlin continues a different kind of protection, a vigilant flirtation, wrapping his handkerchief around her bare waist, and neatly straightening it in a way that she enjoys before they blast off onto the palm tree–lined highway at speed.

Hitchcock's car journeys are little moments of cinema-within-cinema, evocations of an earlier cinematic of attraction and vertiginous thrills where we are anchored within the crazy unstable forward direction of a careening vehicle (see also, for example, *North by Northwest* and *Family Plot*) while the world pivots around its axis and its passengers squirm behind the rectangular windscreen in an allegory of his audience (another visualization of cinematic thought that reaches its artistic apogee in Marion Crane's journey in *Psycho*).[6] Driving means that for the first time they both face us. Alicia tries to scare Devlin out of his nonchalance, but her vision of the road is blurred by her hair in her eyes and, in any case, they are soon stopped by a cop. But these few moments of driving together, her purposeful recklessness, his protective hand near the steering wheel, set up a kind of template for their double act as agents working together for the government to infiltrate and disrupt Nazi plans to build an atomic weapon in Brazil. It, too, is a bumpy ride but this is their first together. The film ends with Devlin driving Alicia away and we see them no more, but for fans of the movie, this moment is a glimpse into a possible future for them, a contented, bickering kind of marriage (where arguments while driving are an essential aspect of the genre), still full of risk and excitement. But what is Devlin doing at this point, what does he want? As we find out, he is a government agent there to recruit Alicia in order that she infiltrate a Nazi network in Rio de Janeiro; *he* has already infiltrated her party undercover and presumably is waiting until she is alone in order to begin his recruitment. But why would that involve allowing her to drive recklessly drunk? In one way he is calibrating her capacity to operate while drugged (she will need this later on), her resilience, her fight, and the depth of her despair. But it is also an opportunity for him to spend time with her *before* she knows who he is and what he wants with her. Perhaps even he doesn't know yet what he wants with her.

When a traffic cop (Garry Owen) flags them down, we meet an emblem of petty officialdom, a slight man in uniform who needs spectacles to drive his motorcycle; Devlin showing his ID allows them to go free and alerts Alicia to his status as a "double-crossing buzzard"; the couple fight in the car, a physical fight, their first time. Alicia acquits herself well, resisting strongly until Devlin punches her once unconscious.

Murray Pomerance has written so eloquently about the film's next two scenes—the first in Alicia's apartment when she awakes, next on the plane to Brazil where Devlin seems to fall in love with her almost instantly—that it is difficult to add more that is enlightening. Pomerance understands that Devlin is far from a sadist callously refusing to soothe Alicia's request that he acknowledge their love, and that the film enacts a cloaked, noirish version of Stanley Cavell's "comedy of remarriage." The first part of the film has them in love, virtually "married," only to "divorce" them when the details of the plan to use Alicia to infiltrate the Nazi group are revealed; the rest of the film is about getting them back together again. Pomerance focuses on the way two scenes early in the film appear to rhyme or resonate with events much later on. When Alicia awakes, hungover, we see her "staring at a glass of juice that has been positioned right in front of the lens."[7] It is not the first time nor the last that liquid in a glass achieves a luminous significance; Devlin instructs her three times to drink it, to finish it (note how as she struggles to get the glass to her mouth a strand of her hair is caught at the left side of her lips; before it obscured her vision when driving—she believed the hair was "fog"; now the hair provides a strong haptic sense of the uncomfortable unfamiliarity of a hungover mouth straining to recover its functionality; a little later, still in bed, she picks out a stray hair from her mouth). Devlin tells her he's been assigned to recruit her because the Nazis in Rio are likely to trust the daughter of a traitor. And that she should do it because of "patriotism." She is skeptical until Devlin plays her a surveillance recording of Alicia and her father arguing, and we hear this exchange between them:

JOHN HUBERMAN: This is not your country is it?

ALICIA: My mother was born here. We have American citizenship.

HUBERMAN: Where is your judgment? In your feelings you are German. You've got to listen to me: you don't know what we stand for.

ALICIA: I know what you stand for. You and your murderous wife. I've hated you ever since I found out . . . I hate you all and I love this country. Do you understand that? I love it. I'll see you all hang before I raise a finger against it.

As we hear this we watch Devlin and Alicia listen too, side by side, and we might wonder, now, more than seventy years later, about how much the vitality of patriotism has changed in the West. While Alicia initially rejects the offer, what she claims to want can only be nourished in a nation that allows democratic communities to thrive: "Good times that's what I want and laughs with people I like . . . people of my own kind who treat me right, and like me and understand me." At precisely this moment the Commodore (Charles Mendl) arrives: an Englishman with a yacht, a parasite who wants to sail this beautiful woman to Havana—is he the unfortunate manifestation of Alicia's "own kind"? It makes her statement look foolish, as if she indeed has no "judgment." For we can only be free to enjoy "laughs," or whatever, in a society that is willing to defend that freedom, freedom from external threats as well as the power of the modern State. In this case, the State wants to recruit her for its own ends, but they are also ones any citizen can share: the containment and defeat of a Nazi threat. Whatever the risk, it is clear to Alicia that sailing with this pompous ass is less appealing than sticking with Devlin. And he has already stuck to her: as the scene fades, she realizes she has his handkerchief still wrapped around her waist.

Next we are on their flight to Rio de Janeiro, another vehicle, this with windows that frame and select views as Alicia watches their approach. Devlin's boss, Paul Prescott (Louis Calhern), is on the flight too, and after a conflab with him Devlin returns to tell Alicia the news that her father died that morning. As she absorbs this, Hitchcock provides Bergman with a close up, and we see her face evolve like a photograph developing; she tells Devlin about her father, how nice he was, how nice they both were, and her realization emerges: "It's a curious feeling. As if something had happened to me and not to him. You see I don't have to hate him anymore. Or myself." And there it is, and Devlin sees it. Self-loathing, self-hatred breeds self-destruction—justified resentment is like drinking poison and expecting the object of that resentment to suffer its effects. Alicia is suddenly free of that, and as they come into Rio she looks out of the window, left, sees the statue of Christ the Redeemer on top of Corcovado Mountain, then looks out the window across the aisle, right, leaning past Devlin as she does so. And at that moment, as he catches sight of her face right in front of his nose (the opposite side to what we can see, since we briefly see him seeing what we cannot), he seems to fall for her. Pomerance suggests the statue suggests "*sacrifice*: exactly what must in some way or other be on Alicia's mind at this instant,"[8] but I think not. Christ the Redeemer has both arms outstretched, not in the typical shape of crucifixion, but a gesture of love, peace, welcome: its openness connotes an ease with accepting the world and its burdens. It is a happy, calm, confidently contented gesture. And something about this travels to Alicia and her curiosity in looking outside, at viewing the world, and in this moment Devlin sees her reborn, new; still having of course the "hard-boiled" attributes he noted about her earlier in her house after she awoke, but calibrated now with something like the beauty of freedom. In another variation of a cinematic moment, Devlin is once again a spectator, witnessing the lightening of Alicia's spirit, and he falls in love. As Pomerance puts it:

> In one beautiful movement and framing, Hitchcock makes it possible for us to know that Devlin has been entranced by Alicia Huberman—entranced because we have been entranced. We are intermediaries of a sort in this romance, since we were entranced first and his gaze came to match ours. It is also exactly at the moment his eyes turn, too, that those tiny white specks, which are the buildings of Rio in the distance, are slowly superimposed, like stars, or like figures in a far-off and alluring world. The future appears

as he catches sight of Alicia in her moment of openness, and we know that she has touched his heart.⁹

Michel Houellebecq, in a less chaste way, offers this analysis of instant love from the point of view of the narrator of his novel *Serotonin* (after a lengthy discussion of the different propulsive fuel for love between men and women) when thinking about his former lover Camille:

> However rarely, among the most sensitive and imaginative men, love arrives at the first moment, therefore *love at first sight* is absolutely not a myth; but rather when a man, by a prodigious psychological movement of anticipation, has already imagined all the pleasures which this woman could provide over the years (and, as they say, until death does them part), so the man has already (always already, as Heidegger would have said on one of his good days) anticipated the glorious ending; and it was that infinity, that glorious infinity of shared pleasures, that I had glimpsed in Camille's eyes.¹⁰

Which is to say, as Pomerance astutely notes in his conclusion, that Devlin too is reborn at this moment as he sees Alicia reborn herself; they land in Rio as new beings together. It is equivalent to the moment where Jeff submits to Kathie's seduction on the Acapulco beach ("Baby, I don't care"), but in this case not a terrible error of judgment, a plausible weakness, but instead something like a foundation that we need to remember in order to find our way through the rest of the film. If we forget the intensity of Devlin's love moment, we will be unmoored for what follows, at a loss to account for his actions, or Alicia's pain: at a loss to say what they *wanted*—the freedom of being in love in a free world.

We see the couple together in Rio at a table outside a café, the publicness of emergent love a thrilling containment. But the talk turns sour quickly; everything pivots around appetite, the driver of action. Alicia wants a maid because she hates cooking; Devlin orders another whiskey, but Alicia has been on the wagon for eight days. She's changed, she claims, but Devlin is rightly skeptical, testing the foundations:

"a phase" he calls it, because "change is fun for a while." "No new conquests . . . practically whitewashed," he says, meaning she hasn't slept with a man or had a drink, and that he (pretends to?) believes that this is a cover, a trick, another Alicia performance. Perhaps he suspects her of being a femme fatale, of adjusting her masquerade to suit her desires and ambitions. He's also testing her resilience under interrogation, and she quickly figures that out, telling him to give his "copper's brain" a rest. This conversation is axiomatic for the rest of the film: it consists in Devlin's immense caution when faced with Alicia's beauty and his evident devotion to her, a caution underpinned by a knowledge of the world as a place where commitment is hard to maintain over time, where vows and promises and treaties are broken and betrayed. It wouldn't be hard to fall in love with her, he says (so we should assume it would be "hard" to pretend not to be). What Alicia craves is a hint, a gesture of faith, something that overrides the skepticism that says, "Once a drunk always a drunk." And, feisty and defiant as ever, Alicia capitulates to that reading:

ALICIA: I think I will have another drink.

DEVLIN: I thought you'd get around to it.

ALICIA: Make it a double.

If you've never been an alcoholic it is hard to understand the strength of this moment: after eight days without drink, every tube in one's body cries out for booze, all the world's objects are perceived as excuses to slake that need; Devlin's lack of faith is stimulus enough. There is a pause where Alicia silently absorbs the thundering agony of her failure to live up to the modest target she set herself. But after making this decision we see Bergman again in close up, "Why won't you believe in me Dev? Just a little." Then, her head drops and she briefly practices the first of the next words silently with her lips before repeating: "Why won't you?"

He doesn't answer and this is a standing question in the film. One obvious reason is that he cannot believe in her without risking her operational utility, without making her "soft" with love, since in any case she was recruited as a "party girl" not as a reformed "daisies and buttercups" kind of item. Any trained agent would be skeptical of those claiming to turn a new leaf, and one compromised by his attraction to her (he acknowledges that it "wouldn't be hard" to fall in love with her) needs to be especially vigilant. The soda siphon (another reminder that bottles and their contents *stand in for* and *emblematize* the pressure of alcoholic appetite) next to his static right arm lets its liquid rock to Alicia's arm movements—she's quite animated, coaxing him, while her black gloves hold her face as if they belong to someone else.

The couple drive to a hill and walk up it for no good reason except the view. What more is there except the privacy of spectatorship? The conversation continues as if they've said nothing in the car since the café. Devlin is testing Alicia, but she pushes at his armor too, by playing up—theatricalizing—*his* doubt about her as a worthless tramp. "People will laugh at you," she says. "The invincible Devlin in love with someone who isn't worth even wasting words on." But he has seen her possess her freedom on the plane as they landed in Rio, and when she makes his putative doubts into words they must seem pathetic to him, vain, pointless. He silences her taunts with a kiss, and they become a couple in love and the film leaves them alone. We cut away, leaving them to their privacy as Prescott assures the room of intelligence agents that Alicia is "the perfect type for the job." From their perspective this means something like a whore, a tramp, a woman unconcerned with maintaining the moral value of her intimacy such that it is another form of transaction, a trade. Prescott's assurance is overconfident she will be a perfect honey-trap for the Nazi Alexander Sebastian (Claude Rains), a body who can infiltrate their secret group, discover what they're up to, bringing the intel back to Devlin. The point of the scene is to underline that Devlin himself has no idea about this plan. What if he did? Everything that went before would play differently. Devlin would be different; indeed, it is doubtful he could be played at all by Cary Grant. Convincing a woman to sleep with Nazis in order to stop their nefarious plans is immoral; it would mean he couldn't be available to notice her moment of freedom on the plane or allow himself to fall in love. Eventually it will be important for us to see that he objects to the plan in front of his bosses but later refuses to tell Alicia that he did.

The couple on the hill are isolated from the world that forms only a pretty background to their moment of union, and the isolation continues in Alicia's apartment, also at some elevation above Acapulco

Beach. Devlin steps onto the balcony and Alicia joins him, locking her arm under his, a gesture that evolves into a kiss. Hitchcock cuts to a closer view of the kiss and tracks even closer as they talk and kiss, kiss and talk.[11] The talk is about dinner because appetite—manifested in our various hungers and thirsts—is so eloquently recruited as a motif in this film. They are physically hungry for each other, and nowhere else in Hitchcock is the happy animality of proximate sex so prominent. We can be in no doubt as to what each of them wants at this moment, indeed this long shot, which begins on the balcony and evolves as they move inside, lasts well over two and a half minutes, only stopping with a dissolve as Devlin leaves the room to meet with Prescott. He does this because he has checked his messages on the phone with hotel reception, Alicia still close, both still kissing. Like all new lovers they may be haunted by the prospect that the current immensity of pleasure in one another's company may be merely transient. And here is, too, a critical piece of dialogue:

>ALICIA: This is a very strange love affair.
>
>DEVLIN: Why?
>
>ALICIA: Maybe the fact that you don't love me.
>
>DEVLIN: When I don't love you I'll let you know.
>
>ALICIA: You haven't said anything.
>
>DEVLIN: Actions speak louder than words.

This turns out to be the crux of the problems they face once they are confronted with the awfulness of Alicia's task. For Devlin what we *do* matters more than what we *say*: any intention stated or otherwise is valueless unless confirmed by appropriately supporting *action*. But for Alicia words matter: they are *actions* too, since they have potential as authentic communications of commitment. We know this because *her commitment* to her country is relayed to us on an audio medium, the vinyl recording that Devlin plays to her in her house the morning after the party. But in what follows, Alicia must learn to use action—specifically her body and its performative act in convincing

Sebastian that she desires and loves him—as well as words in order to effectively enact her mission. What she cannot abide is Devlin's refusal to ameliorate this deception with a vocal commitment to their love, the love we see in motion here and now. Devlin has to learn that while his actions do indeed speak, words matter too. For a long while he does not trust that his words will not *weaken* her *actions* as an undercover agent. And that lack of trust easily bleeds into a sense, at least from Alicia's point of view, that Devlin may never have fully believed in her transformation, her renewal, her freedom.

It is a brutally short happy moment. Just before he leaves Alicia asks him to bring back a bottle of wine to celebrate—and Devlin no longer has the meanness to mention her drinking, he straightforwardly, happily agrees, even buying a fancy bottle (it may be champagne) before his meeting with Prescott.

What Alicia does not see is what we do, Devlin's shock and outrage at Prescott's plan so much so that he leaves the wine and all its sensual connotations behind (Prescott notices this but says and does nothing). "I don't think she's that type of woman," he contests, because he knows she is not. Neither does he know that Sebastian was once in love with Alicia, and as Prescott and another (anonymous, limp) agent tell him to get her ready for the job Devlin paces like a caged beast, struggling to absorb events and their meaning.

When Devlin arrives back at Alicia's apartment it is night; she has set up a candlelit table on the balcony, and we see her hacking away at the cooked chicken corpse before she brings it out to him. Once again he has his back to us, the couple framed by apartment windows, his hands in his pockets unwilling to touch her. "Marriage must be wonderful with this kind of thing going on every day," she says, but Bergman already has a lining of worry in her voice because he hasn't come to her. When she joins him outside on the balcony, the shot of them together reverses the earlier one where they kissed: now night, she stands screen left and has to pull Devlin's hands from his pockets, positioning them around her waist. Still impassive, Devlin's inaction speaks louder, but we see him magnetized to her face and body, incrementally drawn to it yet resisting, studying her beautiful face as if for the last time.

Then the words: when she suggests, as a joke, he is secretly married he brutally replies, "Bet you've heard that line often enough" as if nothing between them had ever happened. It floors her, and when Devlin reveals they have to contact Sebastian, the shot evolves to distance us from them, with Alicia moving into the shadows as she realizes (however partially at first) what must be done.

Alicia asks if he said anything to object to the plan, something in public indicating that he believed enough in her to state that opinion publicly to his employers. But Devlin claims, falsely, that he said nothing, that it is up to her to back out or not. But *that* decision (as far as she is concerned) all depends on him and what he said or didn't say about her to others. "Not a word for that little lovesick lady you left an hour ago?" Costs and debts, payments paid and pending: must love transactions remain always balanced? Maybe in the world of daisies and buttercups: "I'm only fishing for a birdcall from my dream man," she tells him; then, standing next to him again, "Do you want me to take the job?"

DEVLIN: You're answering for yourself.

ALICIA: I am asking you.

DEVLIN: It's up to you.

ALICIA: Not a peep?

It is not a matter of who knows what: Devlin won't tell her what she thinks he didn't tell Prescott and his men, he *can't* say "that you believe I'm nice and that I love you and I'll never change back" as she wants; the "test" is for her, alone. For her, however, it cannot make sense to make that decision without knowing what *he* wants first. And so, they are trapped, pressured of course by the necessity of national emergency (vague and distant although it seems at this point), but also by the intractable nature of each person's necessary demand of the other. For Devlin, that she decides against the job; for Alicia, that he tells her—whether or not she takes the job—that he loves and believes in her. But if he does that she *cannot* take the job for that would mean he *has* to prevent her from doing it; his admission of love may ineluctably weaken her cover as well as his authority and identity as her handler; he must choose between his role as agent—the role that will protect her—and as lover, which may (we can't know as well as Alicia does) make her vulnerable. "I love you and I'll never change back": as we hear these words we cut to a close up of Grant, his handsome face sculpted by moonlight and shadow, not a point of view shot, but entirely *the loving way she sees him*. But that face says, brutally, "I'm waiting for your answer" and the spell is broken. The dependence of Alicia's self-belief on Devlin's spoken public endorsement is made clear as she walks from him ("down the drain with Alicia," she says), toward the bottle again, pouring a healthy amount. But the meal is cold, and as we fade out these two human beings appear utterly apart and desolate, "left . . . somewhere" like the champagne.

The next morning they "land" Sebastian who is out riding his horse; Devlin and Alicia saunter alongside him, where we get an opportunity to calibrate the difference between the profile of Rains and Grant. Sebastian doesn't even recognize her at first, this love of his life. After Devlin engineers it so Alicia's horse appears to bolt, Sebastian (in long shot) rides to the rescue and the job is done. We see only from a distance, watching Devlin watch as she begins her job of seducing this man. The image dissolves into:

Devlin alone at a café table, waiting. What does he want? For the mission to fail or succeed or both, somehow, fail but succeed, for fate to reach down and take him and Alicia out of the awful noirish bind they find themselves in? Grant is naturally at his best when in a playful, holiday mood, but here he delivers a perfectly stilled, cold, contained sense of professionalism lined with scorn and aching resentment. He smokes, thinks. What do you think about when your love is at work "landing" another man? Fade to black.

One part of Hitchcock's brilliance is his capacity to communicate drama such that it registers naturally and powerfully on us without our noticing him doing it, although of course he is the director most famous for *making* us notice technique, too.[12] Devlin's solitude is staged in a particular way such that he sits at a table screen left, a newspaper unread on his lap, a whiskey and soda siphon rhyming with the one we saw at a happier time when they had just arrived in the city. Two waiters busy themselves at a table behind him as another solitary patron leaves the café. To Devlin's left, given equal screen space to him is an empty chair and we hear the clang-clang of a nearby tram signal. Things are on the move, but all he can do is wait. When we fade up, Alicia is also alone in a place for dining but sitting in precisely the screen position she would be if she had been with Devlin at the restaurant. The odd conceit that Sebastian would be late—improbable if we reflect on it for a moment—allows Hitchcock to underline the separation of Alicia and Devlin in an act of composition between scenes.

What is remarkable about Alicia's meeting with Sebastian in a restaurant is the concentrated form that the film's interest in appetite and desire takes on. Rains plays Sebastian as affable and charming (much like his vastly more moral and benign character Dr. Jaquith in *Now, Voyager,* 1942), but immediately and strangely concerned with Alicia's interest in the handsomeness of other men, as if his jealousy is a function of his relative lack of that quality (by his own lights), a drive lit by Alicia's luminous presence (note the shadowless lighting of her face) even as he describes her as a "tonic." We feed on others and their perceptions of us and their world as much as we rely on our own assessments, which in turn are inflected by the lights of others. Sebastian lacks the solid foundation of confidence that allows easy progress through the spaces of the world and its people, and this breeds a natural suspicion of others who—through this lens—might well appear not to suffer from the same affliction. Confidence (not sheer arrogance or recklessness, although these are sometimes useful attributes) is the enemy of suspicion and jealousy. It is the latter that holds Sebastian captive now especially since he has regained the opportunity to win a woman of such astonishing beauty. The paradox is that *her* beauty leads him to speculate on the handsomeness of *other men* rather than get his own house in proper order.

But in the face of this Alicia reveals herself to be a natural undercover—again, immediately she discovers she has this skill. She improvises a story about her father insisting that she leave Miami, but rather than console her, Sebastian thinks of himself, and the rekindling of his desire for her, what he calls "the same—hunger." "Hunger" connotes the necessary, ultimately implacable, survival appetite, as if for him that feeling is so overwhelming, so fundamental that its furtherance demands all his attention. And, of course, its frustration or betrayal would equally demand ultimate force to resist and conquer. Alicia looks down at her drink as if trying to hide her embarrassment at his candor, his feeble tools of courtship that lay bare his desire in an unattractive "foolish" way (something he concedes without her saying anything as if he knows his weakness in this area, as if admitting one's awareness of one's poor performance somehow negates it.) And yet remarkably his weakness wins, produces success. How can he not wonder at the ease with which Alicia agrees to come to dinner the next night at his house? Satisfied but not properly mystified or suspicious, he decides to order tonight's dinner: "Yes," says Alicia, "I'm starved," and Hitchcock finds her face in another way this time, showing her struck by her own word and what it may mean. Starved for love and sex, or for just sex, or loving sex or food or drink or Devlin and all of these things together. *Starved.* This new Alicia is thirsty for a world she suddenly is locked out of at precisely the moment she most desired its pleasures, naturally, straightforwardly, soberly.

What we want is always shadowed by what we need, the more fundamental animal need of human beings to eat, socialize, explore their world; what we want is fueled by desire too, but is more compliant to the authority of the ego to manage it under stress. It is our dual nature as animals and as civilized beings that provides us with the access to judgment that allows such an authority to exist: without an unconscious drumming its beat beneath our conscious egos, we would act like automatons, slavish to whatever the rational (or irrational) beat of the day demanded; but our knowledge of ourselves as needy creatures builds a capacity to manage those desires that would be unavailable otherwise. Alicia's shock on hearing "I'm starved" is a product of her catching herself in one of these moments where conscious control briefly cedes authority to animal desire; and from now on she will do well to notice and monitor when that happens.[13] She is soon to meet a creature who is finely attuned to the weaknesses of those unable to control their desires.

Madame Anna Sebastian (Leopoldine Konstantin) is one of Hitchcock's dark mothers. There are of course the life-giving, vital emblems of motherhood such as Clara Thornhill (Jesse Royce Landis) in *North by Northwest* and Jessie Stevens (Landis again) in *To Catch a Thief*, as well as the strange maternal fragility of Bernice Edgar (Louise Latham) in *Marnie* and Emma Newton (Patricia Collinge) in *Shadow of a Doubt*. Madame Sebastian's severe gaze belongs alongside that of Lydia Brenner (Jessica Tandy) in *The Birds* and Norma Bates in *Psycho*: it seems far too intimately hardwired into the fundamental unconscious of her child for anyone's good. Before Alicia meets her she dresses for dinner, emerging from a room in front of Devlin and Prescott's gaze, dressed in pure white fur, like magical snow ("whitewashed" as Devlin might say). As she gets into costume, Devlin refuses silently to assist with the diamond necklace Uncle Sam has rented for the occasion, affecting to read a magazine. He circles Prescott and Alicia as the former instructs her on what to do, coming to rest with his back, once again, facing us.

When Alicia arrives for dinner at the Sebastian mansion (large and cozy near water twinkling in the moonlight, a dream house like those dangerous ones in fairy tales), her attention is modeled by Hitchcock's camera roaming across the wall and a closed door behind which we hear music and conversation. The silent butler—quite rude—guides her to another room, stuffed full of posh European antique junk, ugly and crowded. But it turns out not to be a room at all but a kind of passageway toward the main hall, where down a long staircase Madame Sebastian comes to meet her. She walks right into close-up, a stage light very briefly flicking an icy sparkle in her right eye. Her hair is worn high and braided like a Norse crown, and she questions Alicia with the authority of a monarch. She regards her son as some kind of specimen.

Talking of which: when Alicia is introduced to Alex's Nazi friends, each one carries their physiognomy of fascism as if in some kind of pantomime for children, and as we hear Sebastian introduce each, they bow into close-up to kiss her hand: Eric Mathis (Ivan Triesault) has the angled features of a burial shovel; William Rossner (Peter von Zerneck) is similarly pointed in an Eastern European fashion, but carries a high domed forehead and thinning hair; Emile Hupke (Eberhard Krumschmidt), by contrast, is a small, rather genial looking man with glasses, although in this company one wonders what slimy perversion fulfills *his* appetite; next is Mr. (no first name) Knerr (Friedrich von Ledebur), a very tall creature, fiercely aristocratic in build and composure.[14] Finally, Dr. Anderson, like Hupke, a short balding man, but with a less compromised face—is the guest of honor.

The dinner is directed by Madame Sebastian, but the drama is provided by the clumsiness of little Hupke, visibly worried that one of the wine bottles should not be on display in front of Alicia. She notices this, as do the Nazi fellows who quickly arrange to dispose of the clumsy Hupke.

We next see Alicia and Devlin meeting at the racetrack, alone together for the first time since the apartment catastrophe, although of course not really alone but in the crowd and under surveillance. Nearby, Alex and his mother are up on a stand, the former watching events through field glasses: we now see what we later find out he has been watching. It is a bitter lovers' argument after Alicia, dutifully providing information about Hupke and the wine bottle, admits that Sebastian has become another one of her "playmates." What this means remains undefined here, but it isn't hard for Devlin to guess. Their argument is partly restrained, under deep pressure because they cannot be seen to behave out of character. But even more striking is the way their woundedness consists of a strange economy of competitive transactions: "you said *this*" versus, "you *didn't* say *that*":

DEVLIN: Pretty fast work.

ALICIA: That's what you wanted wasn't it?

DEVLIN: Skip it . . . I can't help recalling some of your remarks. About being a new woman. Daisies and buttercups, wasn't it?

ALICIA: You idiot. What are you sore about—you knew very well what I was doing?

DEVLIN: Did I?

ALICIA: You could have stopped me. Just one word, but no you wouldn't, you threw me at him.

DEVLIN: I threw you at nobody.

ALICIA: Didn't you tell me to go ahead?

DEVLIN: A man doesn't tell a woman what to do, she tells herself. You almost had me believing in that little hokey-pokey miracle of yours—that a woman like you could ever change her spots.

ALICIA: You're rotten.

DEVLIN: That's why I didn't try to stop you. The answer had to come from you.

ALICIA: I see. Some kind of love test.

DEVLIN: That's right.

ALICIA: You never believed in me anyway so what's the difference?

DEVLIN: Lucky for both of us I didn't.

As she talks Alicia has raised her field glasses to her eyes, obscuring them so that we see two large discs in front of her face, but at Devlin's talk she slowly lowers them:

DEVLIN: It wouldn't have been pretty if I'd believed in you, if I'd figured, "She'd never be able to go through with it, she's been made over by love."

ALICIA: If you only once had said that you love me. Oh, Dev.

DEVLIN: Look, you chalked up another boyfriend, that's all, no harm done.

ALICIA: I hate you.

All the time apart, all the thinking that Devlin has done about what she has done. It's hard not to be sympathetic to Devlin, however cruel he appears at this point. His mistake was to believe that the freedom he saw in Alicia's face as they came into land in Rio was all-consuming, and that in falling in love with her he could complete the transformation such that no job or work—whatever the stakes—could destroy it. But change is fragile and its test is longevity across time, not in a moment's glance, or an afternoon spent kissing. And we must believe Alicia's change to be genuine if we are to understand how devastated she is with Devlin's continued skepticism, especially given what she has done—yes, voluntarily—not just for Uncle Sam but for him, for a man who wouldn't *say* what she needed to hear, and yet even here with tears glistening in her eye, it is clear she still is in love with him. And if depth of hurt can calibrate love, Devlin too is caught by his *want* for her. And his jealousy of the other man.

But to tell her anything about that at this point is to risk not only weakening her own cover (already compromised by his outburst) but his own resolve. He says, "It's a tough job we're on": they are *together* on this job, and this is its cost.

Alex arrives and tells Alicia he was scrutinizing them as if, like us, he could *see* the beats of their despair: "I was watching you. I thought maybe you were in love with him."

It is this danger of her love to Devlin being uncovered that precipitates the next scene where Alicia tells Prescott and Devlin that Alex has asked her to marry him, and her answer is needed immediately. The scene begins with Prescott happily reporting to the local official that his "little theatrical plan is working," but Devlin once more has his back to us, staring through blinds out of the window. We hear that Dr. Anderson is in fact a Professor Renzler, a top German scientist; when Alicia's arrival is announced, Hitchcock cuts closer in to Devlin's back; he seems to physically squirm with discomfort at the prospect of seeing her again. But when he hears a US intelligence official bleat about *his* discomfort with a "woman of that sort" coming to visit, Devlin is stung into an incredible defense; Cary Grant's eyes twinkle to the side, then briefly stick downward, alert to the sound of hypocritical weakness (a gesture he used to great effect in his role as C. K. Dexter Haven in *The Philadelphia Story*) and makes a point which, once more, Alicia will not hear, thirsty for it though she is:

DEVLIN: What sort is that, Mr. Beardsley?

BEARDSLEY: I don't think any of us have any illusions about her character, have we Devlin?

DEVLIN: Not at all. Not the slightest. Miss Huberman is first, last and always not a lady. She may be risking her life but when it comes to being a lady she doesn't hold a candle to your wife sitting in Washington playing bridge with three other ladies of great honor and virtue.

Unlike the woman *you* love, the one I do is willing to risk her life more or less on my say so; yours thrives with pleasure under the freedom people like Alicia enable; however sore Devlin is, he knows that her actions speak louder than words, and however painful it is for him, she is willing to get on with it. Hitchcock gives us the picture of Devlin standing at the window not as an aspect of this scene, but a reminder that much of what he has done up to now is *think* about what is being asked of the woman he loves. Her sacrifice. What he says to Beardsley indicates a growing understanding of its cost to her. But that is about to be tested again.

When Alicia arrives and tells the group Alex has asked her to marry him, Devlin attempts to delay things, citing the inevitable lengthy honeymoon that will result since "Mr. Sebastian is a very romantic fellow." He means Alex will cash out the opportunity he has lucked into by insisting on its repeated physical payment by Alicia: that is what Devlin is saying as he looks into Alicia's eyes. Then Devlin has to leave the room: he can't look at her anymore. Alex too is jealous not of what Alicia might do but what she might feel: he characterizes his mother's "carping" about the marriage as an instance of her jealousy whenever he takes an interest in a woman, despite the fact that he does seem to spend quite a lot of time with her and remains concerned with her opinion (as if it mattered!). But Madame Sebastian does not strike us as a woman preoccupied with such trivial emotion; what she sees is that it is *Alex* who is blighted by jealousy. Her estimation of his weakness is her insight and the source of her questions.

Alex has at least three critical weaknesses, and he seems to lack the resources to address any of them. His sense of his own inadequacy as, in his own words, a "very good-looking" man makes him vulnerable to the kind of jealousy that means he appears even less attractive than the physical attributes genetics dealt him. Marrying one of the most beautiful women who ever lived is a recipe for constant vigilance against the rapacity of other men toward his wife and a constant stimulant for that jealous drive. Secondly, his tiny band of Nazis seem utterly unequipped to launch the merest of threats to anyone except one another: Hupke's drunken mistake and the lethal response to it indicate a group that is near to auto-extinction, never mind reaching the restoration of the Nazi "spirit" that Alex indicates to Alicia is their ultimate end. Finally, he is caught between two women neither of whom have his interests at heart and yet to whom he has ceded authority over his feelings and, ultimately, his actions. Rains does well to humanize such a weak figure so much so that we may feel the tug of pity for him by the movie's end. What Alex *wants* is what disables him, what commits him to his fate.

A punctuation shot that exactly repeats an earlier one: a car arrives in moonlight at the Sebastian home. Some weeks have passed, the honeymoon is over, and the married couple return. Alex is immediately concerned his mother has "shut down" the house, asking the servants to retire and turning the lights off despite his messaging her their return. Note that Rains has no height assistance in the little shot of him and Alicia still near the front door as he apologizes to her for the lack of a "bright homecoming"; Bergman is notably taller, even having to slightly stoop to meet his gaze. Hitchcock is never less than forthcoming, however obliquely, about the physical oddity of that pair and what that might have meant for their honeymooner activities together! The next day Alicia is all wifey, organizing her spaces in the house, but also checking it out—discovering almost immediately a locked door; Mother has the keys, so she goes looking for her husband. A brief scene tells us the Nazi scientist has been successful in whatever it is he is doing (we can take it as some kind of experiment to weaponize atomic material); Alicia interrupts their meeting, and Alex is all too happy to get her the keys (how compliant he is!—is that what women want?). But Mother has the keys, and now we see an echo of what will become, in *Psycho*, the pitiful aural spectacle of a boy arguing with his mother. Alicia listens with patient interest (her spycraft is excellent: she *is* a natural) rather than with Marion Crane's empathic shame; and now for the first time she takes the keys Alex has taken from his parent. What follows is a medley of Alicia opening doors with them until she is defeated by the wine cellar "UNICA" lock: only Alex has that key.[15]

"The wine cellar is the obvious place to look," says Devlin, wearing the hat of a sleuth and sitting with Alicia on a park bench. The mood has changed considerably, time has passed. In closer shot Devlin and Alicia are very close together, far too close for public consumption. "It's no fun Dev," she tells him; he doesn't relent ("It's too late"), but things have visibly softened between them. How do we know this? It is difficult writing about film when one sees what is plain for all to see, and yet one cannot point with certainty to any one aspect that might count as evidence: one feels the impulse to merely say, "Look! Can't you see?"[16] Perhaps things have gone as far as they can such that there is nothing left to be betrayed within their interrupted couplehood. He suggests she prompt Alex to hold a grand party where he is invited, and she reluctantly agrees. But Devlin still watches her as she leaves, another moment of silent watching. He seems to think he is already married to her in some way and that should mean they are now telepathic with one another; he must know that Sebastian, who also believes he is married to Alicia, cannot enjoy the same communication. But the truth is that Alicia is not telepathic any more than he is, and he will have to demonstrate his commitment in word and by his actions in order to make the marriage real.

At the park bench meeting the pair demonstrate their aptitude for the shared duties of infiltration synchronized in action at the upcoming party. There Devlin is no longer an observer but inserts himself into the action of the Sebastian household. Before that, Alicia has to get the key for the wine cellar, and her courage and ingenuity in getting it is an emblem of what she is prepared to do for him.

Gender roles are reversed in this scene: Alicia, already dressed in a jet-black dress, fixes her diamond earing while Alex ponces about in the bathroom still getting ready. While he is in there she uses the opportunity to remove the wine cellar key from his key fob. From the bathroom we hear his nervousness about Devlin's imminent arrival (as if preening himself thoroughly can brush him up to that level of charisma!). But before she can conceal the key, he emerges—all washed and little in his dressing gown—to take her hands, one of which holds the key. Hitchcock comes to the fore: in this and the next scene he will assert a far greater explicit control over what we see (that is not quite the right way to put it: more a matter of the noticeability of his presence becoming marked). The camera pushes forward into a close-up of Bergman's hand as Rain's forces its fingers open to plant a kiss on the palm: no key there. Alicia looks down at her left hand which holds the key and in a fine moment of improvisation throws her arms around Alex, trusting (no doubt from experience) that her wholehearted expression of affection will overwhelm his suspicion. As V. F. Perkins remarks, the gesture of embrace by Alicia "is the image of Devlin's panic . . . This is the 'honeymoon scene,' the scene from the honeymoon that we didn't see, where Alicia proved her aptitude for love. A man who allowed himself to love such a woman might only know that her desire was plausible, never that it was real. (And Devlin is a man to whom such a doubt is, shall we say, paralyzing. It robs him, for instance, of the power of speech.)"[17] The next shot is one of the most famous in all of Hitchcock, a camera maneuver that begins as if from the point of view of a partygoer looking down past the staircase and lit chandelier at the guests below; but it evolves, on completing a right-to-left sweep of the space, to stop on the small figures of Alex and Alicia, moving down and toward them as they greet arriving guests, the camera eventually, once again, locking, in extreme close-up, on Alicia's left hand that holds the wine cellar key. The movement is an *assertion* of knowledge that Hitchcock provides for us, and its elaborate nature elides any question of how Alicia managed to get the key back into her hand from under the table upstairs where she kicked it after dropping it during her confected embrace with Alex; her hand opening on command (in response to the authority of the camera's proximity) indicates a certain nervousness, a need to give it to Devlin as soon as possible. So, we are back in the mood of transactions that were in play in the bathroom scene before: Devlin should not get a "false impression," Alex says, even though it is he who is victim to that; in return Alicia quashes his doubts with her body. Devlin and Alicia's transaction is brokered by an object, the key, and its promise to release them both from the mission to whatever future is left to them. When he eventually arrives at the party and she greets him, Hitchcock shows us an almost obscene image of a close-up of their hands as the key slips from one to the other, a moment almost impossibly more intimate (in a public space) than their earlier extended symphony of osculation.

But why does Hitchcock show us these things in this way? What does he want? Of us? Of cinema? Of anything? Spycraft teaches one to understand that every gesture, action, message, deception, falsehood, statement of truth, half-truth is a mere component of a web of interlinked moves across forces that one may only dimly grasp—because, as an agent, one is after all only another, larger, but still inconsequential component. The novels of John le Carré express this tension between the costs for individual agents avoiding those pursuing or attempting to uncover them and the larger plan or mission that shadows each action, often concealed from reader and character alike. As James Chapman has eloquently argued, Hitchcock loved spy capers because the operational nature of concealment and revelation connects deeply to the aesthetic nature of cinema itself, a medium that, unlike any other, has to conceal its means of production and at the same time present them in plain sight.[18] We have to *see* Bergman acting as Alicia—there is no other way out of it—*and* we have to believe she is acting as Alicia acting as Alex's loving wife in order for her character and Alex's to have any bite or grip on our attention to the drama within which it is presented. There is a kind of economy of belief and control, where Hitchcock controls the currency of our attention and, in a brilliant gesture, thematizes this economy in a way that unifies the central theme of the film itself.

This is not in the way Hitchcock moves the camera or composes a shot, but rather the way the consumption of alcohol gets tied to the prospect of Alicia and Devlin being discovered as US agents in a den of Nazis. We may remember that early in the film Alicia's handling of alcohol gets attached to the question of whether or not she is truly a changed woman, no longer a wanton at the mercy of her nihilistic despair (a situation where alcohol is one's best friend). She does continue drinking at a reduced rate; the party sequence provides her with an operational reason not only to limit her consumption but to hope that everyone else at the party limits their consumption too.

As Devlin and Alicia walk through the throng of guests, they talk covertly: "He's gonna watch us like a hawk," remarks Devlin; "He's rather jealous," Alicia replies. And Devlin quickly connects Alex's jealousy to the drink: "Let's hope the liquor doesn't run out and start him down the cellar for more." Appetite is what fuels Alex, but in a secondhand way—he courts the appetites of others (Alicia's), but his own is so shriveled, so bounded by suspicion and jealousy, it can hardly stand up to the healthier ones such as the straightforward desire for sex, company, and booze. "Start him down the cellar" sounds like the description of a fantasy mouse collecting scraps for its rat master (or mistress). They move directly to where the champagne is being served to guests; there, Devlin meets Señora Ortiz who whisks him away from Alicia after grabbing herself a glass of the champagne she adores. Alicia then looks to the crate of bottles, one being taken at that moment, on ice. That crate is like a clock powered by the drinking appetites of the guest. How ironic, you might say, that Alicia's anxiety is now driven by the consumption by others of the very drug she relied upon to soak her pain. And this is no trivial matter of irony: unless they get to the cellar before the champagne is finished, they risk being captured and executed on the spot. Alicia seems to calculate that waiting for the champagne to be finished is a risk because (a) it may not be and (b) even if it were, it would push their covert investigation far later into the night where their absence is much more likely to be noticed. She even refuses to take a glass of it herself.

Alicia finds a way to rescue Devlin from Señora Ortiz, and they sit together in plain view of the ever vigilant Alex. Because he cannot hear them, he can only observe their *actions*, and their actions are those of lovers arranging a covert meeting *as well as* of undercover agents arranging a covert meeting.

While Devlin investigates the wine cellar, Alicia keeps lookout, and Hitchcock cuts back to the steadily diminishing number of champagne bottles in the crate. He also brilliantly and economically conveys Devlin's poor luck as he flicks through the inventory pages in the cellar, his arm inadvertently knocking to the floor a wine bottle. It contains a "metal ore," presumably the weaponized atomic ore, and Devlin hastily takes a sample, rather cheerfully indifferent to Alicia's fears that someone will discover them there. And why not: whatever happens *they, us, a couple* are in it together, the shared danger is ours. He had so little shared time with her, so little away from the surveillance of others, why shouldn't he be chipper about their little spy caper at its moment of acute danger?

But Alicia is right, and Alex is coming down to the cellar. Devlin kisses Alicia, and Alex sees them outside the garden door in a passionate embrace. Hitchcock shows us precisely what Alex fears and what is real for Alicia as we cut to the shadowed close-up of her loving gratitude to have him ("Oh Dev, Dev. . ."); and Devlin for an instant is himself carried away: a moment of theater becomes real even while its theatrical job is achieved. We see the artifice of the gesture's purpose fuse with its authenticity. "I knew her before you, loved her before you. But I wasn't as lucky as you," Devlin tells a seething Alex. This moment between them, their first privacy since the apartment before the job began, risks everything. Alicia has no time to intervene before Alex will realize his key is missing.

Now it is Alex's turn to perform, greeting Alicia's apology after the party has ended with his own performance of regret for acting "like a stupid schoolboy"; he also refuses to join her ("Are you coming up?"), a little gesture that says he will not be gulled by her charm anymore.

And now Hitchcock wakes us from the night in a series of dissolves including a close-up of a chiming clock, ringing 6 a.m., as Alex opens eyes that were, perhaps, never asleep. But in his mind's twisting and turning over what manner of betrayal Alicia has done to him, he hasn't notice she has left the bed, vanished. What has reappeared is the UNICA key on his fob, and therefore he can be in no doubt: her betrayal of him is as real as that key, as jagged and implacable in its material is-ness, as it lies pointing tail down like an arrow at him. But this is hardly the end of the world's rude material humiliation of him; the director allows us to follow his discovery in the wine cellar of Devlin and Alicia's activities together there. Liquid around a plughole in the sink; the replacement of the wine bottle marked 1940 brazenly out of step with its 1934 brethren on the shelf; that bottle's inadequacy of weaponized ore inside and, finally, its pathetic little cap all loose and undone. How frail is the cover-up, how insulting, how utterly devastating: the broken glass of the original bottle crudely brushed under the wine stand is a mere afterthought.

The mood is grim, mortal, and deadly. Hitchcock now reverses that earlier glittering camera movement along the stairs with which he showed us the beginning of the party to show Alex alone and in shadows ascending those stairs, his face struck by whips of jealousy and spiteful resentment.

We find him next, small and quiet, in his mother's bedroom calling her awake. Madame Sebastian, vindicated and flushed with the power of her own perspicuity ("I knew it. I knew it") assumes the problem is merely "Mr. Devlin"; when he confesses that he'd married an American agent, it takes the wind out of her sails, and she slowly prepares a cigarette as we cut to see Alicia sleeping like a princess, oblivious to her fate.

Madame Sebastian has her cigarette on the go now and claims that she "knew but didn't see" and dismisses Alex's pathetic self-loathing. "We are protected by the enormity of your stupidity for a time"—none of the other Nazis would suspect it. And his mother once again has the measure of this man, noticing his murderous thoughts toward Alicia are as impulsive and childish as his eagerness to marry her was ("You're almost as impetuous as before your wedding"); his desires are unregulated, without sufficient authority, so she must take up that responsibility (and in continuing to do so negates his capacity to develop that resource himself). Against impetuousness, Madame Sebastian counsels patience, a gradual process of removal and erasure.

The final act will cash out the film's theme of contested appetite by having Alex and his mother poison Alicia's drinks. First we see a close-up of her coffee, with Alex encouraging her to finish it before it gets cold. And when we see Alicia next at Prescott's headquarters she is bothered by the light, claiming a headache. In fact she may well be poisoned by the very uranium ore Prescott has identified as the contents of the wine bottle they discovered. He also tells her that Devlin is being transferred to Spain, at his own request. When she meets Devlin for the final time on a bench amidst a busy city back-projected backdrop, she keeps her distance, wounded, dark-eyed, slow, not like before when they were close together in full view. We know that she wants him to talk again, to say he is leaving for Spain. But she is not surprised that he does not say. He notices her looking ill. She claims it is because of a hangover: "back to the bottle again." "It lightens my chores," she tells him; the comfort of the bottle for those who know they waste their intimacy, fake their lives, live in a half-world of unnoticed shadow. Human life reduced to transactions: she gives him the scarf he tied around her naked waist when they stepped out for the first time to drive on that picnic. He remembers but covers its significance with an impossibly cruel comment. "Cleaning house, huh?"—that is, removing all the love tokens from sight and touch as if she were really married and in love with Alex. But he knows she cannot be: what would count for him as evidence of something that he might be responsive to, sympathetic to? He is so caught up in the exhausted remnants of what was panic about Alicia and is now tired resignation that his "marriage" to her can only survive at an even greater distance. Actions speak louder than words: we see him see her covering something, lying about something, not responding fully to what he notices about the way she looks and feels.

Back in the Sebastian household, they continue to poison her drinks, and Dr. Anderson's concerns are not shared by Alex who suggests, like the bloated Commodore at her party in Miami, a boat trip to restore her spirits. Anderson, wanting to help, suggests Alicia join him on his trip to the Aimorés mountains, spilling a little too much intelligence for Alex to bear; ruffled, Anderson picks up the wrong coffee cup, and in correcting him Alex and Madame Sebastian reveal to Alicia their poison plan.

Alicia finds herself poisoned and therefore nearly helpless at precisely the moment she needs most strength and courage. As she begins to lose consciousness the distorted voices of Alex and his mother cloud her brain, while Hitchcock projects their shadows on the door in front of Alicia, merging them as she gets closer to it. We see her fall to the floor from a point of view once again high above the staircase and chandelier, not far from where she once stood with Alex as they welcomed guests to the party. They help her up the stairs to her bed and once again, as she is manhandled to her pillow, Alex and his mother hover above her like birds of prey, the son expertly asking the butler Joseph to disconnect her bedside telephone such that she will not be disturbed in her final hours. Our attention is directed to Alicia's entrapment by her illness, and these vicious killers whose professed concern for her welfare cash out our knowledge of the evil doubletalk of German socialism at its worst.

For the final time we see Devlin alone waiting on the meeting bench, ruffled this time not by the agonizing thought of what he's asked Alicia to do but by her failure to meet him; we see him wait all day, until dark, now pacing back and forth like the sentry outside Alicia's Miami party house.

What follows is one of the most remarkable endings in all of Hitchcock, notable for its oddity, speed, and abruptness. Devlin is speaking to his boss Prescott, no longer in the offices but now lying on his hotel bed (one assumes Devlin has called him up late after waiting at the bench), eating crackers and drinking beer. As Devlin expresses his doubts as to whether Alicia's apparent sickness is really because of drinking, Prescott insouciantly continues his supper, agreeing to Devlin visiting just to check. A matter of national security, the uncovering of a Nazi plot to weaponize uranium ore: it's all cheese and crackers really. Hitchcock never really has much time for bosses or cops or experts; they all come across as pompous, self-satisfied, and dangerously unworldly.

But Devlin does not attempt any sideways approach. He drives right up to the front of the Sebastian house and walks in. Joseph the butler is a weak gatekeeper, spilling the fact that Alicia is ill and allowing Devlin to wait. It takes enormous courage and determination for Devlin to ascend the stairs and enter Alicia's room. She wakes to see him approach her bed, in an echo of the earlier shot when she awoke with a real hangover and saw him upside down: this time he is the right way up. He leans into her, and she reaches out her (rather large) hand to take his:

ALICIA: I'm so glad you came.

DEVLIN: I couldn't stand it anymore waiting and worrying about you. That wasn't a hangover you had that day. You were sick then.

The shot has Devlin's face in shadow and Alicia's lit from the side so that the pillow her head rests on is bright white, like an abstract shape. He lifts her from it toward him, such that the light cuts and sculpts the edge of her profile like a halo, and he is finally able to say what she had to hear before death:

ALICIA: I thought you had gone.

DEVLIN: No, I had to see you once and speak my piece. I was getting out because I love you. I couldn't bear seeing you and him together.

Now, that's been a fact of the matter ever since he saw them meet up on horseback. Why did it take this long and these circumstances before he bothered to mention it to her? *Because we don't do or say what we want.* And that is because we are divided from our own feelings by other feelings that are also ours and hold authority over us, even over our deeper, more cherished feelings, sometimes precisely *because* they are deeper and more cherished. Who would trust them? Certainly not a spy made a fool by love. To her credit, even at death's door Alicia is unwilling to let *that* matter slide by in the moment of rescue:

ALICIA: You love me. Why didn't you tell me before?

DEVLIN: I know. I couldn't see straight or think straight. I was a fatheaded guy full of pain. It tore me up not having you.

ALICIA: (*ecstatic*) Oh you love me. You love me.

DEVLIN: Long ago. All the time. Since the beginning.

One need not be mean or cynical to realize that this is precisely what Alicia wants to hear, the full blossoming of a spoken avowal of devotion that explains everything, his silence, his meanness. But that also raises the possibility that this is all imagined, the final fantasy shots of a woman slipping into radioactive unconsciousness, absurdly imagining Devlin talking to a man eating crackers, one who can—unfeasibly—effortlessly glide into the Sebastian household, full of Nazis as it is, to carry her off in his love-pulsed arms. It's not a bad reverie to end with. Devlin finds Alicia now as she was at the beginning, wrecked by drugs and hardly able to move.

Confronted by Alex and his mother as they try to leave, Devlin uses the only leverage he has, which is to expose the fact of Alicia's treachery to the Nazis downstairs. The group of four descend together, and we see a battle of courage as Devlin forces Alex to comply with the theater or face his fate; even Madame Sebastian joins in aligning herself with her son against the prospect of discovery. The issue is whether Devlin ought to allow Alex to come with them in their escape down the stairs and to the car outside. In these final hurried moments, does Alex notice how longingly the poisoned Alicia clings to Devlin's neck, how she is—always already was—out of her mind while Devlin is close? Alex begs to be taken with them, but Devlin locks him out of the car and drives away. The film ends with Alex ascending the steps back inside his home to face the Nazi's verdict on his love-struck idiocy; and, like Devlin at the start of the film, we watch him from behind, already faceless.

At least we always know what he wants: after discovering the material fact of Alicia's treachery when the UNICA key appears back on his fob, we have a shot of Alex seated on a chair in the bedroom and for a moment we might assume he is waiting near Alicia's bed, ready to have it out with her, perhaps even negotiate with her for some kind of explanation, even reconciliation; at the very least to divine from her lips the extent and depth of her betrayal. But in the reverse shot it is revealed he is at his mother's bedside, like a small boy, waiting for her to wake. It has been noted that Leopoldine Konstantin is only three years older than Rains, and certainly their pact to poison Alicia refigures the relationship such that they appear as evil parents, destroying the weakened fey Alicia-child in their care. Alex and his mother underestimate the compassion of their Nazi friends, who are understandably concerned for Alicia and keep insisting she receive proper medical attention. Some have suggested we feel sorry for Alex at this point, especially when he is locked out of the car Devlin uses to escape with Alicia.[19] Quite how we ought to accomplish this sympathy is puzzling given what he and his wicked mother have done to the film's heroine and the painful way we see her struggle to leave, barely conscious, with the man she has always loved.

More mysterious is the film's combination of two enigmas and their apparent resolution as Devlin tries to raise Alicia from her bed, doing so with spoken avowals of his love that she requests as a kind of power-up or tonic that will animate her dying limbs. We need to confront the fact that the question of where the ore comes from (she weakly tells him that it is somewhere in the Aimorés mountains) is far less important than the puzzle of why two healthy young patriotic people found it so hard to express mutual love, particularly when faced with such a difficult mission. On Devlin's side it remains unspoken that the doubts he may have had about Alicia's transformation were very real, and while it did not prevent him loving her, it surely makes a difference in this moment that the sickness he ministers to is not self-inflicted, not a hangover, any more than it is despair at the nasty task she has had to endure in Alex's arms and company. For the first time he can see her and read her completely but only when she is at death's door; he describes himself as "fatheaded"—a fool, in other words, but that doesn't get us much closer to why he kept that love to himself. It raises the question as to what kind of internal brakes exist such that our deepest desires are thwarted by foolishness, say the idea that our words bind us to a judgment that is forever in authority over us, at the cost of mere humiliation if we are wrong. To amplify these matters in a context of national security, however flimsy the plot, equally suggests that the judgment of our wounded hearts makes love a volatile and dangerous companion, both necessary and potentially lethal for the continuance of liberal society.

Devlin's silence in the face of Alicia's request to express his love is also a way of maintaining the integrity of her performance, a backhanded means of strengthening her resolve such that she is not distracted or weakened in her delivery of a convincing wife by thoughts of Devlin pining or suffering. Like Jeff, his idea of modernity is that it requires a kind of illicit, bad-faith lying to the world, a hustle. But like Kathie, Alicia has evolved an alternate sense of that modernity, one that craves a sustaining commitment from her man, confident that she can still deliver her performance successfully. She has more faith in herself than he does. Hitchcock took the figure of the female double agent that had been depicted throughout the 1930s in movies (often ones set during World War I) such as *Dishonored* (Von Sternberg, 1931), *Mata Hari* (Fitzmaurice, 1931), and *Three Faces East* (Del Ruth, 1930), where the fascination was precisely in the fluid and undulating adhesion of that figure's loyalty to country and/or to love. In *Notorious* both genders have to grapple with the issue of what they should "be": should Devlin be a man (e.g., a lover, a husband) or an agent (e.g., loyal to his country and his calling and his oath)? He is teetering on this all the time in a way that Alicia seems to experience very differently. Her loyalties are in a tension too, but she reaches out to him for stabilization, expecting that they might share mutual unsettlement in the face of what must be done. The clues they found about the Nazi plot were emblems of the more urgent threat to their survival, that of inexpressibility. Fear of never knowing for sure what our loved ones want, or that they may be unable to say or do enough to persuade us that they love us the way we expect them to, threatens to undermine any prospect of human companionship, or love, or community, forever. The park bench rendezvous scenes between Devlin and Alicia where this mutual struggle to get beyond the trap of their own entanglement is, recursively, a seated place of spectatorship where they look ahead toward our gaze as they talk, trying to conceal a public show of the intimacy that has boxed them together.

3

Vertigo

When I feel free it's not when I do something I decided to do myself. It's when something acts within me. Something I don't control.

—Michel Houellebecq, "Michel Houellebecq: Q&A with His Readers"

☙

AT THE END OF *NOTORIOUS* we are at least left with the possibility that the future shared by Devlin and Alicia is a loving one and not vastly damaged by the events that led to her poisoning. But something about the pursuit of knowledge in detective films and its cinematic representation makes satisfied coupledom unsatisfactory; the dominant feeling at the end is to wonder about Alex's fate, and our moral convulsions in response sour whatever celebratory feeling we might have about Alicia's narrow escape. It is as if Alex snaps into focus for us as a human being right at the moment he is most objectified as a risk that must be eliminated. Hitchcock's *Vertigo* ends with a picture of what we might look like watching *Notorious*'s ending: Scottie (James Stewart) looking down at a body from the top of a high tower.[1] He seems transfixed by the sight of the corpse of his lover, a sight denied to us; his arms at his side are slightly lifted, palms turned upward, as if he were trying to raise the dead. The original ending of the film adds a scene cutting from the tower to his friend Midge's (Barbara Bel Geddes) apartment at night where she is listening to a radio report about Gavin Elster (Tom Helmore, playing the criminal mastermind behind the bizarre plot we've just seen unfold) who has fled to Europe to evade police capture, although the announcer assures us he will be extradited "once he is found." As Midge listens she bites the nails of her right hand, seemingly entranced by what she hears but perhaps also distracted by something elsewhere. A noise off-screen raises her from her seat and she turns toward her door—it is Scottie arriving. She turns and makes them drinks with plenty of ice; he says nothing to her as he walks past and toward the windows of her apartment where it is night outside. She hands him his drink, walks away slowly, then sits at her work desk (she is a commercial illustrator), and looks back at him as he raises his drink to his mouth; we hear a car horn, and then the film ends. It ends with them saying nothing to each other (not even a "thanks" for the drink). They are a picture of a couple who are together as merely an audience for a world whose action and excitement lies elsewhere, apart from them.[2]

Most writing about *Vertigo* appears to fall under its spell, and there is something enchanting about its insistence on the reality of psychological haunting. *Vertigo* is a tour de force of "looking at," seeing and not seeing, of being haunted by what one has seen. In particular, one can be haunted by broken or unrequited love (as we saw in *Out of the Past*) which can leave deep tracks in one's being, like rings at the core of an ancient tree. We need to have a confident perspective on such intrusions in our psychic being if we are to lead anything remotely like a satisfied, productive life of our own, lest we be encircled by them. The film genuinely believes that our desires and obsessions can appear like, perhaps even constitute, a supernatural power, akin to the powers of divination or clairvoyance. These are powers that read the world for signs that can guide us: perhaps cinema is a power like that, too.

Vertigo's crystallization of haunting begins with its title sequence. A woman's face appears in close-up as some of the credits emerge to the sound of Bernard Herrmann's spooky, circular music (it resembles a distorted version of a carousel soundtrack, played on strings, aping pipes instead of brass). The music comes before the film and therefore makes what is before the film part of it: the Paramount Majestic Mountain logo where twenty-four stars encircle the words, "A Paramount Release" in front of a matte sketch of a fictional mountain; the words fade to be replaced by a single word, "in," which quickly fades as a vast letter V seems to charge at us from the heart of the mountain as it forms the second enlarged V of the word VistaVision (a widescreen process unique to Paramount studios). While all this is going on the music continues, reaching some kind of punctuation as the V appears, and coloring (although, also strangely, the logo and words are in black and white) the ordinary symbols of ownership and provenance in an unsettling mood. We fade up quickly from darkness to the beginning of the movie's credits. In extreme close-up the left-hand side of a woman's face (we can tell this is a woman because she has full, red-lipsticked lips and soft, cared-for skin). The visible part of her face fills almost half the screen, the curve of her cheek and chin (the ears are oddly obscured as if taped back) resembling the curvature of a planet against the solid darkness of the universe. The camera now decisively moves left, centering those lips in the same position where that V emerged dead center from somewhere deep toward us. But this is not an inspection of a face for clues or evidence of a mismatch between inner truth and outer mask. The film freezes moments after the credit JAMES STEWART appears *from behind the frame* traveling forward to rest above those lips which seem to react in a not-quite-flinching way, as if preparing for the landing of this prestigiously bizarre moustache. The mood, helped by the unsettling music, is one of threat, of a kind of psychological test taking place on a face that exists in darkness and seems unable to move from its position as the canvas for the film's inscriptions. Stewart's name fades from the top lip, and this releases the camera to move once again, decisively this time, vertically revealing the nose and coming to rest so that the screen is filled entirely with the upper face below the hairline and above the nose; dominated in fact by the two eyes, black and shiny, two pinpoints of light which signal the curvature of the eyeballs; a lining of light underneath each reminds us of their vitreous properties, mirrors of the soul, lamps that beam our innerness outward. The eyes move together, screen left, then screen right. We don't see what they do. As this motion happens (remember it is vastly enlarged by the extremity of the close-up) the credit KIM NOVAK appears in the same manner as the previous credit, landing on the bridge of the nose, just as the eyes are turned screen right. As that credit fades out, the camera moves again as the eyes blink twice, to close in on the right eye of the woman, then rest in extreme close-up (so close in fact one can almost count the lower eyelashes individually—just over forty of them), such that the eyeball—entirely black but with its pinpoints of light—dominates. There is just enough space below it to allow a further credit—IN ALFRED HITCHCOCK'S—to land there. The camera now moves even closer—clinically close, one feels the haptic discomfort at being this close to an eye. (Is this the reason lovers tend to close their eyes while kissing? Doing otherwise is just, for mysterious reasons, obscene.) At the same moment the entire screen becomes red, which has the effect of illuminating that eye, which widens in fear as deep within the pupil we see the tiny word, evolving and enlarging as it travels directly toward us from within, VERTIGO. The pupil seems to enlarge to allow this thing to escape from inside it, to birth it, and as it hovers in front of our eyes and floats off, a spiral shape appears within the pupil. The music now warms to another theme evoking a staircase of strings, building higher and higher until the main theme returns again, this time far more emphatically. The shape that emerges from her eye is pink and rotating counterclockwise; its center is oval and black and empty, but around that two spiral arms curl out and around like the shape of a galaxy, and threaded between the arms are smaller lines mirroring the shape and direction of the larger ones. It is the first of ten whorls, often overlapping, their rotation suggesting a flatness like a disk, but their patterning also connotes depth, like a cone.[3] Do they belong in the mind, projected out of our eyes, or are these perfect abstract shapes representative of some other helical psychological entity? A kind of looping visual depiction of thought, or feeling, or compulsion? Are they signs of mentation or ancient formations imprinted deep in the structure of all organisms, echoing with the vast swirls and eddies of the early universe in formation? Round and around, again and again, each one different, but each persistent, generative of the next.

The spirals were created by John Whitney and are the visual expression of Lissajous curves, mathematical equations that describe complex harmonic motions. The idea that deep in the organism lies an interior which generates mathematically complex shapes is mysterious and spooky in itself; but the idea of the human mind under the authority of scientific equations corresponds with the ascension of psychology (and its various disciplinary offshoots, including some elements of neuropsychology) during the twentieth century as *the* hegemonic explanation for human behavior, in particular behaviorism (and its philosophical offshoot logical behaviorism). The basic thought here is that all human behavior can be accounted for by reference to a persuasive description of mental concepts and mechanisms rather than paranormal or extrapsychic notions (soul, spirit, heart, etc.). Sometimes when Hitchcock talks about cinema (say, to Truffaut) it appears as if he believes in this too. But despite this title sequence, *Vertigo* does not. Instead, the circular motion of the already static-but-implying-motion spirals (this nestedness of motion is echoed by the repetitions of the music) tends to further complicate, obscure rather than clarify, whatever innerness might look like. Are they descriptions of feelings, emotions, thoughts? Is the repetition some kind of symbolic gesture toward ideas of repetition-compulsion or eternal return? The mathematically generated precision of the shapes is at odds with any definitive meaning. We see instead their graceful, slightly sinister motion and color, hear the Wagnerian sadness of the music in all its bombastic, melancholic movement.

Then the action of the film begins with another abstract shape, the rung of a rooftop ladder that comes into view, and we pull back with stirring music to find ourselves in the middle of a rooftop chase at night. A white-shirted villain climbs up and runs out of the shot, followed by a uniformed cop holding a gun and James Stewart playing the film's detective, Scottie Ferguson, wearing a brown suit and fedora. The chase across the city skyline of San Francisco takes place just after dusk or just before dawn, when the neon lights still have authority over night. The pursued man jumps to a slated, high-angled rooftop and clambers up and away; the following cop has less luck, slipping on the tiles but managing to haul himself up to safety. Scottie has worse luck, making the jump but slipping down the slates, only surviving by hanging on to a buckled and weakening gutter, as the ground many stories below opens up to receive him. Worse, when he looks down at the ground below, it and the buildings surrounding it appear to distort and stretch in a way that no eye can replicate, but when we see what he sees we take this to be an optical representation of what his mind is doing to his vision. That is called vertigo, a feeling that one is spinning even though one is not and that static objects are in motion when they are not. But what we see when Scottie looks down is not spinning at all, it looks more like a machine's idea of the imagination of falling from a height, something prompted by *acrophobia*, an anxious condition stemming from the irrational fear of heights. The film is named after a medical condition, vertigo, but what it shows us in these moments of optical stress is the stretching of space in front of our eyes such that the only explanation is that the seer's brain is doing the distorting work, adjusting objects and buildings to suit internal pathological demands. We are seeing his hallucination of reality.

In fact, if we take our viewing of movies to involve something like "imaginative seeing"[4] then quite a lot of what we see Scottie looking at seems to be a representation of his *own* "imaginative seeing," as if he treated the world around him as a kind of movie, replete with patterns and objects that one needs in order to find meaning in it. The shots that represent his inner experience of vertigo are merely one species of this kind of representation, and that we get an example so early in the film ought to alert us to the generalized pathology of his perception.

The uniformed cop turns back and heroically, very bravely reaches down the steep roof to offer his helping hand to the stricken Scottie. But the cop falls and we, once again, see Scottie see the strange little body grow smaller as it plummets to its extinction. Pertinent here is Hitchcock's lighting of Stewart's piercing blue eyes; in the instant the cop falls and we see his body begin to turn over in its descent, we cut back to Scottie's face and arms, suspended still from the gutter: he cannot turn his head fully down, but his eyes follow the direction of the fall, a key light picking out his right pupil in a bright dot as he looks down in absolute terror. His eyes remain trained on the catastrophe below as we fade to black. We don't see how Scottie is rescued from his predicament, but cutting away has the effect of leaving us with the lingering trauma captured in Stewart's horrified eyes. The eyes are signs, portals that radiate meaning to us, but they speak in the language of sights which we cannot translate. Stewart's eyes beam terror at us.

The next scene is in Midge's bright yellow apartment with her working at her angled drawing desk and Scottie (still) balancing his walking stick on the end of his right index finger. It is a lovely, messy little workplace-cum-home, with lots of sketches on the walls, fresh flowers at the window, easy classical music, and a modest cluster of modern framed prints on the wall. A lining of anxiety crouches among the mess, but the bright light of the room flooding through the broad schoolroom windows keeps it at bay. Their conversation is easy and fluent, not a hint of the erotic promise of a man in a woman's house, just friendly talk about Scottie's imminent freedom—today is the day his medical corset is removed. Their small talk is about big things in the past; Scottie has quit the police force, and Midge reminds him that he was once a bright young lawyer with the ambition to become chief of police "someday." The reminder seems to trouble Scottie, and he rests both hands meditatively on the handle curve of the wooden walking stick. Midge reassures him the death of the cop was not his fault, while he complains about his acrophobia that leads to his vertigo.

Everything we see about Scottie up to now emphasizes the relationship between physical constraint and his stance toward it: hanging from the gutter, the focus on his large eyes soaking in the height, and seeing the tragedy below draw a picture of his mind's reaction to it; in Midge's apartment he winces at the awkwardness of a medical corset (which we see him feel) and brandishes his walking stick with contempt. These emblems of physical discomfort have a direct relationship to his irritable mood, his restlessness, and this idea broadens out to encompass the entirety of her apartment (including her) and his prospects for the future. He pointedly refuses to consider a desk job back in the police service by making a joke about the perils of his vertigo using the stick as a prop. When Midge says this is "where you belong," we see that this too is a kind of restraint on his restlessness, this opportunity to be free (from his job, from his identity as a cop, from the past):

MIDGE: Well, what'll you do?

SCOTTIE: Well I'm not gonna do anything for a while. You know, don't forget I'm a man of independent means as the saying goes. Fairly independent.

When Midge suggests that he "go away for a while"—she clearly means a holiday of some kind—he mistakes this as a kind of maudlin gesture ("You mean to forget? Midge, don't be so motherly"), one of the many times he will mistake Midge's ordinary concern for him for something else—an overtuned maternal concern that borders on the pathological. He hurts her, momentarily, by calling her motherly, and he doesn't notice, as he leans the rubber base of his stick against her clean, pale yellow wall.[5] He is even rude enough to ask her to turn off the music, and she complies as a dutiful host (not a mother).[6] Scottie moves around the apartment with an ease and command that seems unaware of the pleasure he gives Midge by being there, but we are aware that she needs to keep working as he pontificates about his "predicament" and questions her about the cantilever brassiere she is sketching. We need not look to the extreme moments of suffering and darkness that James Stewart is well known for in Hitchcock's films to already see something not at all right with this man and his treatment of a friend. Michael Wood claims that Hitchcock "already in *Rope*, had found in Stewart a darkness that was not supposed to be there, as if his patient thoughtful manner were not a comfort to him but a quiet mode of torment."[7] That torment and his capacity to play tormentor is evident in *It's a Wonderful Life*, especially when the bankrupted George Bailey returns home and is vicious to his wife and children. When Scottie leans in to study the bra (Midge reminding him that he's "a big boy now"), we see a hilarious picture of what the title credits might have looked like to its creators: a wire and cloth contraption, pink and curved, aping the organic but not born of it.

This odd object prompts Scottie to ask her about Midge's love life, which she claims is "following a train of thought." Are we meant to assume that Midge loves Scottie, or at least sees him as a good match, a companion in life? He asks her if she will "ever" get married, and Hitchcock offers two extreme close-ups of Midge looking over the frame of her large spectacles as she hears him say that it was she who broke off their romance in college after three weeks. There is an emphatic contrast between the casualness of his recollection and the seriousness of that close-up, which implies there was more to this story than he recalls. Scottie's relationship with the past is already in question, long before the film gives us better reasons to worry about it. Midge's clear independence, straightforward friendliness, and the insistence on working through their conversation marks her not so much as a mother but as a reliable and intelligent companion and, more importantly, an independent woman unafflicted by a stereotypical desperation to be married to a man. By offering them as types, an aspect of the movie's cleverness is to disarm our curiosity about Midge and, later, Judy Barton by making them legible when they both have more depth and mystery to them than it seems at first glance.

Scottie attempts to cure his affliction "progressively" by practicing stepping up to greater heights incrementally (this takes place after Midge has clearly indicated how busy she is). The little stepladder she provides (also yellow) is as smart and neat as she is, but he swoons on reaching its top step, collapsing in her arms after unwisely looking out of the apartment window to the streets below. When we see his point of view from its top step, looking out of the window down the side of the adjacent building, we also notice the vase of flowers, white and red but oddly desaturated, lower screen left. The organic is juxtaposed to the mathematical, vertical lines of the wall and the rhomboid shapes of the windows, as the building falls away in perspective (there are two other plants further below, one with yellow flowers, the other casting an organic, gently moving shadow on the flat gray of the exterior wall). We see Scottie's eyes widen in terror as if filled with the magnitude of absorbing this sight: we see that what he sees overwhelms him like a hallucination.

The next scene has Scottie meet with Gavin Elster, a former college pal, now head of a large shipbuilding company. The sequence is, in miniature, an evocation of cinematic manipulation as much as it is a depiction of actual, fictional, manipulation of Scottie by Elster (and by means of fiction). It begins with an exterior shot of Elster's shipbuilding headquarters that allows the director to make his cameo (he is carrying an oddly shaped container for what looks like a musical instrument). Scottie walks past Hitchcock on the sidewalk, and then between two large columns in the center of the frame away from the camera toward a guard who "directs" him by pointing further into the complex. Screen left, on one side of the columns, we see a bright yellow crane vehicle, while to the right, on the grey wall of the building we can make out one letter and one partial capital letter: "LA" in bright green. Near this is a stand containing three newspapers. Cinema, going to the cinema, being directed, LA, the media industry, the labor and construction of that industry near but just out of sight: all of these elements are gently, almost subliminally, evoked and not insisted upon as meaning-making elements. We are much more likely to notice the fact that Hitchcock has made his cameo than to ponder on the resemblance of our own habits of walking into large nondescript buildings within which industrial-scale fiction will be presented. And yet all these elements are there rather than something else (any other letters would have done as well as LA). At first Elster is seated in front of a large cinema-like window through which we can see the mechanical operations of the shipping company he runs (a large dark crane dominates the foreground of the view behind in which we see the vast partial skeleton of a massive ship's hull being constructed). His office is elaborately decorated with framed paintings, photographs, and ornaments, some of which Scottie fiddles with as he listens to Elster's account of how he married into the business yet finds it boring work. Scottie "reads" the objects decorating the room but fails to realize he is being set up. Elster ponders how San Francisco has changed since he came back from the East, and Scottie picks up his thought, pointing to a painting just above a large glass case containing an impressive model ship; the painting's caption declares it to be "San Francisco in July 1849" and depicts a modest, homely looking settlement beneath mountains. As he moves toward it and looks at it, we are positioned *behind* Scottie so our visual information is approximated but not exactly corresponding to his; we are behind his gaze, tracking it. Like the large window behind Elster and the little raised floor he steps up on later in the scene, these are moments that evoke spectatorship, the form of studied viewing. This is also the scene in which we see Elster's manipulative force. He begins his pitch that his wife has been possessed "by someone dead" after Scottie has sat down and then deliberately moves to stand behind him on a part of the room that is elevated slightly (one step up) as if it was a stage, and he is shot near its "wings" as he elaborates the tale he claims he wouldn't know how to make up, even though he has precisely done that. By talking to him from behind, he makes Scottie squirm in the high-backed chair: "Scottie, do you believe that someone out of the past, someone dead, can enter and take possession of a living being?" he asks. Elster claims that his wife, Madeleine, suffers from this delusion, and Scottie's initial skepticism (take her to the "plain family doctor") prompts Elster to say, "You're still the hard-headed Scott aren't you." And this ought to make us pause also: nothing we have seen, even his dismissive attitude to Elster's claims about his wife, gives us a picture of Scottie as "hard-headed"; instead he seems rather ineffectual and low-energy, not just physically (a much older, heavier cop is able to make the jump across the rooftop that Scottie bungles) but mentally too.

Elster's story about his wife's fantasy is striking for the way in which it figures a lonely individual vulnerable in her isolation to possession by little more than a figment of the past: a fiction haunted by a fiction. It is a good picture of Scottie himself later in the movie. As an example of the danger of Madeleine's delusion, Elster describes the time he followed her to Golden Gate Park, and once again we hear a picture of spectatorship that is doubled—Elster watching his wife sitting by the lake staring at the pillars of the Portals of the Past monument. Again, this spectatorial relationship will be replicated later in the film when Scottie watches Madelaine looking at the portrait of Carlotta Valdes, the dead woman she is haunted by. In painting a fiction where a person is hostage to the sights of the world and its past, Elster creates a spooky reflection of Scottie's own predicament, pathologically unable to continue working because of *his* past, but easily defeated in the face of small setbacks (the neat little yellow stepladder's top step). Elster describes his anxiety about his wife's wandering around looking at objects and places and then asks Scottie to follow that person, to do the same thing:

ELSTER: I want you.

SCOTTIE: Look, this isn't my line.

ELSTER: Scottie I need a friend, someone I can trust. I'm in a panic about this.

SCOTTIE: I'm supposed to be retired, I don't want to get mixed up in this darn thing.

Scottie's reluctance surely matches our intuition that something is askew, fake, about Elster's story. Indeed, Hitchcock tells us to be on our guard when he overemphasizes Elster's delivery of the line (that Madeleine is haunted by) "someone dead" with a very Hitchcockian camera movement that pushes the frame into a close-up as he says it. He immediately cuts away again to frame Scottie perturbed by this (as if he is too close to someone not quite stable) and then pulls the camera back so that the two men are framed (audience and author) by the frame of the upper part of the office (itself bedecked with an almost embarrassing proliferation of framed pictures). The density of the framing motifs, shown to us at just the moment where Elster begins his first conjuring of the story about Madeleine's obsession with her past, is juxtaposed with Scottie's initial skepticism ("Take her to the nearest psychiatrist"), but then as Elster continues, drops away (although the setting does not change obviously) as a prominent feature. The frames crowd the shots that contain them, dividing them into segments. When Elster is pushing his plot at the moment of maximum force, we see him facing away from us toward Scottie who is at the screen right, "pushed" to the side of the shot and seemingly "boxed in" (Elster says they are going to "an opening" at the opera and dining at Ernie's Restaurant first. When I hear the words "opening" and "opera," am I alone in thinking instinctively of the word "box"?)

The next part of the film is anchored primarily to Scottie's vision, his watching, following, observing Madeleine. In what is yet another evocation of the cinematic, the detective and camera are aligned as agents of (or devices for) the discovery of knowledge through observation. The voiceless forty minutes of screen time detailing this detective work begins with an already mobile camera floating toward the exterior of Ernie's Restaurant, an already dreamlike state, as if Scottie has—between Elster's office and here—already brought himself into a state of high expectancy. Hitchcock fully involves us in his imaginative visioning of Madeleine. We have already seen "through" Scottie's eyes with the trick device of approximating his vertigo via a camera zoom adjustment at the start of the movie. Here, we are folded into his vision again, but it is one that seems to blend effortlessly (yet strangely) with the guided automatism of the movie camera. In the shot of Scotty at the bar of the restaurant leaning back as he looks right, toward the seated part of the restaurant, the camera takes its cue from his movement (more precisely it seems to take its cue from its focus on Stewart's shining pale blue eyes), and the shot evolves, drawing back and shifting left at the same time, and then resting briefly on the crowded guests eating in the large red room. Next, it follows another kind of cue, Bernard Herrmann's music which already seems to describe feelings of loss and death and love in some awful configuration.[8] And yet, like the camera movement, like the dress Madeleine is wearing, it is graceful and achingly seductive. A cut back to Scotty (who could not have possibly seen this view of the restaurant from his position at the bar) shows us he is nervously aware of his own heightened expectations on seeing Madeleine; she gets up from her table to leave and walks directly toward him, framed by the wooden posts that separate one part of the restaurant from the bar; she walks ahead of Elster, who is waylaid by a waiter, and directly into a close-up of her profile. She is immensely beautiful in this view of her, a view that Scottie cannot see optically but seems to intuit anyway (he appears to remember it later on); as the music reaches its climax, an implausible brightness bursts onto the red wallpaper behind her and she turns her head toward Scottie, just as he turns away, coy, as she looks toward and then beyond him, back at her husband. He watches her leave, and she seems to glide away, reflected again briefly in a mirror before vanishing. Again, we are left to watch Scottie's eyes (in fact his left eye) as he watches her leave and turns back to the bar.

This brief scene is enchanting because it rhymes with the earlier scene in Elster's office. The "rhymes" are both evocatively cinematic, gestural and compositional all at once. As Madeleine leaves she stops behind Scottie at the bar, and he has his head very slightly, discreetly, turned right (toward his right shoulder), with the tail of his right eye observant. This shot of him echoes the view of him that Elster would have had at the end of the previous scene, where we saw Scottie hemmed in against the wood paneling of the office as he was pleaded with (where Scottie has a sense of standing defiantly against the wall in a way that Judy echoes a little later when he is buying her clothes). Scottie slightly turns his head to the right when Elster tells him they are dining at Ernie's before going to the opera opening, as he does here as Madeleine hovers behind him. It's as if Hitchcock's camera replaces Elster's head in its proximity to Scottie in this subsequent sequence; and once again we feel as if Scottie is somehow being addressed or pleaded with, but this time it is by Elster's use of Judy Barton's attractive disguise as Madeleine the haunted wife. A picture shown is more convincing than a story told. When in the next shot Madeleine begins to turn her head toward her right shoulder to look back into the restaurant to where Elster is, there is a cut-back to Scottie turning his head back toward the bar. There is a rhyming sense of these movements as if both turns are somehow geared to one another or synchronized. When Madeleine and Elster leave, we have a final shot of Scottie from over his left shoulder turning his head smoothly to watch her leave and showing us (as Madeleine showed us and him) the other side of his face. These shots are of course eloquent in showing Scottie's discreet, immediate fascination with the evident beauty of Madeleine. Because of these rhymes we have a further sense of systematic organization and manipulation injected into the detailing of space and gesture. Aligning our previous view behind Elster's head in his office as he asked Scottie to observe Madeleine at the restaurant with the view of Hitchcock's camera as Scottie observes her could simply be an assertion of the equivalent of two kinds of master manipulators: the director and Elster. There is also the sense that Scottie's reluctance in the office and the evident spark of interest ignited by the sight of Madeleine in the restaurant are associated as cinematic events, that hesitation to get involved and the arousal of interest rely specifically on the *spectacle*s set before one's view, the hint (in the awkward attempt to be discreet as he catches a glance at her) that there is something disreputable about looking at objects in this way, and the automatism involved in the very act of looking and positioning oneself (tiny adjustments of neck and eyes) and one's perceptual apparatus such that seeing the sight on display is possible. The fact that, as we find out, Madeleine as played by Judy Barton is moving herself precisely to allow such a view of her by Scottie only compounds that sense of the way spectator and spectacle seem intimately geared to one another both optically and aurally: we see both James Stewart's and Kim Novak's ears from both sides as if the director was concerned to make it clear that what they could not possibly hear (Herrmann's music) was, nonetheless, a pertinent if impossible diegetic element in their overall sensorium. The movement from a picture of Scottie's reluctance where, surrounded by framed pictures of old San Francisco in Elster's office, he looked off-screen at an unidentified view to the beginning of involvement where what he sees is emphatically, sensually, arousing for him, is articulated cinematically for us but also for Scottie: it is a performance enacted by Judy playing Madeleine designed to arouse Scottie who plays his part by sneaking a view of her, as he is meant to without, so he thinks, it being known by Madeleine that he is doing so. But he must surely know that Elster sees him there and would see him, perhaps, sneaking this view? That is not what is emphasized at all in these shots which instead involve us very much in the enormity of him seeing her for the first time, rather than the plot about following a haunted spouse.

Finally, there is nothing at all mysterious about Judy's presentation of her Madeleine: she simply walks elegantly to the door, pauses just behind Scottie's position at the bar, and turns back to look after Elster. We see her as she is, clearly: it is instead a theatrical device of bringing up the lighting on the red wall behind her profile that is mysterious. Cinema is more mysterious than a woman.

The next part of the film depicts Scottie following Madeleine's car in his: the camera remains mostly anchored on a view of him watching and observing. The work he is doing is *detecting*, trying to find out through his observations what is going on. By the end of the film he finds out that what he is watching is theater, a fiction played in real time by the woman playing the role of Madeleine, Elster's wife (we never know where his real wife is until the moment we see her corpse). He follows Madeleine as she provides him with credible evidence that she is in fact obsessed (not yet quite possessed) with the past. What is the nature of this evidence? Apart from her visit to buy flowers, the evidence consists of his witnessing of her involvement as a spectator with specific sights in the world, sights that he shares: the gravestone, the portrait in the gallery, the view from the room. When we follow him he provides us with evidence that, like the "fictional" figure he tracks, he too is prone to entanglement with a mysterious woman. She is modeling for him the behavior that Elster's plot demands of him—that he become obsessed with rescuing Madeleine from *her* obsession. The entanglement is circular, vortex-like in its motion and dizzying fluidity. He is watching a performance put on just for him by a master actor, and as we see him doing this, Hitchcock's camera and Herrmann's music created for us a picture-in-formation of the evolving nature of his involvement with her. There is a great sense in these scenes of following of the infectious nature of *study*: that what is of interest to Scottie *is her* interest. The attention and focus of others necessarily becomes *our* interest, captures our attention, and is what *we* begin to focus on too. We are in a world of optical reverie, of watching and seeing and contemplating, of being a watching, seeing being.

Murray Pomerance has convincingly argued that the origins of the detective—the embodied subject who detects in the world—can be found in the increasing visibility and accessibility of a public world such as promenades, pleasure gardens, parks, and so forth from the mid-seventeenth century onward. Such spaces concentrated people and aroused curiosity in "the sights" of the emergent modernity; the spaces provided occasions for looking and seeing and being seen:

> That taking a promenade could furnish a curious person with leisure and opportunity to examine similarly occupied strangers, to gaze at their presentations of self and furnish speculation as to their class, ethnic, or geographic origins, suggests one clear source—embedded in a concrete social organization of the seventeenth and eighteenth centuries—of the practice of detection formalized in modern life. One might argue that detecting began with taking a walk; that, operationally and figuratively, the detective, icon of modernity, "walked through" his world and appreciated its sights from a walker's perspective.[9]

Something happens around the mid-nineteenth century, exemplified by Poe's short story "The Man of the Crowd" that this process of detection becomes secretive, hidden, and caught up with criminal and other kinds of pathology. Certainly among elites (including the literary elites such as Flaubert) following the European revolutions of 1848, where national bourgeoisie were confronted for the first time with the arrogation of their values by organized working-class political movements, there was a sense of the *disenchantment* of the world which is the moment of, or impulse toward, modernism, the time when aesthetic modernity turns against bourgeois modernity, exemplified in the works of Manet and Flaubert. The sights of the world are now haunted by the impersonality of crowded spaces and the empty hypocrisy of bourgeois industry, culture, and politics. Into this world the detective-narrator of "The Man of the Crowd" pursues an unnamed man hoping to read his actions, movement, and outer existence as an avatar or cipher for his inner intention, his inner life (Anscombe uses the figure of a detective following another man "going round town with a shopping list in his hand"[10]). What has changed is not the thirst or appetite for sights, but the way in which they tend to indicate something secretly wrong either in the world or in the doer's action in the world.

The modern detective emerges in the city which becomes a place haunted by the fact of the unborn ideals of the bourgeoisie, reminded by the force of the 1848 revolutions that their lives are founded on the sweat and misery and labor of numberless, anonymous others. And folded into this disenchanted vista for detection are the earlier senses of detection as a form of *tracking*, of reading signs the better to divine outcomes, to find prey, or locate friends or enemies. Tracking in the modern world of distraction means most of all attending to the ordinary and the familiar, precisely those things that are beneath notice. As Carlo Ginzburg reminds us: "For thousands of years mankind lived by hunting. In the course of endless pursuits, hunters learned to reconstruct the appearance and movements of an unseen quarry through its tracks—prints in soft ground, snapped twigs, droppings, snagged hairs or feathers, smells, puddles, threads of saliva. They learned to sniff, to observe, to give meaning and context to the slightest trace. They learned to make complex calculations in an instant, in shadowy wood or treacherous clearing."[11]

One could read these tracks in two ways: as symptomatic of a past consisting of clues about the movement of prey or, in medicine, the origins and progress of a disease; and secondly, as divinatory signs pointing toward the future, such as the destination of prey or a prognosis about the resolution of illness. There is an endless spectrum of imprints on the world available to be assessed by the skilled detective. Scottie's tracking of Madeleine mixes these senses of the symptomatic and divinatory: he wants to know what she is doing and what that means about what she is going to do. The directed intention of disclosure of information that is part of any cinematic aesthetic can feel like signs or symptoms being tracked, too. Hitchcock in this film makes this process feel like magic, a kind of clairvoyancy or cinemancy. It is especially those everyday things in plain sight that we typically fail to notice (although we may register them unconsciously) that emerge as critical. As audiences we are seekers (querents) like Scotty, avid followers of skillful aesthetic entities as they travel through time and space, eager to divine the meaning of traces, signs, objects, habits, words. Signs can be alchemic too, transforming from mimetic indexicality to representation, to allegory, to symbol. As Pomerance describes Poe's story, "The follower acts as though believing, without the least shadow of a doubt, that his prey's small gestures, his stops and starts, his moments of manifest *behavior* will furnish solid indication of his personal intent. We see walking as watching; and watching as calculating . . . since the hero of our story . . . is nothing if not a reader himself, a man given over to reading the actions of a stranger for indications of intent."[12] The sights that face us are transformed by cinema, the tracking/hunting/searching activity of the follower/detective is cinematized; in cinema everything sheds light, radiates signification.

Vertigo offers a picture of the pathology and dynamic of detection-as-hunt while expressing the debt of the detective to the flaneur-like wanderer, but there are significant adjustments for the modern twentieth-century setting. Firstly, Scottie's following of Madeleine is privatized: his car follows her car, they get out and get back in and drive again. They are, while driving, cut off from the world but tethered together by Scottie's responsiveness to her vehicle's movements along the San Francisco roads. What he is confronted with by watching her is someone who, isolated and alone, appears driven to visit particular *sights* and to spend time looking at them. Scottie watches Madeleine's viewing of the world as if there was something wrong with *her*, something out of the ordinary in what she is doing, some underlying pattern that would shed light on the items that she grants her spectatorship to and the reason for her attention to them. The answer seems to be that she is herself following the historical traces of another woman—Carlotta Valdes—around the city.

So, a lot of what Scottie has observed concerns watching Madeleine's performance as a watcher, a spectator. She waits at the flower store looking at the stock, she ponders a grave respectfully, she is sitting opposite a painting. Madeleine represents a keen audience for the objects she visits; and later when we realize that this is the performance, we see Scottie not as the audience watching an audience, but simply as a man being entangled in the skilled performance of Judy Barton. A worked-up, controlled audience: what we see is how Scottie is being manipulated. This cinematic evocation of the detective's growing involvement is so layered and thick in *Vertigo* that it even outclasses *Notorious*'s presentation of intelligence agents playing a part for their targets and for one another at the same time. *Vertigo* layers performance within performance, and the evocation of cinematic spectatorial relationships is layered and dense throughout, creating a kind of spiral of overlapping complexities. Wanting to know the truth of the world seems to be deeply entangled with the fakery and fiction of playing a role in the world, playing a part and watching others play that part (knowingly or unknowingly); and layered above and within all that entanglement is the framing of this role-playing by the sights, sounds, and movements of the camera's musical eye.

The film does something very strange with this spectacle of seeing: it converts it into a representation of fascination, then an embodiment of it not as a cinematic translation of what it feels like to think or be fascinated with something. It shows us what fascination *is*: a strange, supernatural force that captures the being who is struck by it, stills and holds them, rapt. It is something that lasts longer than noticing or registering that something is happening. It is the very terms by which we must understand Scottie's involvement. The film does not show us or represent to us that he is involved: it involves us in that involvement so that we *share* (not identify or align ourselves with—these are too weak as forms of engagement) what it is he is doing. And there may not be a word or term for what that is: it is something that happens in the film *Vertigo* during these scenes of tracking Madeleine during her daily pilgrimage to Carlotta's places in the city.

In *Vertigo* the detective's involvement emerges gradually in steady stages as Scottie tracks his prey rather than in those all-at-once moments of sudden rapture, such as Devlin's notice of Alicia as she peers out of the plane window as they land in Rio, or Jeff's first sight of Kathie in the bar in Mexico. *Tracking* reminds us that the detective is formed not only from the legacy of our ancient hunter-gatherer past but from a more recent sense of the necessity for the divination of meaning enabled by the sheer shattering spell of modernity itself; that in this world of shattered meaning, everything radiates signification, and hence everything is resonant as an object to be known, tracked, filmed, framed, shown.

When we find out later that Madeleine's interests are performed in order to convince Scottie that she is indeed obsessed with a dead person, it only reveals that her real focus and interest was precisely in maintaining Scottie's interest in the illusion she was creating. When she stops at a store Scottie follows her inside via a gloomy back entrance which offers a strange ambient hint of threat as he sneaks behind her and peeks through a door at Madeleine purchasing some flowers. She is dressed in a smart gray jacket and skirt, holding an expensive-looking fur in her hands. Once again, fake Madeleine parades herself for his view and once again Scottie suspects nothing. Because he is following her, a lot of the views of Kim Novak are from behind. Are we to assume that Scottie notices, as we might, how well-fitted Madeleine's skirt is, the firmness of her behind that it shapes?

Next, Madeleine parks at the Mission Dolores church, and Scottie discreetly follows her inside (the soundtrack has assumed an eerie electric organ melody for this part, as if the creakiness of the tall tale being told is being underlined for us); he follows her outside to a small colorful cemetery, which is shot in extreme soft-focus that makes the brightness of the day and its colors assume a sickly, blurred aspect. It is as if Scottie is watching her through the gloomy fog of bright sunshine, and the bright yellow flowers that frame his view of Madeleine keeping vigil at a grave might also remind us of Midge's genuinely bright and happy apartment. This is *not* a happy view; it is a view of a woman romancing the stones of death, keeping company with them. We may associate the music we hear with some mood happening within Scottie. He is at the sickly start of a romance, of being seduced by the fact of a woman who claims to be possessed by another woman, both of whom are more or less fictional anyway: Madeleine an actor in Elster's plot, and Carlotta Valdes—the woman whose grave Scottie sees Madeleine beside—perhaps mostly a folk tale more than a real historical figure. The yellow roses Scottie passes as he shadows Madeleine in the graveyard remind us of Midge's sensible brightness; they might remind us of less occultic ways to attach ourselves to reality in the modern world of the present (like the innovative bra in her apartment). The headstones and the larger monument that Madeleine disappears behind catch the midday sun so that their edges are bright white, almost etched into the frame of the film. The gravestone Madeleine was fixated on is marked "Carlotta Valdes," and Scottie hurriedly takes down the name in a white notebook that we never see him use again. But it is important that it is there as an emblem of notation, of study, and of record.

He follows her green car to a stately art gallery, the Legion of Honor museum, a grand place whose exterior signals the historical significance of the fine works it contains. We see him walk toward it, and then inside the gallery we see him walk from the darkness of the foreground of the shot where he is framed by two large columns (and the figure of a nude sculpture in black marble to our screen left), and Madeleine seated at the center of the frame in a room of paintings, herself contemplating one we cannot yet see. We are behind Scottie, and there is a strong directionality to this shot (and the eerie melody that starts up on the soundtrack at this point), leading us toward Scottie and on to the lit area where Madeleine sits.

First, we cut from behind Scottie to a closer frontal shot of him, from slightly below and to the left of him, so that we have a good view of him looking; he turns his head to the right, frowning as if in concentration (the gesture tells us he is looking studiously, slightly puzzled at what he sees before him). The next shot shows us Madeleine seated in a large gallery space, seated and seemingly transfixed in the distance looking at a painting ahead of her on the wall. Then we see Scottie taking this in, shaking his head a little bit and looking from Madeleine to the portrait as if not quite understanding what he sees. Then he seems to decide to walk closer to get a better look at what is going on. Closer should mean clarity; he moves along the far side of the gallery room, affecting to look at the paintings, and we are behind him again; then he looks back and the next shot reveals he has edged his way directly behind where Madeleine is seated. We now get a much better view of Madeleine's back as she is seated in front of the painting. In this shot we can get all at once the pertinent features: the painting is of a youngish woman in a dress, holding flowers that are similar in shape and coloring to the bouquet of flowers next to Madeleine on her seat

Madeleine contemplates the portrait of Carlotta Valdes, and we see the representation of the person who is named on the gravestone. Carlotta emerges by steady stages in the film, accruing substantiality: a name on a gravestone, an image in a painting, and finally a real actress playing the role of Carlotta in Scottie's nightmare. Scottie "reads" this scene, and this interpretation is given to us by Hitchcock's camera, tracking his eyes as he notices that the flowers Madeleine bought resemble those held by the figure in the painting, Carlotta Valdes. The camera then moves in a way that shows us how Scottie notices that Madeleine and Carlotta share a similar hairstyle. This movement feels overemphasized as if the mere fact of the similarity is not really what the camera's movement is for at all; a simple cut between the hair in the portrait and Madeleine's hair would have been sufficient. The movement is rather doing to us, the spectators of the film, what Judy-as-Madeleine is doing to Scottie: it is showing us one thing by pretending to show us something else. What the camera movement is showing us is not the fact of the similarity, but the fact of Scottie's noticing of it as an index of his overentanglement, his "cinematic" ensnaring by the seductive visual rhyme and echoes of flowers, hair, real, representation. As Michael Wood describes it, this is not at all Scottie's optical point of view:

> As he looks the camera zooms in on the bouquet she has beside her on the seat, then continues to the painting, ending on a close-up of a similar bouquet there. We see Scottie again, standing at the same distance, and we cut to a swirl in Madeleine's hairdo, zooming in and then moving on to the same swirl in Carlotta's hair, this time in a close-up that almost puts us into the painting, a visual proximity that Scottie could have achieved only by climbing over Madeleine and using a small ladder. Some version of this effect happens in movies all the time—how often is our vision simply aligned with that of a character?—but here it is truly extravagant. It's not that Scottie can't see what he sees and make his deductions. It's that he can't see it in this way, and our literal viewing becomes a metaphor for what he thinks.[13]

Shortly after this account Wood remarks that the film is "so purely a movie . . . it beautifully and scarily exploits the possibilities of the medium, makes our dependence on them something like an addiction"; indeed this little moment in the gallery is extraordinarily eloquent in its expression of the film's presentation to us of the means by which we are prone to entanglements and manipulations both as an audience for movies and in the real world. It is also mechanistic, automatic in the decisive ostension of its movement (*this* is like *this*), reminiscent of something a machine might do when it was learning about the similarity between things based on shape and other aspects of raw appearance. We might remember, sophisticated flaneurs of the modern city that we are, how fundamental to organic development and animal learning imitation is; that as Aristotle reminds us *mimesis* is the basis of our enjoyment of the dramatic arts. "This is like this": the flowers are like the flowers in the portrait; she does her hair the same way as the person in the painting. Human beings see patterns in the world: imitation is one way of marking, even theatricalizing, a pattern of repetition. And yet seeing is not the same as distilling, as clarifying. Noticing the clue, finding the track, does not necessarily lead to the prey. False tracks, false leads, made-up clues. The fundamental things of the scene are reflected back to us through the astonished picture of Scotty's *confounded* face, as if these simple correspondences disguise in their simplicity something more profound, more terrible and awesome than he can fathom. The fact that he is confounded by what he sees feels *uncanny*, and its uncanniness is further underlined by the way Scottie seems to regard Carlotta in the portrait as somehow looking back at him: herself becoming another spectator in this complex grid of looking, seeing, watching, and being watched.[14] As Scottie looks between the portrait of Carlotta and the seated figure in front of it, we see behind him the frames of two paintings, as if the edges of reality have parted like a curtain as he watches and he has stepped out of this world into another. The sense of supernatural danger is only deepened when we consider how strange it is that we never see Madeleine's face during this scene, only her back.[15] The directed-facingness of this position, similar to those noted in *Out of the Past* and *Notorious*, here functions as a kind of *erasure* of her face altogether so that it feels "replaced" by Carlotta's. If this thought occurs to us we could begin to believe, as perhaps Scotty does, that the dead can come back out of the past to possess the living. Of all the seers in the scene, Carlotta is the exception since she seems confident, composed, and not at all troubled. As when we see her embodied by a live actress later on during Scottie's dream sequence, this is not a picture of Carlotta as hysterical or mad. Her gaze meets the troubles and sights of the world evenly: it is those living in it that somehow cannot cope with what is beamed into their vision.

Detectives are supposed to be athletes of perception and are hence peculiarly vulnerable to the deadly or seductive sights of the world. *Vertigo* is congested with visions of lookers stunned or confounded or seduced by what they see; and one can imagine that notion of the macabre dangers of a world whose sights entrap and enthrall. The sights of the world are transformed in this movie into deadly, danger-ful things: the visual field is *pointed*. As Murray Pomerance eloquently observes:

> The *Vertigo* gallery sequence metonymizes cinema. We are led on (1) a moving journey through (2) a group of intensively composed pictures, and offered opportunity for

(3) reading not only those pictures individually but also the whole picture sequence as an unfolding chain of revelations. If any film anywhere accomplishes this metonymy to some degree, Hitchcock here takes pains not only to make indication of this state of affairs but also point to himself doing so, making express *indication* of that effect: movies unfold syntactically, *but here and now I am pointing this out*. Perhaps he means us to think of Gallery 6 [where the scene takes place] as metonymy for not film generally but for *Vertigo* itself, a film about facts pointed out; thus, as a pointer to *Vertigo*'s recursion.[16]

This recursion seems to be both an intended and an unconscious features of the detective films considered so far in this book. It a constitutive risk of the business of detection that when the detective-hunter searches for and tracks "pointers" they need to be aware, as Scottie here is not, that the world may be deliberately pointed in the way it is in order to mislead. That this is a feature not only of detective fiction, but also the subjective life of any perceiver, is articulated by this exchange between the two trench-coated "Mysterious Men" in the final episode of Dennis Potter's metafictional masterpiece *The Singing Detective* after they find a scrap of paper at a bloody murder scene and come to the realization they are plot devices, mere entities in a fiction:

> FIRST MYSTERIOUS MAN: That's it. That's the point. You put your finger right on it.
>
> SECOND MYSTERIOUS MAN: Have I? How do you mean?
>
> FIRST MYSTERIOUS MAN: We don't know a bloody thing about our . . . You never use my name do you?
>
> SECOND MYSTERIOUS MAN: Do you ever use mine?
>
> FIRST MYSTERIOUS MAN: There's blood on this paper, all over it.
>
> SECOND MYSTERIOUS MAN: What does it say?

First Mysterious Man: It says, "Who killed Roger Ackroyd?"

Second Mysterious Man: Who?

First Mysterious Man: Christ knows. Is he a foreigner?

Second Mysterious Man: Do we know him? Is he on our list?

First Mysterious Man: I don't know him from Adam. But . . . it's a clue. Everything—all things—*mean* something. All things point.

For Scottie that all things point is his torture: his eyes cannot stop seeing the sights the world has ranged against them. The agony is not that the world's appearance is misleading but that it is infinitely interpretable; he is prone before the pointedness of a world spikey with signs, traces and tracks that entrance and ensnare. When Madeleine leads him from the gallery to the McKittrick Hotel, an old shabby building run by a strange bird of a lady, this aspect of the visible world is once again pointed to in a close-up of a chandelier; when he questions the hotelier, he discovers Madeleine uses the name Carlotta Valdes and has literally vanished despite the fact he saw her open the curtains in her room upstairs where we see her look out of the window and we see him get another framed view of her (pointed at him).

Preoccupied with his first day's work, Scottie visits Midge's place and fixes himself a drink. Midge is perched on her work unit that abuts a fabulous view of the city through the four large windows of her corner apartment; she is whitening her shoes, and in response to his question about who would know the folk history of the city tells him that the man to ask is Pop Liebel (Konstantin Shayne) who runs the Argosy Book Shop. In an impeccable performance of storytelling, Leibel fills out the historical tale of Carlotta; this is a man dedicated to details, who has many pens and a notebook in the top pocket of his ill-fitting silk smoking jacket. Unlike Elster he tells his tale with charisma and no manipulative shenanigans: Carlotta was a showgirl, picked up by a rich man, they had a child, and then he abandoned her. She becomes "sad," which evolves to mean insane; walking the streets, she calls for the child that was taken from her. What we might pay attention to, particularly on later repeated viewings, is his comment about the man who "threw" Carlotta away: "He kept the child and threw her away . . . you know men could do that in those days, they had the power and the freedom." Remembering he used these same words with Scottie earlier, we might see Elster himself in this story, literally throwing his wife "away" by tossing her off a bell tower. Perhaps we ought to consider too that it is Scottie who is abandoned by Madeleine/Judy until by chance he discovers her again, unknowingly, on the street. And Judy too, has been abandoned by Elster, and that is all before we get to the situation of Midge equally "thrown" by Scottie and his obsession with Madeleine and her little mysteries. It is not just "in those days" that people abandoned one another with little sense of their responsibility or loyalty to them. "The idea is that the beautiful mad Carlotta's come back from the dead and taken possession of Elster's wife. Oh, now Johnny really come on!" Midge's healthy skepticism leads her to probe for what she considers the real motivation behind Scottie's interest: "Is she pretty?" And after she leaves, Scottie consults the brochure he picked up at the art museum: the black-and-white print of the portrait of Carlotta gets mixed with the profile shot of Madeleine at Ernie's that Scottie could not possibly remember as he didn't see it; but now he appears to (which is to say a shot of him looking at the brochure is followed by one of its pages with the portrait printed on it which in turn has Madeleine's profile at Ernie's superimposed over it: what else can we assume except that Scottie is somehow "remembering" what he didn't see?).

There is no doubt Scottie is receptive, vulnerable to the strange tale and the absorbing, puzzling sights it provides. He meets Elster at his club where it is revealed Madeleine has inherited several pieces of Carlotta's jewelry which she "handles . . . gently, curiously" before wearing them in front of a mirror. Elster tells Scottie that she has never heard of her great-grandmother Carlotta. Nor does she know that Carlotta went insane and killed herself. "Her blood is in Madeleine" he says, and the implication is that insanity can be inherited, passed along the bloodline to drive behavior outside conscious decision making, beyond volitional control. Her blood has authority over her actions in Elster's telling, and once again Scottie seems to buy it.

For the next part of the film Hitchcock binds us so closely to Scottie's perception of what he sees that we find it difficult (especially given the luscious views and beautiful things put in our sight) to diverge from his wish to assist Madeleine. In particular we get a sense of inescapable repetition (like that of a spiral in animated rotation) when Scottie follows her again to the art museum, and then she leads him ahead, this time to a new location, the Presidio park and out along the road next to the bay, to park directly under a stunning view of the Golden Gate Bridge. Never has this incredibly beautiful piece of engineering and design seemed so portentous, its reach from the city to the valley and parks beyond seemingly spanning the distance from civilization to the jagged crust of the planet, from present to past. It is little wonder that by the end of the film Scottie is so incensed by this particular moment of deception; Madeleine/ Elster have chosen this spectacular location for a sad spectacle of faked suicide: a major part of the "production" in which Scottie has been unwittingly recruited as a major character. She slowly walks to the edge of the bay, allows the wind to artfully billow her skirt and scarf as she disappears behind the edge of a building momentarily out of Scottie's sight; when he catches up with her she is deftly dropping flowers from her little bouquet of roses into the water. We see them floating in it—her point of view or his imagination of what they look like? Then, apparently bored with this process, she drops the entire bouquet in the bay before dropping herself with some grace into it too.

There is an explosion of sound, a violent uplifting of music as Scottie has his opportunity to save her, leaping into the water, embracing her for the first time as he effects to carry the putative drowning lady to safety through the petal-filled water. Placing her soaking body in his car seat, an equally wet Scottie implores her to respond to his husky, "Madeleine? Madeleine," and her dreamy half-conscious reaction creates an odd sense of a couple moments after mutual orgasm. Everything is in reverse: we move from an orgiastic state to Scottie undressing her, putting her in his bed, then making his apartment warm and cozy for her, before she awakes and joins him for coffee and conversation.

His apartment blends some modern design—venetian blinds, the steel coffee pot and sugar bowl, portable television—with more traditional elements such as the log fire, brass fireplace tools, wooden coffee table, and burgundy leather chair. His curtains are labia pink which contrasts to his green sweater and the taupe long sofa. Madeleine's clothes are hung to dry in a little bland kitchen, and next to it a drinks cabinet squats beneath a strange golden mandala-shaped object hanging on the wall, echoing the shapes of the title sequence. The camera's pan ends on the frame to Scottie's bedroom, his extended single bed occupied by Madeleine. He has been monitoring her sleep for some time from the sofa, drinking coffee and reading a newspaper (other reading material including the men's magazine *Swank* can be seen on his coffee table). He gets up to watch closer as she murmurs in her sleep. The phone rings in his bedroom (it is Elster—perhaps signaling Judy to awake for her next scene) and she "awakes."

Scottie is loyal—for the moment—to his "employer" as regards the care of his wife. As she dresses, Scottie collects a cup and some milk from his kitchen and then Judy-playing-Madeleine makes her second entrance for him, emerging from the bedroom and taking some cautious steps toward the man who undressed her a little while before. One of the striking things about the film is that once we meet Judy Barton it is very hard to reconcile her Kansas small-town outlook with the extremely skilled actress she clearly needed to be in order to pull off the incredible feat of inhabiting what Bourdieu calls a *habitus*—an entire embodied presentation of all the inherited habits, life experiences, and cultural capital that we have accumulated across a lifetime and which Judy, for sure, did not inherit but *learned* (we are meant to think Elster "taught" her these things by the end of the movie, but even this seems hardly credible; is she just a "natural" deceiver? So malevolent that she can hardly realize the enormous evil in which she participates so seemingly effortlessly?). A similar problem occurs when we read a novel such as *The Great Gatsby* where we are left with the puzzle of how a bond salesmen from the Midwest achieves the altitude of lyrical eloquence Nick Carraway's narration presents to the reader. The only feasible explanation (beyond the convenience of not worrying too hard about the preposterous plot) is that our credulity is entangled in our proximity to, and trust in, Scottie's perception of her. In fact it is testament to Kim Novak's considerable skill as an actor that we *can* detect a lining of the practiced nature of Madeleine's persona, a very slight overemphasis on rectitude in the handling of vowels and consonants as she speaks, that appears slightly—almost imperceptibly—at odds with the way her mouth hangs too far, too hungrily, open over her teeth as she listens to Scottie explains how he fished her out of the bay and dried "her things." After a shot of him speaking, the cutback to Novak has her mouth now tightly, properly closed, and it is in these fractionally brief instances we may detect the deceit at work.[17] As she warms by the glorious log fire Scottie questions her about her movements around the city, clearly seeking to establish her reasons for doing what she does and, more to the point, how these declared reasons intersect with what he knows about her relationship to the influence of Carlotta "in her blood." He's clearly unsettled by her mistaken recollection of her movements and by the straightforward falsehood of her claim never to have been inside the Legion of Honor art museum. And yet he is also clearly attracted to her considerable assurance when she directly questions him; she carries an authority over the spaces she inhabits, even unfamiliar ones such as his apartment, and easily slips into confident declaration: when he tells her his name is John Ferguson she voices the judgment that that is "a good strong name." As she fixes the pins back in her hair, he settles down on the sofa to gaze at her in a kind of wonder. We might imagine this is not an apartment that has been too often troubled by the presence of a woman, and she steers the conversation to just this point: she asks what he does and his reply, "wander around," gets the semi-ironic response "that's a good occupation." Scottie says that some people prefer living alone, but we see Madeleine, leaning on the coffee table bedecked with the rounded organic shapes of the sugar pot and a cigarette dispenser, assert that it's "wrong"—not sad, not "not for me," but "wrong"; she adds, "I'm married you know."

Scottie does know and Judy-as-Madeleine knows that he does. But he does not respond to this comment, as if the enormity of it—morally and professionally—is an intrusion into what it is he *wants*. At this point that seems to be more than the kind of random sexual adventure promised by the letters pages of a publication like *Swank*, however fortuitous events up to now have been to fictions in that genre: it is much more driven by what seems a genuine concern for the health and safety of a beautiful woman with a sad condition that Scottie wishes to heal in a whatever way he can. Part of the betrayal that Judy visits upon him in creating a fake person for him to care about is how much he has to ignore in order to find that species of compassion, not least the immorality of entanglement with an old college friend's stunning young wife. But, equally, we can take

Judy-Madeleine's comment about the wrongness of being alone as the expression of a genuine stance that conveniently suits the fake Madeleine's performance of estrangement from the world in her possessed mode as the abandoned Carlotta *and* Judy's real estrangement from it as an agent in a murder plot now facing a kindly man who wants only the best for the fictional woman she is bringing to life in front of his patient, concerned eyes. Adding to this complexity is the fact that Scottie, too, is lying about his role in all this to Madeleine and that Judy knows very well that he is. His guile and deftness in negotiating this tricky moral territory while remaining disarmingly compassionate and clearly already in love perhaps fascinates Judy since he, too, appears as someone able to step outside the ordinary constraints of ethical moral life.

These fraught worlds compress into one another at the moment Scottie offers to bring Madeleine another coffee, his hand landing and interlacing briefly with hers and a kind of electric charge implied between them as their bodies stiffen and evolve in acknowledgment of the moment. And however many times one sees this film there is something that cannot be denied about the scene, however much we are aware of its webs and spirals of deceit, irony, and ellipsis: its fundamental tenderness. Scottie's actions, however morally compromised on clever, close, detailed inspection after the fact, are *right*: it was right for him to rescue her from the bay, to care for her carefully (while updating her husband on her progress), and we can hardly blame the man for developing, alongside his evident compassion, a further evolution of this compassion, this worry for her, into the beginnings of the spring of love. Likewise, however much we know—on further viewings—that Judy's act as Madeleine is to entrap Scottie, it is hard to deny she *does* respond to Scottie, particularly at this moment, and especially because he seems so genuinely concerned for her as well as interested in her. It is not unfeasible to assume this is the first time, or one of the few times, "Judy Barton from Kansas," whoever she *actually is*, has been treated with (paradoxically) genuine compassion and care.

She watches him closely as he goes to answer the phone that had interrupted their hand-touching, as if Elster somehow could see into the apartment and has waited for a moment precisely like this before landing his call (this is another spooky dimension that further crystallizes that clairvoyant sensibility embedded in the film's fiction). The call also is a signal for Judy to leave the apartment, and she vanishes as she did at the McKittrick Hotel, still putting on her clothes as she exits his apartment complex just in time for Midge to see her leave. There is a bravery to Midge's attempt to cover her hurt response to this sight (she is in fact seeing Judy leave as part of Elster's plot, seeing *Judy* not *Madeleine*), as if Scottie's keeping her out of this part of his life is an index of its importance to him, and thus her diminished status as his confidant and friend.

    The next day we have the final movement of Scottie's following of Madeleine by car, which ends on the surprise for him that she leads him right back to his own apartment. The bright beauty of the city is emphasized in these shots, as if the couple's dunking in the bay has cleansed it; yellow cabs shimmer in the sun as Scottie follows her car in his, and one believes for a moment that this calm city with secrets tucked away in its hills would indeed be a fine place to wander for a person of independent means; even driving around under the crisscross of power and telephone lines with the blue sky and blue bay ever in the background seems calming. Madeleine has come to deliver a thank-you note, and Scottie meets her on the steps outside the red door of his apartment; she is wearing a gorgeous ice white woolen coat over black clothes, gloves, and handbag—a picture of elegance—and as she leans against his wall talking to him, she has never looked more beautiful. She is even playful when Scottie slips that he "enjoyed" the evening, agreeing that she did, too. There is something just close to the idea of flirtatious in the direct way she smiles at him and leans easily back against the stair rail as he reads her note. It is little wonder that Scottie, faced with this astonishing creature, pursues her to her car and, as Jeff Markham did with his employer, Whit, breaks any agreement he may have had with Elster by suggesting to her that they "wander" together. He is asking her to join him as a companion, and as he rushes to close his front door, once again we see Judy watching him move with genuine interest.

    Instead of wandering the city, she drives them into the wooded hills, far away from other people and into the ancient heart of the natural world, a dark secret place dominated by towering redwood forest. For Madeleine these trees calibrate the cycle of human life and death, and while Scottie attempts to ground her musings with scientific facts about them, she seems in a theatrical mode, touching the rings of the cutaway redwood trunk with a black gloved hand while incanting, "Here I was born, there I died. It was only a moment for you. . ." (presumably the "you" is the tree). And this performance is where Judy is least convincing, resembling Blanche Tyler's fakery in *Family Plot*, but played in earnest, without irony, for Scottie's credulous consumption. Hitchcock assists this theater by mixing in a kind of spooky music as the ghostlike Madeleine wanders off into the trees and vanishes again in front of Scottie's eyes. Anyone who has played with a dog knows this game: it's called, "come and find me." And when he does, the performance is even more creaky, but Scottie's drive to know is insistent because what he wants is to know what it is that drives her, and that is precisely the question her performance "points" at him, radiates toward him, emanates. "Why did you jump? [into the bay] Why did you jump? Why did you jump? What was there inside that told you to jump?" This is an odd formulation of the question: not just why did you do something but what thing, what entity *inside*, instructed you to take that action, as if our movements in the world can be explained by the identification of something "inside" that compels us against our will (the thing we might usually associate having authority over volition) to do something. Scottie is thoroughly absorbed—been possessed—by this lark about her "possession."

More than this, the forest setting gives his questions and her frantic, melodramatic responses ("Please don't ask me again, please promise me that"—as if Judy is tempted to identify the actual living entity, Elster, the authority "inside" who has in fact told her to do what she does) an immoral context, for the dark forest is precisely the place that adulterous lovers might choose for their lovemaking (as we shall see in the opening shots of *Chinatown*). Once again everything feels in reverse, with this secret setting a place for interrogation while the open space of the wave-swept shore is the place we see them finally kiss. What is shared between the condition of vertigo and that of being in love is a kind of dizzying sickness, a nausea fueled by the stabs and whips of adrenaline and anxiety, a feeling that can literally knock one off balance, leave one "wandering" almost blind in the streets. Technically the condition is called *limerence*, the strange obsessive euphoria that encircles fresh lovers such that the rest of the world seems unreal like a back projection. The forest seems choked by death, by the sordid vegetative grimness of "everlasting" life; the windswept shore that they drive to next captures the broiling sense of love uncontrolled and annihilating at the edge of the world. As they stand near it, Scottie tells her he is responsible for her now that he has saved her life, that he is "committed" and that he has "to know." And now we get a remarkable, very brief shot of Madeleine from behind, showing the spiraled Carlotta knot in her hair as she says, "There's so little that I know." Hitchcock returns to this framing throughout their conversation as Scottie attempts to excavate the fragments of what she claims to remember about the fugues she experiences; in fact these fragments become components in the nightmare we later see him having (he takes these signs and makes them his own)—walking down a long corridor with darkness (death) at its end, looking into an open grave, sitting in an anonymous room, a tower with a bell in Spain. "If I could just find the key, the beginning and put it together"—Scottie struggles with these words as if he realizes their inadequacy, and he is now hostage to Madeleine's trump card, her claim that if she were mad that would explain what he cannot. She runs off toward the sea, and they embrace in the moment at which she lies most effectively to him: "I'm not mad, I don't want to die, there's someone within me and she says I must die!" Her entreaties are accompanied by her open mouth close to his, virtually begging him to kiss her, which he does.

This torrid melodramatic scene played with a straight face is contrasted with the giggles of Midge in her apartment where she is working on an as yet unseen painting. It is night and the room is cozy, Midge wearing a red blouse and black skirt, slightly more formal than usual as if painting were a serious business despite the hilarity it is causing her; she, too, is preparing a scene. Like Madeleine she left a message at Scottie's apartment asking to see him, and as she mixes him a drink she tells him she will make him dinner if he takes her to a movie. Scottie knows that she wants to know what he has been up to, but he remains evasive, claiming he has been "wandering." He's only there because she asked him to come. Midge is his friend, a close enough friend that regular, easygoing contact comes as a natural punctuation in one's day or over the week. Whatever we think of our friends, the beginning of a new romance for either party is a moment of crisis; we rightly wonder if our own relationship with the friend might be obliterated by it—a selfish impulse, no doubt, but nonetheless a time of anxiety. She brings him his drink and sits down near him as she tells Scottie that she has gone back to her first love, painting; we get a profile shot similar to those we have seen of Madeleine (in Ernie's, at the flower store, in the car) and, without being unkind, Barbara Bel Geddes—attractive though she clearly is—cannot compete in profile with the altitude of beauty that Kim Novak has available to her. She has painted a comic portrait of herself modeled on that of Carlotta Valdes in the art museum; it is genuinely funny to see this modern woman with an arch knowing look staring right back directly at us; less direct, more playful, but as confident as Carlotta in the portrait. We get a juxtaposition of Midge and Midge-as-Carlotta in a shot that frames the seated Midge and the painting side-by-side. It is the Midge in the portrait who has the capacity to seize Scottie, confront his idiotic infatuation, and shake some sense into him, not the fragile, slightly mouse-like woman we see already distraught at the pain she has caused Scottie. "That's not funny Midge, no. . ." (but it is, we feel, unsettled though we may be by Scottie's distress), and he leaves quietly in a kind of embarrassed, hurt way that some of us might recognize as the marker of a relationship coming to its end. Perhaps there is no coming back from such an exit and no salve for that kind of hurt, however dumb it might be, however lovestruck Scottie is. Midge's distress after he leaves is one of the more painful parts of the film; her anger at herself for what is *his* failure to appreciate the comedy of the painting is also a recognition of *her* failure to appreciate his vulnerability to the seduction of such a conventional tall tale, one she might want to imagine her dear friend would be far too sensible to fall for. The harshness with which she pulls her own hair indicates self-directed anger that might be better deployed outwardly.[18] And that does not mean Scottie can avoid the weight of this friendship-at-an-end; we see him alone at night walking the streets under the clang of stoplights; coming home he apparently falls asleep on his taupe sofa, awoken by Madeleine ringing his doorbell; the fire burns low in the grate, and he looks as if he's slept a tangled night in his clothes. When he opens the door, for an instant we see only a dark shadow (not dissimilar to the shadow of the nun in the bell tower just before the film's ending), the light revealing a distressed Madeleine, now dressed in gray. She hardly looks as if she has had a troubled night of dreams, as she claims, instead immaculately made-up, icily perfect; once again she plays "come get me" with her tale of the bell tower arising in her dream, and Scottie follows as she now provides so much detail he couldn't fail to realize the place she means. And he tells her: "Madeleine, a hundred miles south of San Francisco there's an old Spanish mission, San Juan Bautista it's called, and it's been preserved exactly as it was a hundred years ago as a museum." For him, this is the key that unlocks everything, the sheer empirical fact of something from the past existing now, that one can visit. Conveniently, it is also a tourist spectacle, a piece of public theater that one can visit. All Scottie has to do, he reasons, is take her there and doing that "will finish your dream, it will destroy it." And presumably she will be cured. What he does not know is that in telling her he will take her to the mission that afternoon, she now must tell Elster so that he can murder his wife; what Scottie does not know, and Judy must, is that his realization seals Mrs. Elster's fate.

We see Scottie's car driving through forested roads toward the mission, and inside Madeleine in her gray suit watches the road ahead and then looks up at the treetops and the blue sky above the car as they glide along the road. This shot is one of the few from her point of view, and I take it to be *Judy's* point of view, something confirmed when we see the shot repeated during their return journey to the mission at the end of the film. It is perhaps the most melancholy, romantic (in the technical sense of a mood in lyrical despair in the face of modernity) shot in the film, the trees gliding by a different kind of clock marking time from the redwood in the forest. Their sweeping by describes and evokes trembling anxiety, the rushing past of time and space, a building urgency.

The climax of the first part of the film takes place at the San Juan Bautista mission; we see its cloisters and the green courtyard in front of the saloon and stables, a solitary nun crossing it reminding us that the mission remains operational, not a mere façade. Then we see Madeleine once again riding shotgun, this time in an old four-horse carriage in the stable. As she did in his apartment that morning, Madeleine launches into her hokey trance-talk, and Scottie good-naturedly points her to a full-size papier-mâché horse, rapping its hollow neck and remarking, "He'll have a little trouble getting in and out of the stall without being pushed . . . you see? There's an answer for everything." What Scottie wants is for her to simply *see* the fact of the matter, but what he does not know is that she already can see what is real, far more than he since what is coming will blind him for a good many months before the truth of this moment becomes apparent to him. Which is to say, Scottie's insistence that one just "sees" the world for what it is cannot be accomplished by simply looking at it a bit harder. One needs quite some time to feel one's way under and inside the fabric and texture of that reality as it channels through our daily lives; moments of realization are rarely sudden, and when they are they can happen so fast that one is liable to respond poorly to them.[19]

They kiss for the final time, a "kiss shot" from behind Scottie's head so that we see when Madeleine breaks it off that she has seen some signal from outside and above them (no doubt Elster waving from the bell tower—"get a move on!"): and Scottie's wholehearted declaration of love only makes the moment more agonizing for her—we see in a spectacular way her face evolves back and forth like images appearing then vanishing on photographic paper, shifting between Madeleine and Judy. Everything is "too late" in melodrama, except this is only a fake melodrama, a play within a play for Scottie to witness: if Madeleine *were* real would she have been cured by Scottie at this point? The question seems absurd given what we find out shortly, but surely it was one uppermost in his mind at the time, the sense that he could not rescue this woman he loves from vague forces that occupied and propelled her up the bell tower. He does try his best to keep her, but Judy in a desperate moment pledges her love to him while at the same time manipulating him (with some kisses) to let her go into the church. She ascends the tower, and he is blocked from following her by the onset of his vertigo. At that point what he takes to be Madeleine's body falls outside the little gray window of the tower and, once again, his wide blue eyes absorb the horror looking out once to see the broken body on the rooftiles below and then again; and then seemingly keyed to more internal forces as he raises his left hand to his mouth. It is a picture of extreme stress, as if he's been caught or sighted himself doing something foul and evil. He has failed to save the woman he is infatuated with, a human being in his "care," so to speak, who despite his best efforts destroyed herself. Suicide is devastating precisely because self-annihilation threatens to rip the fabric of society apart: how can we live with ourselves as moral agents if we allow a world where our fellow humans desire to erase themselves from our company? Those left behind by the self-killers have to deal with that shame, that disgrace, the agonizing reflection about whether or not they could have done more to prevent it.

The rest of the film darkens its mood even further from this low point; it implies that if we accept the authority of our trauma there is no way to escape its repetition. Indeed, this final part begins with repetition, the left-to-right pan from the cloister across the green courtyard at the mission, where a coroner's inquest is being held. The coroner exonerates Elster and forcefully lays the moral if not the legal burden of blame on Scottie who indeed *was* too weak to save Madeleine. The coroner's words bite into Scottie: "He did nothing," he did not make a greater effort to save Madeleine's successful suicide even knowing that she was clearly suicidal: this is all right, and yet it feels all wrong, it feels somehow *unjust* even if we struggle to find reasons for thinking so. Perhaps because we have seen and felt the genuine compassion in Scottie's efforts to help Madeleine and what appears to be her real struggle with a nightmarish intrusion into her dreams of a possessing entity. As we learn from the inquest, Scottie too is now vulnerable to such moments; he left the scene of the "suicide" claiming he had a blackout and remembered nothing until he was back at his apartment hours later. Once the verdict has been reached, Elster approaches Scottie near a window and tells him he is leaving the city, assuring him it was not his fault, that "we both know who killed Madeleine." The latter says nothing, and we see the early stages emerging of what becomes a kind of paralysis, as if the challenge of the world, of surviving within it after the object of one's love has died, is simply too terrible to bear, so unbearable that the carrying out of everyday tasks and routines seems like blasphemy. He now wants nothing, and in that state the world can wreak a terrible vengeance on the mind.

We see him visit Madeleine's gravestone (undated it merely says her name and "Wife of Gavin Elster"), and then we experience Scottie's nightmare. This is the hinge at the center of the film, the ultimate fusion of Scottie's optical point of view with the imaginative one that Hitchcock has presented to us up to now. It also consolidates and extends the film's interest in the *graphical* representation of consciousness, one that began with the eerie spirals of the title sequence, and continued with objects like Midge's drawings and sketches, the portraits in the art museum, Carlotta's headstone, Midge's portrait of herself (in particular the shot that combines it with Midge seated in front of the checkerboard flooring in her apartment), and the cutaway tree trunk with its indicative historical events glued to it.[20] For all its garish excess, the dream depicts Scottie's presence within it as a *determined force* always moving forward. The dream begins with a shot of him restlessly thrashing around in his bed covers before a close-up of his head suddenly turns to blue, flashes back to normal color, then back to blue, then to a mauve alternation (as the music builds up a kind of thrilling, strumming momentum as if something is about to crash into his vision) as his eyes open. To call it a dream or a nightmare is problematic since early on in the sequence Scottie appears to "wake up" and look directly at the camera with terror in his eyes. Is he waking up to "see" the dream as it is about to unfurl, or is he already in a dream where he is dreaming he is looking at what follows? The fact that he looks square at *us* with fear is unsettling enough: there is something in us, in our viewing of him that is terrifying; or—perhaps worse—there is something unfeasibly *behind us* that he can see and we cannot. The next shot is a color drawing of the rose bouquet that Madeleine bought in the flower shop, the one which resembles that held by Carlotta in the portrait. It is set against an ochre background (similar to the color of Scottie's walls), but in a green flash it morphs into an animated version where the organic flowers take on abstract forms, exploding toward us in a fast gliding movement that further distorts their shape; central but briefly seen is a solid "rose"-like core. It resembles a hostile alien cell sloughing off its earthen form to envelop the viewer. But then it vanishes into blackness, and we are back at the mission inquest with Scottie once again standing silent at the window (a yellow filter flashes over this shot), while Elster stands next to an actress playing Carlotta. Her costume emphatically gives her an air of the theater as if Elster did not just bring to life "Madeleine" as played by Judy Barton, but also the core inspiration for the part, Carlotta Valdes herself. She so resembles the figure in the portrait that she must have been its actual model, or so it seems: whatever the truth, it is close enough to feel extremely uncanny just in terms of the *sheer optical wonder* of imitation, of mimesis: a portrait coming to life. (Portraits are drawn, typically, "from life," hence their indexical power.) And this is part of the reason why the dream is not exactly a nightmare, and not quite something that is happening to Scottie, more something he is directing and arranging for himself, as the fragments of the past trauma are struggling to pattern themselves in some kind of legible order. For sure, as Robert Pippin shows us, there are "clues" Scottie brings to his own attention, not least the proximity of the "living Carlotta" to Elster, as if they are in collusion (or that she is emanating, spectrally, from his presence), as well as the "artifice" of the bouquet.[21] Carlotta looks up *to* Scottie in a gesture which is, brilliantly, the first—unspoken—moment where a character says to Scottie, "Can't you see?," and it is immediately doubled by Elster, once Carlotta has met Scottie's gaze, *also* looking at him as if to communicate the same thought. The plant of this thought (and hence its eventual payoff at the end of the film when Scottie sees Judy wearing the necklace) is next emphasized by having the Carlotta actress—her name is Joanne Genthon—pose in a way very close to that in the painted, still, portrait, with Hitchcock's camera tracking in to the necklace she is wearing, as if Scottie's conscious unconscious has now been totally interpellated by Hitchcock's art; it gives him *direction* and *focus* that he could not bring to bear on his entanglement with Madeleine. It reminds us of the key moment in the gallery where he appeared confounded: but it was not the necklace that caught his attention then. Now, he is no longer confounded by the false signs in a way that entraps him into the fantasy talk of an actress; he is confounded by real signs, real tracks that promise to lead his mind to the solution to the enigma. And, in doing so, Hitchcock unhitches his camera from its slavish description of Scottie's imagination and now becomes less a collaborator in his visions of romantic doom, and more a critic pointing to its death-dealing deficits. This design adds up at this point in the "dream" to a collective bidding by the cinematic elements for Scottie to see better. The next shot has Scottie apparently following this cue, walking toward us against a black background with a puzzled yet determined look on his face. Confounded by what he sees, he continues his pursuit; he wants to know. This is the purest picture of a detective driven not by the promise of erotic freshness, but by a thirst for meaning, for truth, whatever the cost. As he continues to walk patiently, the wind gently tousling his hair, the cemetery where Carlotta is buried appears behind him (once again there is a red filter flashing); it is as if he has willed it, in his pursuit, into existence. Then he looks down at the empty grave, long and dark beneath Carlotta's headstone: she is no longer there, perhaps was never there, perhaps is a blank figment in an evil plot, the black open grave an allegory for the unlit cinema screen or an empty film gate, both waiting to be filled with fantasy. Somehow, since this is Scottie "dreaming," at this moment we experience a frisson of what might be called his death drive (Pippin reminds us that fear of heights may be a combination of fear of falling and fear of wanting to fall, an acknowledgment of our desire for self-annihilation[22]) and that is caught up, entangled too, in the desire for meaning and knowledge. The thrill, the rush of incoming death, if we could capture it, eternalize it, *live it*, would be a precious feast for the beautiful soul, a chance to experience all meaning at precisely the moment of its obliteration from the world. Whatever that means, it gets close to my experience of the following scenes. For in plunging into her empty grave we do not fall with Scottie, but instead have his face, disconnected from the world and body at the center of a vertiginous, animated pattern, where the lines of motion travel toward the center of his head; he looks back at us almost impassive, vanishing briefly, then traveling closer to us, as if the lines are filling him with ultimate power, the authority of all meaning, all knowing knowledge. He seems calm, exulted, like a god. What does this god see? We see the shape of Scottie's body, dark and little, falling unreal toward the roof under the bell tower, and then that setting is removed and the shape travels through beautiful white oblivion, gliding away, alone.[23] Now Scottie wakes up, violently sitting up, staring once again at us now with terrified wide-open eyes as if he has seen the terrible awesome face of God itself, who is all meaning, after all.

What is the impact of this dream and its clues on Scottie? Does it stimulate him into action? The very opposite: he is catatonic. We find him in a well-to-do institution for the mentally ill, visited by Midge. I think one does Midge a great disservice to confuse her friendship with some kind of deficit on her part because of her affection or love for Scottie. It is extremely difficult, and terribly painful, to watch a friend or other loved one suffer in this way, apparently stuck like Scottie, in the grip of their own pathological mentation. His room is bright with just enough institutional compression of space to deny it a sense of the cozy; he could look out of the window past the ivied wall and the railings to look at passersby, but he is turned inward, still, in his chair, unresponsive. Midge has brought some Mozart for him to listen to, a lovely gesture (not at all an emblem of her tin ear because he once objected to Bach in her apartment: one should insist on Mozart, especially to those with a Wagnerian soundtrack in their head), and there is something painful in her clarification as if to fill the dead air with words, "Wolfgang Amadeus"; he is "the boy for you," the one who will "clear the cobwebs away." At this Scottie turns his head toward her, and we see her as he might see her. It is an astonishingly scary picture, and coming so soon after the unsettling "dream": Midge is all smiles (her wide grin almost grotesque) standing beside a vase chock full of red roses that appear threatening as if part of a Lucien Freud painting; we might feel this only for an instant, because Midge can only hold the cheery look with a struggle, especially when Scottie sweeps his pained eyes toward her. She makes a great joke about what might happen if the musical files were mixed up with dipsomaniacs getting the melancholiac treatment. Midge also acknowledges she has to be more than a friend ("Mother is here"), and perhaps she always has been that: a protective reality check on whatever it was Scottie thought he was before his accident; perhaps intuiting that this lonely man was always someone lost amidst the fierceness of the world, ill-equipped to face it except in a fantasy of omnipotence. And now the fantasy is over, he appears as a frail man roped to an armchair; and, in keeping with the tone of the remainder of the film, all roles become reversed. Midge is to Scottie as Scottie was to fake-Madeleine: she cannot help him because the depth, the reality of his trauma, is beyond her understanding. He is not sad because he is still in love with a woman; it becomes clear he does not know at all what is wrong with him or what he can do to make things better. For that, he will have to go out into the world and discover what is still awaiting him.

Another division, another "curtain": this time a pan across the cityscape of San Francisco accompanied by uplifting music suggesting recovery, a new dawn. But instead we find Scottie revisiting the places and objects associated with his job following Madeleine; we might take him as still suffering from the trauma or, as he is dressed in the right garb, trying as a detective to piece together the terrible thing that has happened to him in order to somehow assemble it into a coherent, meaningful shape. He is driven, committed, to revisiting the spaces and things that are or resemble those that remain significant components during his job as a detective following Madeleine. This is another version of the "same but different" motion we saw in the gallery when he noticed the resemblance of things between the portrait of Carlotta and Madeleine: these things are almost the same but slightly different: close enough to show the intention of imitation— what does that mean? When he sees a woman dressed like Madeleine leave her house and move toward Madeleine's lovely green Jaguar, what does he think? He asks her (at close range, she looks nothing like Madeleine) where she got the car, but we should ask what it is he thinks he is doing. In some way he seems to be tracking traces of Madeleine as if he already suspects she has not vanished from the world at all. At Ernie's he sits at the bar where he first saw her and immediately, like a magic spell, sees her again (it is as if his eyes are projecting her presence *into* the world where she is absent), but the woman (in fact Kim Novak dressed as Madeleine) as she walks closer to him suddenly becomes a different actress, a different woman. The uncanniness of the medium is made blatant, coarse and frighteningly brutal in front of us with a simple cut. It can rob men of what they want to see. He visits the art museum, and a woman is seated where Madeleine used to sit in front of Carlotta's portrait: he walks right up to her as if she will *be* Madeleine merely at his bidding. He sees the pink and white rose bouquet favored by Madeleine and Carlotta in the window of a flower shop and then, looking up from it onto a crowded San Francisco street, he sees Kim Novak, dressed in green walking and laughing with three of her workmates. She is now playing Judy Barton, and Scottie is right to look closely: how could he miss her and how could any audience not realize that this is the same actress? The representational psychosis of one actress playing two fictional entities (arguably three) in a film is not unique, but we usually accept the conceit with the proviso that it not disturb our sense of the credulity of other characters. But right up to this point Scottie has been imagining Madeleine out of the blue in various ways: has he conjured this being too into life, not quite perfect but the clay from which this god can model the object of his desire? More than this is the sheer mystery of her remaining in vision, uncorrected by editing or a change in shot-scale. There is, if one looks closely, the briefest of hints that she sees him too, first in the long shot that introduces her character when she looks in his direction and her steps miss a beat, and again just as she leaves her friends and the shot and seems to glance to her side. That would explain why she is less than surprised when Scottie turns up outside her hotel door and why she has the evidence of her identity readily to hand. What it does not explain is how slowly she walks away from him along the street as if inviting him to follow her. Again everything is in reverse: before Scottie trailed Madeleine to the McKittrick Hotel and watched her pull the curtains open in her room upstairs, but when he followed her inside she had vanished. Now Scottie trails Madeleine-as-Judy to the Empire Hotel and watches her open the curtains of her room, but when he follows her inside she is right there.

Now, Scottie is a detective, not a fool, unless we take the final shot of the film as an emblem of The Fool, perched precariously at the edge of disaster he has led himself to. That seems to shortchange his capacity for wondrous suffering in the face of a brutal and cruel realization he was the victim of a sleazy murder plot. To get there we have to ignore Scottie's treatment of Judy as an emblem of the puzzle he feels compelled to solve. To be sure, this is caught up in, or seen through the lens of, his pathological romantic entanglement with whatever we take the entity "Madeleine" to be. But one of the reasons he seems to cultivate a distance from Judy, even as he affects to enter into a relationship with her, is that he must pursue, wants to finalize, or seal the meaning of, the strange thing that has happened in his life. However wounded, he is back on the job.

Another strange thing is Judy's reaction when she opens her hotel room door for him. If we accept she spotted him earlier staring at her on the street, then she's had long enough to think about how to react to the possibility, probability, that he's followed her here. If we are to grant Judy any sympathy then her resistance to him, her insistence that she doesn't know him, can only be explained fully not as an act of self-preservation but akin to Devlin's love test of Alicia: only if he is persistent enough, enough to face the truth, can he earn her trust. The hard thing for her is that she is competing with a version of herself, the better version created by Elster and her; if she knows anything then she must realize the exterior habitus was in large part the thing that attracted Scottie to her Madeleine; she will gamble that the habitus at its core—inherited rather than acquired—will be enough to keep him again. But how do we know *this* Judy is any less fabricated? Do we take a base level of habitus—working-class origins, manners, forms of speech—as necessarily more authentic than any other? Why? Part of Hitchcock's genius is to understand and present social class as the continuous process of sorting and distorting moral order; but it can also be faked, theatricalized, and used for evil ends—class can be a costume one wears and preserves for advantage. Notice the way, when she is showing Scottie proof of her identity, Judy follows the writing with her finger like a child in the early stages of reading. As Edward Gallafent has eloquently noted, the casting of Novak is apt as she was up to this point known for roles where happy coupledom was always avoided or frustrated.[24] It is quite plausible to read her playing of Judy Barton not merely as another performance, but one chosen this time by the woman Novak is playing, a means not to hide but to flush Scottie out; to get him to lose his deadly illusions and, by offering a version of a woman without mystery, bring him face to face with their limitation.

All of this is conjecture. As she puts her wallet down, she turns to her dresser, and we get a shot from behind Scottie looking at her in its mirror and she looks at him *through the mirror*: we see her doubled and reflected, and it is in *his* reflection in the mirror that Judy notices and remarks, "Gee, you have got it bad, haven't you?" and turns to him more sympathetically. The cinematic screen is evoked again in the mirrors, reminding us of the way we frame reality that—long before the invention of moving images—was "cinematic" in nature. She shows him a photograph of her father, who died, outside his hardware store, beside another of her and her mother back home in Salina, Kansas. She says her mother remarried, but she didn't get along with the new man and came to "sunny California" three years ago: no doubt hoping for adventure and distance from whatever kind of man her stepfather turned out to be. She's proud of her accomplishments, her independence, leaning back on her dresser and looking at Scottie with a smile: "honest." They agree to have dinner, and the camera moves to rest at the back of Judy's head. Then, in another chilling moment she turns and looks directly at *us*, just as Scottie did during and directly after his dream. She stares for a long time as the shot is mixed with the view of the bell tower that was Scottie's just after Madeleine ran into the church. Now it is Judy who can summon views for us, and we see shots repeated from earlier in the film: Scottie following her into the church, up the stairs and then, an extraordinary new shot, breathtaking in its conceit: Madeleine bursting out of the trapdoor at the top of the bell tower where Elster is holding Madeleine already—another Madeleine, the real Madeleine, dead but presumably untroubled by Carlotta's possessive influence before that—shockingly dressed in exactly the same way and in fact who looks exactly like the Madeleine who has just arrived at the scene of the crime. (She is played by Jean Corbett who appears slighter slimmer than Kim Novak.) As Elster hauls his wife out of the tower, we get a very strange sense that one person has been killed while her double remains there and alive, enough to scream although we do not hear it in Judy's version of events.

We then return to Judy still staring at us, the lights now restored to her little room.

It is a mistake to think only of Elster's plot as preposterous because the fact is that up to now, however unlikely its success, it has worked. To murder one's wife by confecting a story about her, placing a double in the same town, and trusting that that double's activity would not be contradicted by anything or anybody the real wife did or met, while convincing a detective the double is not only real but possessed by a figment from the past is quite a feat. It is in some ways an elegant, elaborate, and graceful plot, perfectly executed. Elster was particularly fortunate in finding two people so apt for their roles: Scottie's vulnerability for a mystery that promised to restore youthful romance, where he could act as a rescuer as well as a sleuth; and Judy's performative agility in playing a woman who embodied such an enigmatic promise.

Judy's flashback ends and the music—heavy, consequential, sad—suggests she bears if not guilt then considerable regret for what she did. She goes to pack, and we see she has kept the gray suit, the one that is the same as her double died wearing. She then sits and writes a letter to Scottie (in a wonderful touch this means we get to notice that Novak is left-handed; for some of us lefties it is an embarrassment to be seen writing by hand since we appear, so I'm told, to do so awkwardly, childishly, wrongly) while we hear her voice say the words she is writing. She tells Scottie that he can give up his "search" (although how she knew he was doing this, if this is what is what he was doing, we don't know), that he was the "victim" and she was the "tool" of Elster's plan. Hitchcock's camera gently, patiently works around Novak's extraordinarily beautiful, young face as we see her think about what she is writing and saying: "I made the mistake, I fell in love. That wasn't part of the plan. I'm still in love with you and I want you so to love me. If I had the nerve I'd stay and lie hoping that I could make you love me again. As I am, for myself. And so forget the other, forget the past. But I don't know whether I have the nerve to try." Anyone who doubts Novak's capacity as an actor would do well to study this incredible scene: she handles the business of writing (below, off-screen) with a steady effort of her shoulders and upper body as if pushing the lines out, and then on "forget the other" she looks up, wondering if such a thing is possible, and on "have the nerve" her upper body begins a different movement, rapid breathing as if steeling herself or mustering the will to find "the nerve," the courage. It is a common aspect of our young mentation that we resist challenges that occur to us, believe in our capacity to act and overcome with the hopeful confidence of youth and inexperience. If love means anything to her, she might think, then it has to have earned "the nerve" to defend it, to own it. In any case she has already written that she would have to lie to "make" him love her "again": she pulled off "Madeleine" for someone else's evil purpose; surely she can pull off "Judy" for Scottie? Unless he is so shallow, so unwitting, that what he fell in love with was not, somehow, "her" at core "for myself" but part fiction. This is a highly unusual situation and not at all a common thing that any romantic partners might encounter ordinarily, however many masks and false selves they deploy throughout their partnership. As an actress her bad luck was that her intended audience fell in in love with her; it was worse luck for her to fall in love with him.

 The decision is made as she rips up the letter with determination, resolution, and we hear a sour note; then Judy hides the gray suit at the back of her wardrobe, picks out a mauve dress, and walks toward us with it, thinking, hugging the dress. It feels like a calculation: if Scottie is merely a man who gets off on falling for rich women in elegant stylish clothes then she will need to press hard against that, coax him into a reality that accepts her for what she is—the accomplice to a murder, the person ultimately responsible for making him fall in love with the thing she created. If he can accept that and remain in love with her, and if their coupledom can survive it, they would be formidable. But Scottie at the end is inflamed by the fact he is only a poor creator of his object of desire, a mere amateur; as he says to her at the top of the tower: "You played the wife very well Judy. He made you over didn't he? He made you over just like I made you over. Only better, not only the clothes and the hair but the looks and the manner and the words." Looks, manner, words: he means the *bourgeois habitus*. Elster trained her to do that, to pass as a *bourgeois*. And this explains the oddity, if we think about it for a moment, of having Judy as a working-class girl rather than anything else. It means that class can be faked, that the solid inherited characteristics of class that thinkers like Pierre Bourdieu argue cannot be counterfeited are critical as the ingredient of "Madeleine" that seals a crucial aspect of her attraction for Scottie. Like Jay Gatsby's love for Daisy Buchanan in *The Great Gatsby* there is a strange mystique for working-class men about possessing, "having," rich, privileged women, making them fall in love with those unworthy in class terms to meet them outside of delivering the groceries.[25] The genius of *Vertigo* lies, in part, in the insight that that mystique goes both ways, that bourgeois women can become fascinated with the idea and reality of romance with those of the lower orders and that Judy somehow knows this, and plays Madeleine that way. Notice how Scottie checks himself when he lets slip to Madeleine that he "enjoyed" the night after he rescued her from the bay, thinking no doubt she would see this as improper; but she lets it go easily.[26]

But now Judy has to bank on Scottie's capacity to transcend that preference, not to look beyond her appearance but take her as her "for myself." I can't be alone in thinking that is a terrible, unworldly misjudgment: "I walked into danger and let you change me because I loved you" she tells him at the end, but that is hardly enough, is it? What is there to Judy Barton, of herself as "she is," that could possibly move Scottie to love her *except* her mysterious resemblance to Madeleine?[27] To know that we only have to attend to her as she is and not as we think she is.

Judy's agreement to eat dinner with Scottie in no way cures his propensity to "see" artifacts of Madeleine; in fact it seems to amplify this tendency. As they eat at Ernie's his attention is drawn from his meal (he doesn't look at Judy) to a woman dressed in the Madeleine gray suit, an elegant rich woman to be sure, and Judy notices his notice and he is chastened that she does. She looks at him evenly, realizing the pull of the bourgeois body, one that she herself played so well; and she must know her simple mauve dress—more revealing of her body yet cheaper—is inelegant, deliberately so, fussily cheap. "See better!"—but Judy then looks down at her food, perhaps realizing that this will be the cost of being with him, his continuous roving eye, his endless dissatisfaction with her as her, unless she becomes what she once was.

Scottie takes her back to her hotel, and there is a little rhyme with the post–bay apartment scene as he helps her unlock her door and their hands touch as they did when he went to offer Madeleine more coffee as she sat near his roaring fire. He tells her not to go to her job, and he offers to take care of her. "I just want to be with you as much as I can, Judy," he says. Why?

In some ways Scottie's relationship to Judy parallels our relationship to the film on repeated viewing: in some unspecified, vague way, we know that Judy represents the key to whatever it is Scottie is suffering; he wants to stick with it, to be with it constantly in order, perhaps, to get inside or underneath the puzzle; for us, continued viewing of the movie often feels as if we are close to an infinitely escaping object of desire, something that should add up but instead repeatedly feels odd, disturbing, offering none of the usual satisfactions of art. However much time Scottie spends with Judy, he doesn't get at the heart of the problem, and even the truth about what it is she did is so grotesquely banal, so blatantly manipulative and exploitative, that it doesn't satisfy the ache—however sentimental,—that draws us repeatedly to her, to Madeleine, to *Vertigo*. It is as if we find out every aspect of the film's production, visit its locations, talk to surviving crew, avail ourselves of the most comprehensive picture of how it was made, and still we are left with the raw fact of the film itself, its rigidity and inflexibility in its "is-ness" that no amount of research, no amount of knowledge can salve. We either succumb, like Scottie, to the dark romantic spiral of the film's aesthetic in which case we are condemned, like him, to admit our folly and its dangers and the prospect of forever more repeating the mistake, falling for the bait; or we reject it with clear-headed skepticism and hence condemn ourselves at the same time to rejection of art itself, its very possibility.

For a moment it looks as if Scottie's plan will not be unpleasant. We see them walking next morning in Golden Gate Park, near the Portals of the Past monument, and the soundtrack offers a thrilling, upbeat melody as if refreshed in the healthy sun under which they stroll. There is the possibility of a relationship there, but it is immediately soured by Judy noticing the regular appetites of two lovers kissing on the grass nearby. Her reaction to his is opaque: it is not a future she can imagine for herself, perhaps; certainly not with the man beside her. She may not at all envy the young lovers on the grass. Perhaps the sheer complex, convoluted nature of her entanglement with Scottie is the rarest of rare relationships, unthinkable and unrepeatable. Scottie doesn't act like a man who loves her, or even desires her. What can she do except go along with what he wants until he is satisfied? Until he comes to a point where he does want her physically? He takes her dancing: she nuzzles against his chest, smelling him, but he remains stiff and formal. He buys her a flower, a white lily, from a street stall and then takes her to buy clothes at Ransohoff's. And so begins Scottie's process of making over Judy so that she appears more like the bourgeoise Madeleine. Of course, both he and Judy know exactly what he wants—the gray suit that she wore and still has in her room—but Hitchcock shoots Novak from below as she realizes just how pathologically he wants to recreate what he has lost. Frustratingly that is, of course, her, but she cannot become that without making it clear what she has done to him. The suspense that lines the rest of the film depends on Judy's realization that giving this man what he most wants will spell the end of their relationship. She confronts him with the plausible objection that she won't wear something worn by the now dead woman he is clearly still in love with; she runs to the corner of the shop like a child with her hands behind her back as if banished there by a teacher in the classroom. And equally plausibly if rather aggressively, he argues that it can't matter that much to her and that in any case he wants her "to do this for me." Remember they've only been seeing each other for a couple of days at this point, so it is quite a large statement of confidence in her pliability. There's a lining of class condescension in his comment too, as if a woman of her education and intelligence could not possibly understand the magnitude of what he, as God, with all the power and freedom over her that he can muster, is about. "You certainly do know what you want, sir," says the shop assistant after he asks her to get a black dinner dress, the kind Madeleine wore at Ernie's when he first saw her. And Judy adopts the same sullen, petulant pose when we see them back at his apartment, leaning head down over his desk. Their conversation reaches a kind of honesty: "These past few days have been the first happy days I've known in a year!" He admits he doesn't know what "use" his dressing her up will do: his idea is that once he sees her as Madeleine, he will recover something, by meeting someone who in his eyes approximates the thing he lost. That sounds all wrong: except how many of us do just that, replacing a dead pet with a new one, a lost spouse with another marriage; if we strip away the morbid, macabre dimensions of it, this is not as unusual as we may like to think. But Stewart's performance is so magnetic, his obsession so all-encompassing, that we feel the sheer *menace* of that desire, as if it is necessary to *erase* the "new" person in order to recover the one from before that one wants. As Judy pleads with him to love her for herself (after an awkward moment when his assurance to her "that there's something in you" he finds attractive goes sour: he can barely tolerate the feel of her flesh), he looks past her words with pitiless blue eyes: "The color of your hair. . ." And again, that condescension: "Judy please it can't matter to you." How can he be so selfishly callous, so laughably unaware of the humiliation he demands? The hair color moment is typically the point in the film, if I am at a screening with students, when their credulity hits its limits: there is often mass laughter. But the film will not release us from it, it offers a close-up of Stewart's unblinking eyes like lasers drilling into Judy and us: he has gone beyond obsession into a kind of automaton-like, programmed focus. There is another, gorgeous rhyme as Scottie maneuvers her near his fire and drops a pale green cushion to the floor (reminding us perhaps of the one he dropped there for Madeleine). And then we wait with Scottie at her hotel for her transformation to be completed.

He is in suspense. Waiting for *what* to emerge? A woman from the dead, a ghost, the embodiment of his love, its manifestation? What does that look like, feel like? He's waiting for a new experience intended to recreate an old one. It is a lengthy pause: Scottie has read his entire newspaper, fiddles with the packaging for some of the clothes, keeps checking the window for her approach. Somehow despite his window vigilance he misses her arrive, but she does come; we hear the ping of the elevator, and then Judy in the gray suit but with her hair down walks the corridor to her room and past him, ignoring his complaints—she's had enough now—as she uses her mirror to brush it. He begs her and she turns to look at him, full in the face, evenly, with a kind of *knowledge* as her eyes scan him. Once again we are positioned behind Scottie so we see her face but not what she sees in his: is there disappointment in hers, a realization about what he is, what kind of man?

Another moment of suspense as she exits the room to change her hair in the bathroom. And, again, we're asked to contemplate him and wonder about his expectations; there's a particularly woeful shot of him against the white nets of the window suffused in the neon green of the hotel sign; he looks small, almost childlike, a little boy alone with his love and his yearning.

That boy, perhaps, grew up to the sound of tales of his Scottish ancestry, or knew about the bleakness of Hebridean islands, their perfect windswept isolation, and imagined the fullness of life exploding over him in a perfect accident of love. That he might pursue the secret of the world, discover its name. A quiet, gifted student, his college days were blighted by his exuberant love for Margaret, so overwhelming in its sentimentality she had to end it for his own good, for their own good. A crisis, legal studies abandoned, instead he joins the local police force and his quiet, patient efforts propel him eventually, slowly, to the rank of detective. But he never has a partner (uniformed cops have to assist when needed), never learns to navigate the currents of political turbulence such that he might achieve his egotistical dream of becoming chief of police and bringing order to this degenerate world. Margaret remains a steadfast and loyal friend, ever watchful for a relapse in the crisis that overtook his younger days. And when it happens again she is powerless to assist since it happens beyond her sight, beyond her control. So enormous is his fantasy of being rescued by love that he cannot abide mockery of it and must submit to its control over him, its ordering of an otherwise untethered life. Does Scottie even know what love is, can he contain it, possess it at all? His experience of love is as an unbalancing, sickening, dizzying force like vertigo itself, one that throws his body into sweating paroxysms, shaking emotion, an epic emotional landscape that threatens to tear the fabric of reality to pieces. (As Daisy says to Gatsby, "You want too much.") This is the man we find trembling alone in a hotel room in San Francisco waiting for the answer to emerge from the bathroom. Like Jeff and Devlin we see a picture of all this history, all these muddled thoughts and emotions *from behind*, the camera directs us *through him*, until like a stage curtain parting, he rises and turns as the door opens and we see the majesty of his wounded face, its eyes wide and absorbing the fantastic figure as it walks toward him, Judy's eyes steady and anchored to his, watching closely as she realizes *her* triumph in making *him* come to life in front of her and—as happened in his apartment when she walked toward him in the red dressing gown—her lips part in a smile and she tilts her head longingly to the left (a gesture associated with Judy's desire). He can finally touch her for herself—what self? What does it matter what self? And when they kiss, the rightly famous sequence begins, where once again we are tucked behind Scottie as the room revolves (or the couple do, or both. . .), and as we crest in the rotation to see his face, the old-timey horse-drawn carriage from the mission stables appears behind, as if this emblem of past transportation signals its wholehearted return, that the consummation of love is hallucinogenic (he can't *see* this carriage because it is behind him, but we see him *feel* its odd presence). Judy herself appears to swoon, to lose consciousness in his arms, as she absorbs the full spectrum of his attention in its hungry, desperate expression. It is an entirely grief-laden moment. We might be asked to hope such love exists, but at the same time we have to see its dizzying sickness, its powerful association with death and dying.

The next scene is all smiles and recovered breath. Dressed in her black dinner gown, Judy prepares herself for their dinner at Ernie's: she's clearly worked up an appetite ("I'm gonna have . . . [glances at him knowingly] . . . I'm gonna have one of those big beautiful steaks!"), and then she attempts to put on the necklace that we have seen Carlotta wearing in the portrait. When Scottie assists her (and has trouble with the clasp mechanism) he asks, "How do you work this thing?" and she replies, famously in a film laded with ironic lines, "Can't you see?" This man whose eyes are vulnerable to all the sights of the world notices in the mirror the fact of the necklace, remembers its provenance, and realizes, all at once, what has happened to him. The necklace is one of the signs of the world that calibrates it, and that in our tracking of them allows us to measure time and space which is to say their meaning; like the rings in the tree's core that Madeleine points to, the necklace measures Scottie against the cosmic forces that swirl beneath virtually every moment seen and heard in the film. Scottie could ignore it, go along with it, and it would become an unspoken emblem (in an incoherent film) of their mutual pact to forget and enjoy their good fortune to find each other. But Scottie's way is more moral, smaller. For him the world, instead of a place of secrets and mysteries and oceans of love and death and desire, is rather a nasty little place dense with deception and evil and smallness. A dirty world of betrayal unfit for the adventures of his imagination. We get a very close shot of Stewart looking directly back at the camera as he works this out and as Judy fusses trying to locate her lipstick. Part of the realization has to be that he is in a room with a bad person, a collaborator in a murder, someone with the "nerve" and the courage to go through with setting him up *and* to "make him" fall in love with her again despite the risk of being uncovered. Stewart's rightward look with his eyes feels malevolent: he, too, is very dangerous, the Wronged Boy, his romantic hopes for the world dashed, humiliated, and mocked.

When one is wounded so severely, the sheer scale of it can take some time to absorb, can take a while to get its pants on and get moving at the appropriate speed. Silence and time are needed in order for it to amass the necessary tools for retaliation. He suggests they take a long drive down the peninsula, and during that drive he assembles the battalions of his moral outrage. They are armed no doubt by the humiliating fact that Elster not only banked on his incapacity to climb the tower, but on his failure as a detective in other respects, notably to spot such a bizarre cover story. That a working girl like Judy was the tool that enabled his victimhood is not very complimentary either; he is a love-fool sold on a fantasy of bourgeoise womanhood, a sap who was played like a fiddle by a cheap pair of murderers who were also screwing each another. All of this must occur to him during that drive to the mission. His plan is to take Judy to the place where he last could credibly experience the entity he must still call "Madeleine" (what other name is there for it?), the insubstantial thing he fell for not once but twice. As if confronting her with what he knows she knows will help anything: it communicates the depth of his blame and marks its beginning, but he will also be denied the chance to forgive her for what she did.

From Judy's point of view we see once again, this time at dusk, the moving shot of the treetops as they drive toward the mission. The rocks of the planet seem ancient and glistening in the moonlight as they crouch beside the road. She must know too that the reckoning is near, that only begging for forgiveness (which she does not do) might help. Once they reach the mission Scottie claims he wants to stop "being haunted" and intends to step back one last time into the past in order to be free of it. Quite how or why he imagines this would work is left unclear: we might remember Midge's remark that only another trauma could cure him of his acrophobia. He seems to want someone in the world to acknowledge the sheer depth of his suffering about everything that has happened. But even if they could do that, what next?

As he ascends the tower stairs, pulling Judy with him, he reveals he now knows about her role in Mrs. Elster's death. He is exceptionally angry, murderously enraged. It is surprising he doesn't strangle Judy there and then, but what seems more important is wreaking enough emotional hurt as possible, laying himself bare in his woundedness. It feels like a kind of calculated apocalyptic desire to lay waste to everything around him; Stewart stalks Judy as she ascends in front of him, like a lethal cat focused and barely contained. He is very rough with her, even dragging her entire weight up the final few stairs to the bell tower itself. As they fight going up, the core of Scottie's anger revolves around the accomplishment of Judy's performance under Elster's tuition: he was just better at making a "Madeleine" than Scottie ever could be, perhaps because his reasons, though no less urgent, were far less noble, less constrained by anxiety about rectitude and morality. He focuses on the one flaw in her performance—her scream just before Mrs. Elster is thrown off the tower: "Why did you scream? You played the wife very well . . . those beautiful phony trances . . . and you jumped into the bay didn't you? I bet you're a wonderful swimmer aren't you? Aren't you?" She faked a suicide attempt, and we might remember that moment, one he later remarked sealed a debt between them.

In the bell tower there is little Judy can do except watch. He has taken them to a little stage, a small movie theater for their last encounter high above the world. It is hard to imagine another actor exhibiting the depth of suffering and hurt that Stewart does. "You shouldn't have been . . . you shouldn't have been that sentimental": he is shaking, sweating with rage and pain. In my experience those who believe they are compassionate and virtuous tend to respond disproportionately to slights and hurt. The kindest thing to do would be to deny his hurt the extended drama that more time to blame Judy might offer. When a nun appears—another woman in costume—Judy takes the opportunity to throw herself out of the tower to her death, screaming once again (as if the first time was a rehearsal for her own death). And Scottie is left with the nun ringing the bell, standing at the edge of the tower, his arms slightly outstretched in a manner similar to that we saw taken by the falling shape in his dream. "It's too late, there's no bringing her back," he says to her seconds before she dies: he means there's no bringing Madeleine back, no forgetting what has been done to him, but she pleads that he keep her "safe" and kisses him, and he responds in kind as if there might be a way, after all. But to live in a human world is to live in a moral world or none at all: the nun reminds us that morality, faith, commitment, honesty, and all the distortions and corruptions that trail in their wake are necessarily part of that world and cannot be bracketed off. The last word spoken in the film is "mercy," and one can only hope that Scottie has enough of that left to treat himself with more compassion than he was able to show her.

The unnumbered Tarot card called "The Fool" depicts a young man stepping perilously close to a cliff edge looking up and unaware of the imminent danger; Alejandro Jodorowsky asks, "Where is he going? Straight ahead? It is possible, but it is also imaginable that he is turning endless circles around his staff."[28] Scottie by contrast stares down directly at Judy's body, and we have in this pose a picture of elevated spectatorship, of superior knowledge, all traces and signs tracked down and finally interpreted. But what does he have with all this hard-won understanding? Devastation, empty hands. Julian Jaynes argues that the emergence of consciousness can be measured—timed—through the history of divination, the records of omens, auguries, and sortilege;[29] here the final lot has been cast and Scottie—resolute, still, committed—remains its sole spectator alone in the cosmos to read its message.

4

Chinatown

> To emphasize the point that the audience is seeing everything from Gittes' perspective Roman Polanski often put the camera behind Jack Nicholson, so the audience sees his back and shoulders.
>
> —IMDb, "Chinatown (1974): Trivia"

Gavin Elster enjoys considerable good fortune: not only does he find a woman who closely resembles his wife, he also discovers his old college friend has recently quit his job as a police detective and is "available," should he be properly tempted, which he is. In *Chinatown* Jake Gittes (Jack Nicholson) has also quit the police force where he worked as a uniformed officer in the Chinatown district of Los Angeles, and when the film begins we see him at work in his office as the head, and chief investigator, of his own private detective firm, J. J. Gittes and Associates.[1] The primary work he attracts, his "métier" as he later calls it, is "matrimonial," and we see immediately what that means as we watch his client Curly (Burt Young) examine photographs of his wife engaged in sex with another man in a forest. In *Vertigo* Judy was Elster's girl for a time before he threw her away, and no doubt part of the hurt Scottie experiences is in the realization that he was in love with a woman who, however much she claimed to have fallen in love with him, remained in

Elster's hands until *he* decided to give her up, paying her off with some clothes, jewelry, and money. We should not underestimate the powerful forces unleashed when people feel that their love and commitment has been betrayed: it undermines their sense of the shared past they lived with their loved one, now realizing that that time was in fact not what it appeared but something darker, full of deceit, a kind of robbery of one's little time on earth. As we saw in *Vertigo* the eyes in particular are the anchoring organs of perception, portals between inner and outer but vulnerable too to what is put in front of them. In a witty juxtaposition of sound and image Curly groans over the photos of secret copulation, and Gittes averts his eyes as if in embarrassment for the poor cuckold. He affects the bored tolerance of the experienced detective who's heard it all before. Curly himself seems oddly concerned with showing Gittes how upset he is, hurling the photos up in the air and scrunching the venetian blinds with distressed hands—it's as if this photographic news is no real surprise, and both men have to go through the motions of witnessing his upset ("Enough's enough," says Gittes). We should immediately notice how well he is doing—the blinds are new, and his office seems cool because of them even in the heat of the LA summer. His cream three-piece suit, silk handkerchief, and "sunray" striped tie exude cool elegance and controlled, expensive style. He is framed seated in a leather chair so as to magnify Nicholson's extraordinarily handsome profile, his teardrop nostrils, thinning but still sleek hair. "She's no good," says Curly after Gittes pours him a generous bourbon—but they both know that: what's to be done? ("When you're right, you're right, and you're right.") Gittes is also at pains to exhibit his sense of social justice, letting Curly know he can be flexible on a repayment scheme ("I don't want your last dime, what kind of a guy do you think I am?" he asks escorting Curly from his premises). A lot of what we see depends on our grasping Gittes's desire to be seen to be doing dirty work with elegance, virtue, or "finesse," as he later explains to one of his workers, and our understanding that this is some kind of social conscience, a moral respect for doing things with a sense of justice. *Chinatown*'s detective is quite different in this respect from the other sleuths in this book; unlike Alicia or Devlin, for example, he does not work for the national good but the moral good. He cares about appearances, but we would be wrong to take this as an index of moral shallowness. He must feel the current of Curly's humiliation, his upset at being cuckolded and at being, now here in this office, a bang-to-rights cuckold in front of another man.

In the script their conversation is longer than we see in the film. Curly pours himself another drink and says, "You know something Jake? . . . I think I might kill her." Now, there's enough hesitation in that statement to calm a worried listener, but it points to a feature we saw at the end of *Vertigo*—the issue of what kind of punishment, and what duration of blame, an egregious act committed against you deserves.[2] I suggested that Scottie ought to be merciful on himself, forgive himself as he could not do after Mrs. Elster's death. Hannah Arendt in *The Human Condition*, following a thought of Hegel, notes that human beings have no way of undoing actions they take in the world and everything they do constitutes an action; except we can choose forgiveness. The act of forgiveness opens up the possibility of freedom since it releases us from what we have done unknowingly or hastily:

> Forgiveness is the exact opposite of vengeance, which acts in the form of re-acting against an original trespassing, whereby far from putting an end to the consequences of the first misdeed, everybody remains bound to the process, permitting the chain reaction contained in every action to take its unhindered course. In contrast to revenge, which is a natural, automatic reaction to transgression and which because of the irreversibility of the action process can be expected and even calculated, the act of forgiving can never be predicted: it is the only reaction that acts in an unexpected way and thus retains, though being a reaction, something of the original character of action. Forgiving, in other words, is the only reaction which does not merely re-act but acts anew and unexpectedly, unconditioned by the act that provoked it and therefore freeing from its consequences both the one who forgives and the one who is forgiven.[3]

The bell tower debate between Scottie and Judy raises the question of whether forgiveness is plausible for someone in Scottie's position, so soon after the discovery of his betrayal; emotions are clearly, necessarily, running high. The alternative—punishment, either throwing her off the tower himself, or handing her over to the police—is certainly in the air too; forgiveness in that context would be an act of creation, a counter to Elster's evil theater of doubles and haunting, a gesture of free will. But the enormous, Christlike fortitude it would take to do such a thing, and so soon after finding out, is almost totally implausible; the sheer weight of the humiliation Scottie has to absorb has to be got through somehow before he can reach that option, if he ever will. Gittes by contrast reminds Curly (in the script version) of the social and political reality of killing in revenge:

CURLY: They don't kill a guy for that.

GITTES: Oh they don't?

CURLY: Not for your wife. That's the unwritten law.

(*Gittes pounds the photos on the desk shouting*)

GITTES: I'll tell you the unwritten law, you dumb son of a bitch, you gotta be rich to kill somebody, anybody, and get away with it. You think you got that kind of dough, you think you got that kind of class?

The lesson Gittes teaches Curly is that social power—wealth and class—provides a shield against the usual moral constraints most of us have to face in ordinary life. Everyone knows that. But it would be wrong for us to hear Gittes talking so wisely so soon into the movie: indeed, he has to come to face the truth of this excised statement by facing the events of the movie itself. Otherwise it would be quite strange to see a detective who knows this, believes this, fail to spot Noah Cross (John Huston) as the central villain earlier than he does. Gittes's mistake is to underestimate the sheer evil mechanism of which he is merely a component part, a tool.

Gittes's secretary, Sophie (Nandu Hinds) now tells him he has another meeting, with Mrs. Mulwray (Diane Ladd) who is waiting with his operatives, Mr. Walsh (Joe Mantell) and Mr. Duffy (Bruce Glover). The firm is doing well, but Walsh and Duffy have to share a far less well-appointed office space; Mulwray has dressed up for the occasion but, as we shall discover, it is a costume worn by an actress posing as the real Mrs. Mulwray (Faye Dunaway) and sent there by the evil center of the film Noah Cross, a rich water supply magnate, in order to discredit Mr. Hollis Mulwray, the chief engineer of the city's Water and Power Department. Like Elster, Cross uses one's ordinary trust that people who one meets are in fact who they say they are, and as we have seen even experienced detectives fall for that. Discovering he has been deceived Gittes will, like Scottie, want to correct the world's perception of him (his self-perception) as someone who can be had so easily. As with his meeting with Curly, the content of their conversation provides the sense that marriage betrayals are so common Gittes can hardly muster the enthusiasm to pretend to care. When she tells him that she believes her husband is seeing another woman he affects interest, but eventually asks her to forget the whole thing:

GITTES: Mrs. Mulwray do you love your husband?

MULWRAY: Yes of course.

GITTES: Then go home and forget everything.

MULWRAY: But I. . .

GITTES: I'm sure he loves you too Mrs. Mulwray. Do you know the expression, "Let sleeping dogs lie"? You're better off not knowing.

MULWRAY: I have to know.

The scene further establishes our sense of Gittes as respectable, unwilling to harass a fisherman client for his fee, or take on any work that happens to walk into the office: he appears principled.

Chinatown was released in 1974 but it is set in the past, Los Angeles of the mid-1930s, and it weaves a psycho-political drama about corruption and power partly based on real events.[4] As in any great film these gestures toward historical specificity are contained within broader universal themes where the pursuit of, and hunger for, knowledge is brokered by an almost biblical sense of the fragility of survival even in the modern world of suits and cars and cold cocktails on a hot day. The city seems to be on the brink of apocalyptic drought so that two kinds of appetite—the thirst for sustenance which compresses such things as family, work, and love, and the thirst for knowledge—are played in parallel.

Gittes's first step in the Mulwray investigation is simply to turn up at a city hall meeting where Mulwray is due to speak. The topic under discussion is the building of a new dam that will provide a reliable water supply since the nearby ocean is useless (in the days before desalination plants): "You can swim in it and you can fish in it, but you can't drink it and you can't irrigate an orange grove with it," the speaker says as Gittes, seated among a rapt audience of yeomen and petit bourgeois, yawns in boredom. The speaker finishes with a vivid flourish that contrasts the barren dryness of the desert with the plentiful balm of water (this fusion of wet and dry is captured for us visually as we see Gittes consult his horseracing newspaper: the headline mentions the famous thoroughbred Seabiscuit): "Now remember we live next door to the ocean but we also live on the edge of a desert. Los Angeles is a desert community. Beneath this building, beneath our streets is a desert. And without water the dust will rise up and cover us as though we never existed." When Hollis Mulwray stands up to speak, however, he offers another equally biblical view of the proposed dam: that its construction on unsuitable bedrock risks a catastrophic flood like the one he admits he was responsible for once before. That Gittes imagines he is condemned to listening to stale municipal discussion is further undermined by the entry of many sheep into the hall followed by their shepherds wielding crooks. One accuses Mulwray of somehow being caught up in the stealing of water from the valley, the ruining of grazing, starvation of livestock (again this has resonances of some apocalyptic plague): "Who's paying you to do that Mr. Mulwray, that's what I'd want to know!" The assumption of political corruption is as baked into the social world as sand in the sidewalk paving.

Gittes follows Mulwray into the desert, the parched landscape of the LA river; he watches him through binoculars as he walks amidst the rocks and dust and talks to a young boy on a pale white horse. Mulwray bends down and grabs some earth in his hands: what is he looking for, what is his investigation? He goes to his car and takes out a large book of what may be charts, or maps of the area, and appears to study them: we notice how still and dry it is, the thin pages untroubled by wind. Inevitably the depiction of detective work will evoke the cinematic relationship of spectator-object/seer-seen; depicting Gittes following Mulwray shows us one investigator following another, one enigma tracking another.

This investigation uncovers the investigators' different methods. Mulwray (perhaps stung by the accusations of the shepherd) is tracking something Gittes does not see—the journey of fresh water through the LA system and into the sea—and he does so by actually visiting sites that carry the signs, the imprint (dampness) of that travel; in contrast Gittes observes with optical or technological assistance—binoculars, the wing mirrors of his car, the watches hidden under Mulwray's car tires that indicate how long he kept vigil before driving away. There are the beautiful cluster of shots where Mulwray walks along the rocky seashore in the late afternoon while seagulls squawk above him, picking up a starfish, seemingly contemplating something while Gittes watches from above next to the end of a storm drainpipe that juts out from the ground. In one of the shots he is distant and alone at the very tip of the rocks, virtually in the sea; a place where adulterous lovers might meet with the promise of solitude, but not Mulwray. The shots conjure a haptic sense of thirst such that it is a relief when we hear the gurgle and then see the shock of water exiting the drainpipe next to Gittes; below his quarry looks up with a kind of despair, as if this is the confirmation he was waiting to see. This doubling is a feature of the film, its thirst for repetition that is so ingrained it appears to be unconscious (although it has delighted eager fans of the movie for decades) such that everything arrives in our view in pairs, the double a corrupted version of the mold that formed it. Like a rhyme it is a repetition of part of something, falling just short of being a repeat of it. This happens aurally as well as visually.[5]

The next day when Walsh shows Gittes freshly developed photographs that he took covertly of Mulwray and Noah Cross arguing outside the Pig 'n' Whistle, he says he only heard one thing, "apple core." "Apple core?" repeats Gittes. We later find out he has misheard and the word is "albacore"—the fish that we already heard Curly talk about as he left the office as he describes his financial difficulty (the fish he mentions are all technically tuna). Why would anyone argue about apple cores? Or albacores for that matter? Gittes is annoyed at Walsh's ineffective intelligence gathering, reminding him that the job requires (as he wipes his hands with a silk handkerchief), "a certain amount of finesse." A good director will play a scene so that its ironies register in the viewer without being rammed down their throat: the scene is notable for its beginning, where we hear Walsh off-screen (presumably in a darkroom nearby) as Gittes picks up a cup and saucer of coffee, a fresh copy of *Racing Record*, and sits in a nice armchair, takes a sip of his drink, crosses his right leg over his left as he flicks the paper to attention, and with his left hand unflaps the corner of his suit jacket so that it is free to drape over his thigh. He is very neat, almost affected in adjusting his comfort to read the gamblers' daily report. He is after all a mere private eye, spying on those caught up in the degenerate desperation of adulterous play, a bedroom peeper (notice how the Paramount logo at the film's start is shown to us as if we are peeping through bedroom windows at its naughty elevation); Walsh by contrast has no airs or graces about what he is doing. It is Gittes who is so concerned about how he appears to the world, not as a sleazy man for hire tracking the copulatory shenanigans of the populace, but a professional with finesse, all the latest "discreet" technology, all the best clothes (he's wearing a gorgeous glen plaid three-piece suit) but not the intuitive capability to realize the importance of the photographs he is looking at. As he picks each one out of the water of the rinse tray he fails to ask who the man Mulwray is arguing with actually *is*—and he is so keen to reprimand his older associate he asks no follow-up questions about the argument, the most obvious being how did it end? For what Walsh has photographed is (one assumes) the final time Cross attempts to convince Mulwray to go ahead with the dam construction (and possibly to allow him access to "the girl," Katherine [Belinda Palmer]). Polanski allows us to enjoy this reprimand and Nicholson's fine carriage of clothes as if Gittes were a politician protecting his public image; compared to, say, Jeff Markham or, better, the oily Jack Fisher, Gittes models himself as a cut above the average LA gumshoe. But in the very next scene Polanski will show him snapping covert photos of Mulwray and a girl in a rowboat.

One more thing: living in a very hot location one becomes attuned, in the height of summer, to all liquids particularly those that promise cooler temperatures. The very sight of them commands attention. Gittes chooses to drink coffee with milk, but the brown stillness of the office and the presence of a radiator in the wall behind him magnify our haptic sense of heat; the water tray springs alive as a wet salvation, but its contents depict, in wet shiny ways, the heat of an argument in the heat of an afternoon outside a pub (we see two men argue about two men arguing, another rhyme, another double of a double).

Gittes's other operative has in the meantime tracked Mulwray to Echo Park where he is taking a rowboat ride with a "cute little twist." And once on the boat with Duffy, we see another dimension of Gittes, the covert peeper, his elegant clothes and dashing devilish smile a fusion of pretension and guile. Here, for the first time we see events from just behind Gittes's head, the camera placed to follow the line of the lens's look in front of his snooping eye. He snaps the couple as they row toward his boat, and then he follows them (without Duffy) to the El Macondo Apartments where he climbs up to the roof—a little bell tower—and photographs the couple from that vantage point, as Katherine comes out of the door to where Mulwray is waiting at a little table. He covers his eyes with both hands and then removes them (like stage curtains) to see her new dress and shoes, and she twirls a little bit for him. We see the end of this motion, impossibly reflected at the end of the lens of Gittes's Leica III 35mm rangefinder camera. In another rhyme he dislodges a slate tile from the roof (as he knocked some rocks down below when following Mulwray the day before) and alerts the couple below, implying that this meeting—unlike the rowboat outing—is somehow covert, underhanded.

In one of the great ellipses of cinema, we immediately cut to the result of Gittes's investigation, a front page jammed with saucy headlines that destroy the reputation of Mulwray: "DEPARTMENT OF WATER AND POWER BLOWS FUSE"; "Chief's Use of Funds for El Macondo Love Nest Being Investigated"; "J. J. Gittes Hired By Suspicious Spouse," as well as a photo of Mulwray and Katherine framed in a heart shape. Gittes is in a barber shop for a shave by Barney (George Justin); outside we see a car radiator steaming and broken; "the heat's murder," he says. It's 9:20 in the morning and Gittes has become a minor celebrity, "practically a movie star." Another customer, a banker (Doc Erickson), seeks to pour cold water on the moment: "Fool's names and fool's faces . . . You got a hell of a way to make a living," he tells Gittes. They get into a minor fracas, the way strangers do in a barbershop: Gittes insists he makes "an honest living" helping people in "desperate situations": in this game of moral one-upmanship he points out he doesn't throw families out on the street if they can't pay their mortgage. "We don't publicize it in the newspaper" is the response, as if Gittes had merely tipped off the press in order to amplify publicity for his firm. Gittes's reaction draws on an aspect of Nicholson's star persona, his latent vulcanism, a propensity to explode at any moment. For Gittes has been played, and his reaction is a casual almost blasé treatment of the fact (he's gone for a morning shave and appears to lap up the publicity until its questionable moral valency is raised in public). He struggles in raging irritation out of the prone position he's adopted in the barber's chair, leaning over the banker: "Who is this bimbo, Barney, is he a regular customer or what? Hey listen pal I make an honest living, people only come to me when they're in a desperate situation. (*Jabbing his chest*) I help 'em out, I don't kick families out of their houses like you bums down at the bank do! Huh? Maybe you'd like to step down out of the barber chair and maybe we can go outside and discuss it, what do you think?" "Finesse" is confused, or complicated by, Gittes's belief that he is doing honest work about dishonest behavior, and the social conscience he exhibits provides the foundation for righteous, combative, indignant outrage. But he rapidly admits a kind of helplessness, confessing he had no idea how the story of Mulwray's corruption and adultery got into the newspapers, meaning he was played by other forces he had no idea about. His temper is only salved by Barney telling him a dirty joke which tickles Gittes so much he forgets the newspaper headline, and bounds into his office eager to repeat it to Duffy and Walsh.

It's hardly feasible that Gittes even hears the beginning of the joke since he seems so agitated by the banker's taunts, but once in the office he has it down perfectly. The joke is about how a husband, in seeking his own relief from boredom in lovemaking with his wife, discovers in its punchline she is much more experienced than he might like. The husband, tired of "screwing his wife" is advised by a friend to proceed as "the Chinese do," interrupting intercourse at frequent intervals in order to prolong the event and introduce more interesting, nonphysical elements, such as smoking or reading. But as Gittes tells the joke he is oblivious to the objections and discomfort of his operatives who know, as we soon do too, that Mrs. Evelyn Mulwray (Faye Dunaway)—*the real Mrs. Mulwray*—is already in the office and in fact standing behind him as he tells the joke. It is a joke about spectatorship and knowledge. Once again, we see things happening to Gittes beyond his realization, literally behind his back. Quite a lot of the film up to now has the camera angled to show Gittes frontally or at least in profile (with one notable exception, see above); here a frontal shot is used to demonstrate that his awareness is critically limited to what is precisely in front of his nose. He has no peripheral cognitive perception and this, as with Scottie's limited view of what is happening to him, turns out to be a crucial flaw. The punchline is that the husband's wife, preferring the uninterrupted all-at-once kind of lovemaking effort, finally objects that her husband is "screwing like a Chinaman." The line reveals a kind of cuckoldry at one remove, the wife's experience with a racially marked lower class, who will be shown in the film to work as the servants of rich white masters. Hence, "China" is situated as a place everybody knows, secretly, but avoids confronting because the consequences are uncertain, disruptive, humiliating. We later learn that Gittes himself worked in Chinatown for the district attorney as a police detective but that something went terribly wrong there: his desire to protect a woman there ended up putting her in the worst kind of danger.[6] Has he learned nothing? He should be able, as we are, to read the exquisite evolution of pained expressions that wash across Walsh's face as he politely listens to the dirty joke, gradually turning his head toward Evelyn behind Gittes and mustering the faintest of embarrassed smiles.

Gittes's explosion of laughter at his own joke—not well told in fact—admits its own defeat as he turns laughing, notices Evelyn, and is stilled into stunned silence. They tried to tell him she was there! Once again we have a detective dealing with a woman who is not who she appears to be: the "original" Mrs. Mulwray was a fake, a tool to instigate the investigation of Mulwray, expose and embarrass him, no doubt a threat made to him and made good by Noah Cross during the argument outside the Pig 'n' Whistle. Evelyn is icy and cool much like Madeleine, a woman from a class higher than Gittes, and like Scottie, he seems immediately taken by this, fascinated by her manner and poise. But she is there to confirm that they have never met, that Gittes was set up, and for her lawyer to serve him papers.

Gittes goes to Hollis Mulwray's office and bluffs his way past a secretary gatekeeping its inner sanctum: there he notices a framed color photograph of Evelyn smiling and very happy in riding clothes next to a horse; it is the one of the few times in the entire film we do see her happy, and Gittes seems briefly absorbed by it. He rifles through the drawers of the office desk: Mulwray is neat and nothing more (a checkbook, a leather-bound pedicure kit, an empty drawer); on a larger desk he opens the large book we saw Mulwray consult on the LA riverbed, and it turns out to store his notes ("Tues night Oak Pass Pier–7 channels used"), and then he is interrupted by the entry of Russ Yelburton (John Hillerman), the deputy chief, another gatekeeper, who leads Gittes to his own office. This is a darker, smaller room with a large marlin mounted on the wall above the desk and another on the opposite wall. Gittes is snooping around, looking for Mulwray, and gradually absorbing the room's objects. Yelburton says Mulwray is at lunch, but doesn't know where he is. When Gittes leaves he meets Claude Mulvihill (Roy Jenson) waiting by the lift, and for the first time, in contrast to his poor joke telling, we see a classic Chandleresque display of witty sword fighting:

GITTES: Mulvihill! What are you doing here?

MULVIHILL: They shut my water off. What's it to you?

GITTES: How'd you find out about it? You don't drink it. (*Presses lift button.*) You don't take a bath in it. They wrote you a letter! But then you'd have to be able to read.

Mulvihill, easily taunted, approaches Gittes with menace: he is the kind of hired muscle that gives real thickness to Gittes's claims to have finesse, to work an honest living. The thug has been hired by the city to provide protection against threats to blow up the reservoirs, and Yelburton blames the farmers, hostile because of water rationing in the valley (although quite how blowing up reservoirs is going to help with that is left unsaid); Gittes allows us to experience his deeper knowledge of corruption, telling Yelburton that when Mulvihill was sheriff of Ventura Country the bootleggers delivered their booze to the beaches with impunity. He's either corrupt or incompetent.

In the next scene Gittes arrives at Evelyn's grand house; his car sweeps up the drive past a gorgeous well-irrigated green breast of lawn. He rings the doorbell near a large wooden front door, painted in glossy black like something one might find in a castle, and the camera is positioned behind Gittes so that we see his back and shoulders, and a slice of his profile beneath his pale tan fedora. A Chinese butler called Kahn (James Hong) opens the door but keeps silent as he takes Gittes's card and closes it again. We can tell the world appears to be operating as if it is hiding a secret thing nearby. And nearby the squeak of another Asian servant finishing a beige car with a chamois catches Gittes's attention before the door is opened and he is ushered somewhat rudely inside. Notice the way Gittes attempts to command eye contact with the butler who avoids it and tells him rather brusquely to "wait." But Gittes will not be stilled; Polanski uses a handheld camera behind Gittes as he wanders out into the garden which is dominated by a large pond filled with rocks; its gardener fusses around it, poking into the water with a rod and pulling out a wet clump of grass, dropping it and the rod down in a kind of exasperation, and standing back with this hands on his hips as if to say, "Look at this disaster!" We get the sense he's been working at it for a while. "Bad for glass," he tells Gittes, but what we know he says if we've seen the film is really "bad for grass"; Gittes repeats what we hear, "Yeah, sure, bad for glass," even though it makes no sense at all that pond water might be "bad" for either glass or grass. Then we have an astonishing shot of Gittes peering into the water, his eyes lit by something glinting within it, and when the point of view is revealed, it looks like some exotic organic crab-like creature sunning itself on the submerged rocks in some picture of primeval, Devonian life. Gittes fetches a rod to fish it out but he's interrupted by the arrival of Evelyn, bright in white blouse and tan jodhpurs.

We know by the end of the film that the haunted quality of the house—the odd way its servants are invested in earnest cleaning and closed-mouthed order—is a function of the fact that a murder has taken place in this very pond. Noah Cross drowned Hollis Mulwray there, losing his glasses in it as he bent down to keep Hollis's head submerged. That happened a few hours before Gittes notices the spectacles gleaming on the rocks; if Evelyn knows about it, it is hard to say and the film never resolves this. When they sit down Gittes tells her that "whoever set your husband up, set me up" and that in order to protect his reputation he needs to know who did it. Evelyn responds by telling him she will drop the lawsuit. That is a misstep: why would she want to do this, why does she worry about Gittes wanting to talk to her husband unless she already knows he is dead? Gittes tells her that her husband's girlfriend has disappeared, but she already knows this: once again he is behind, as we are, with the fact of the matter. When he claims that his insistence is not personal, she contends, "It's very personal. It couldn't be more personal. Is this a business or an obsession with you?"

That is a fine question to ask any detective. On the one hand it seems Gittes wants to protect—to rehabilitate by his own lights—his reputation by finding out who it was who set up her husband, but that is *not* the reason for his persistence. He tells Evelyn, "If I can see him I can help him," which is to say he wants to collaborate with Hollis in exposing the underhand forces that set them both up. It is not exclusively a matter of business, and when Evelyn realizes this she loses her composure, telling Gittes to look for Hollis at some reservoirs, and is ruffled when he leaves abruptly. If she did know at this point that Hollis was already dead that suggests her father's—Noah Cross's—malign influence over her is immense, as is her fear of him. There is considerable tact in the direction chosen here: as Gittes enters the home and walks around it feels *febrile*, hot and busy (as Murray Pomerance has observed, even the sounds of the car outside being detailed connote sexual activity[7]), and when we see Evelyn she is no longer the cool and controlled customer we met in Gittes's office, but sweaty and flushed and her claim to have been riding "bareback" vaguely suggests the kind of outdoor sexual activity we observed in the photos at the film's start. It's the kind of feeling one gets walking into a room or a house very shortly after some vigorous sex has taken place there: you can point to nothing in particular that would count as evidence of the fact, and yet all of one's senses confirm in some undefinable way that what has happened, happened. Brilliantly in these scenes Polanski captures that very feeling. Gittes is alerted to something (not quite *that*) too in Evelyn's manner, and he becomes far more assertive toward her, taking on the rather aggressive stance he will hold up to the very moment he discovers her true secret.

A common way to understand the film's title is to take the district of Chinatown as standing in for all that is unknowable in and about the world; in the plot, at least, a place where one does not ask questions or attempt to influence because the intentions would be at best misunderstood and at worst lead to catastrophic outcomes. That goes too easy on the *China* part of the word: there are Chinatowns in big cities across the Western world, and apart from being tourist destinations, they also point to the historical failure of Western societies and their Asian immigrants to fully integrate at a comprehensive scale. Racial and cultural stereotypes crowd around a lingering truth that the way "the Chinese do it" remains in its totality beyond the knowledge of the West. There is partial knowledge, glimpses through the frame of the bedroom window, but unlike the experienced wife of the joke (which is a joke about men's failure to find knowledge they find disturbing; instead they must stumble upon it), the viewer cannot grasp a full picture unimpeded by a frame. That is the position Gittes finds himself in at Evelyn's house.

He leaves and drives to the Oak Pass Reservoir Evelyn mentioned; we see him arrive at it through an angle behind and near his shoulder, looking through the windscreen of his convertible so that we see the full waters of the lake ahead equally framed by the bland concrete holding its vast volumes in containment, all lit by blazing sunshine that glints off the many chromed details of the car and the water beyond it. There are uniformed cops guarding the place. Why? Gittes doesn't wonder. Once again he bluffs his way past, posing as the bureaucrat Russ Yelburton, and drives through. He sees Lou Escobar (Perry Lopez) ahead talking to two young boys in swimwear but is stopped by his sidekick, Loach (Dick Bakalyan): "Gittes! For Christ's sake! Get out of here before he sees you." What is this about? Some history between them such that Loach needs to protect Escobar against what he might do if he sees Gittes? This is evidently the case since they greet each other like two old friends who have fallen out catastrophically a long time ago; long enough past not to fight at first sight, but not that long, not long enough to keep avoiding whatever it was directly, wisely doing so and yet hinting at what went on. There remains affection and that seems to win the day here. When Gittes pulls out a cigarette, the uniformed cop nearby warns him that there is "no smoking here," but Escobar allows it and takes his first opportunity to refer to something in the past they both know about, "That's alright officer, we can make an exception this time. I'll see he's careful with the matches and doesn't burn himself."

> ESCOBAR: (*looks at Gittes's suit*) You look like you've done well by yourself.
>
> GITTES: I get by.
>
> ESCOBAR: Well sometimes it takes a while for a man to find himself. Maybe you have.

LOACH: Yeah, going through other people's dirty linen.

GITTES: (*to Escobar*) Yeah. Tell me, you still putting Chinamen in jail for spitting in the laundry?

What on earth does it look like for a man to "find himself"? What Escobar means is knowing how not to act in ways that hurt yourself. Escobar says he's "out of Chinatown" since he was promoted to lieutenant, and when Gittes reveals he is there to talk to Hollis Mulwray we once again realize this is a situation where Gittes is behind everyone else. Mulwray is being dragged from the reservoir, the top of his body pulled into frame upside down (as if he is looking up out of the upper frame of the film), eyes stark staring open, soaking wet as if this is a drowning kind of "birth" into the film (this is the first close-up of his face we get), roped and unwilling into our view.[8]

Once again we get a rapid intelligent ellipsis, a cut from Hollis's vivid wetness, to him dried out and wrapped in a candlewick cover at the point his wife identifies the body to Escobar. He begins to question Evelyn about the affair, and this leads her into some confusion—the police don't know *she* didn't hire Gittes, and Dunaway plays her rapid disintegration under questioning, hemmed in by three men (Escobar, Loach, and Gittes just beyond the door) with a stuttering, stammering gait. It is an extraordinary performance of a woman accustomed to dealing with the powerful blows of male domination, the whips and punches of controlling questioning, of logic, of swarming certainty; Polanski even pushes his camera toward her to complete the circle of pressure. She *feels* it crowding her, and Dunaway shifts her body while planting her feet still and modeling her words on the body's movements, halting, struggling to compete with rising levels of deception and doublespeak. Gittes comes to her rescue, playing into the lie that *she* did hire him and getting her out of a tough spot. And she seems to want to play the game with him, outside saying she will send him a check to make it "official that I hired you."

That is odd, of course, because unless something was untoward, and Evelyn knew it, why would the deception need to get to that level of detail? Gittes then goes to the morgue where he engages the rotund and jolly chief mortician Morty (Charles Knapp). The latter points out the irony of the water commissioner drowning in the middle of a drought ("Only in LA!"); oddly Gittes hangs around as Morty and his team pull out another body, Leroy Shuhardt, a local drunk who lived in a one of the city's storm drains, "quite a character"—he says as one of his assistants eats a sandwich and drinks a cola nearby:

MORTY: Yeah, he drowned too.

GITTES: Come again?

MORTY: Yeah. Got drunk. Passed out in the bottom of the riverbed.

GITTES: The LA river?

MORTY: Yeah. Right under Hollenbeck Bridge, what's wrong with that?

GITTES: Well, it's dry as a bone, Morty.

MORTY: It's not completely dry.

GITTES: Well he ain't gonna exactly drown in a damp riverbed no matter how soused he is.

MORTY: We got water out of him. He drowned.

This is a fine piece of sleuthing, hanging around long after anything apparently relevant to the case in point and yet finding a critical component that sheds light on the matter. Somehow an unknown drunk drowned in a region of the city that is dry, and we have seen already the instances of the sudden appearance of water in dry conditions. The control of water flowing through pipes during a drought indicates considerable control, and that points to those with power to exercise it. So we have another sense in which the world is pointed toward the detective's existing interests.

The next scene in the film is redolent of those in *Vertigo* where Scottie revisits the places he went during his pursuit of Madeleine; we see Gittes return to the LA riverbed that Mulwray visited and under the bridge where he first observed him talking to the boy on the horse and consulting his notes on the hood of his car. It is as if

Gittes returns there in order to physically experience what the riverbed is actually *doing*, if it might be capable of drowning someone. We notice first of all a residue of water, a mere puddle under the bridge, and when Gittes gets down there we see it shimmer in the afternoon late sun, surrounded by the detritus of the city—abandoned crates, furniture, signage, random things cast away. There are more puddles. The boy on the horse is there again, and Gittes questions him and the boy tells him exactly what he told Mulwray, that the water "comes in different parts of the river, every night a different part." Gittes as detective is painstaking and patient in the pursuit of knowledge and in the face of the bare inscrutability of the world, here framed cosmically—a riverbed where the detritus of civilization has fallen, where only animals are transport, and a boy with no family wanders around on his horse.

Gittes returns to the Oak Pass Reservoir where Mulwray's body was found, and it is now dark, shadowy, *noirish*, and deeply quiet. Two loud generic sounds, like gunshots, cause him to duck for cover, but this aural doubleness is another kind of fake: it is the alert that signals the storm drain is about to empty. Gittes is swept up in the gushing water, pinned against a fence where he manages to struggle over it sodden and upset—he's lost one of his expensive shoes. What might have been a waste of a night now pays evil dividends with the return of Claude Mulvihill and a small man dressed as a kind of cross between a hood and a pimp (Roman Polanski). Gittes is unfazed: "Hello there Claude, where'd you get the midget?" The hood pulls a knife and threatens him because Gittes is a "very nosy fellow," slitting his left nostril open, the blood leaping up his face and mixing with the wetness already there. It's a warning of more violence to come if Gittes continues his nosiness.

Something of Nicholson's potent defiance, his irritable resentment (familiar to viewers of *Five Easy Pieces* or *The Last Detail*) is brought forward into view now, as we find him bandaged—publicly marked—seated in his office as he discusses a response with Duffy and Walsh. But revenge does not look promising: even if they expose that "a contractor" is making payoffs in order to get a dam built ("the big boys that are making the payoffs"), it is hard to see how this benefits Gittes or anyone else. Is public exposure justice? Walsh mocks Gittes's plan to "sue the shit out of them": "Sue people like that they're liable to be having dinner with the judge who's trying the suit." What has the death of Mulwray got to do with this?

The conversation is interrupted by a call from Ida Sessions (Diane Ladd), the woman who posed as Mrs. Mulwray at the beginning of the film. The call is the stimulus for the film and Gittes to move beyond his idea of a lawsuit, since Sessions wants to ensure Gittes knows she "never expected anything to happen like what happened to Mr. Mulwray," and this indicates that at least she believes her deception and his death are somehow connected, hence her attempt at exculpation. But she won't tell Gittes who hired her, instead directing him to the obituaries in the *LA Post-Record* newspaper where she assures him he will find one of "those people." What she means are people who are not in fact dead, but made to seem so in public notices: people like "Jasper Lamar Crabb" who we see named in the next shot of Gittes reading the newspaper, a memorial service held for him at the Mar Vista Inn, an aged care facility Gittes and Evelyn visit later in the movie. He tears out the column of obituaries and turns to the front page where we see the headline "Water Bond Issue Passes Council." He's in a restaurant, an expensive one, waiting for Evelyn to arrive at his request. He interrogates her about the check she's sent him (at first she thinks he is trying to extort her, but he's after something else), telling her that she's "short changed" him on the story: "Something else besides the death of your husband was bothering you. You were upset but not that upset." This is a line that refers us back to their second meeting at the Mulwray house, the one where Evelyn appeared breathless, distracted. Gittes made no indication at the time, but we felt something was askew. This scene now connects us back to our earlier feeling which Gittes—unseen to us—has caught up with. He is apologetic with her, as if something about her class unsettles him, creates an awareness of himself as not quite making it—by her lights—in the finesse department. But he is equally resolute in trying to find out what she is concealing. Gittes lied to the police on her behalf, and now the check represents evidence that he was withholding evidence in a murder case if Mulwray was killed:

EVELYN: But he wasn't killed.

GITTES: (*takes a breath, smiles patiently*) Mrs. Mulwray, I think you're hiding something.

When we cut to Evelyn she looks terrified as if realizing she cannot conceal what she hides, and so she does what children do when their parents seem to look inside them: gambles on telling a covering lie, a confession less than the truth but intimate enough that it might get over the threshold of suspicion. She claims she knew about her husband's affair and was "grateful" since she, too, was having affairs. None of this is true: her husband was not having an affair at all, merely keeping his stepdaughter company—there is clear affection between them that we see and mistake for something else—a girl, Katherine, who is in fact Evelyn's daughter and her sister, the product of incestuous rape. *That* is one secret she is hiding, the most momentous—but we never find out how much she knows about her husband's death. Gittes with all his thinking about city corruption and the nefarious conspiracies of the "big boys" doesn't come close to figuring this out until she tells him the secret near the end of the film. The cause of Evelyn's secret and the core of the corrupt-but-productive forces that Gittes pursues for the rest of the film are, of course, linked—they are one and the same man, her father Noah Cross. The generation of productive forces, the film seems to say, is intimately linked with corrupt evil, that one cannot make a mark on the world so deep as to claim a presence in the future beyond death without destroying fundamental aspects of family and community life. Evelyn's stammering hesitation undercuts her stylish exterior; she seems in the old-fashioned sense of the term "neurotic" at this moment: "I think you know all you need know about me," she tells him. But he has to know about her rape in order to stop suspecting Evelyn of her husband's murder. As they ready to leave, he has one more question: it relates to the initials Evelyn has put at the top right corner of the envelope containing the check she sent him:

> GITTES: Oh, by the way, what does this C stand for?
>
> EVELYN: C-C-Cross.
>
> GITTES: It's your maiden name?
>
> EVELYN: Yes. Why?
>
> GITTES: No reason.
>
> EVELYN: You must have had a reason to ask me that.

GITTES: No, I'm just a snoop.

The C that he points to is curled, coiled like a snake at its upper bend, almost spiraling. That she hesitates in revealing its secret, and yet takes such care detailing its sinuousness, suggests a doubleness of attitude toward it. As they leave the restaurant Gittes updates her and the audience as to the tally of the plot events and what we can make of them, up to this point:

> GITTES: OK, go home. But in case you're interested your husband was murdered. Somebody's been dumping thousands of tons of water from the city reservoirs and we're supposed to be in the middle of a drought. He found out about it and he was killed. There's a waterlogged drunk in the morgue. Involuntary manslaughter if anybody wants to take the trouble which they don't. It seems like half the city is trying to cover it all up, which is fine by me. But Mrs. Mulwray, I goddamn near lost my nose. And I like it. I like breathing through it. And I still think that you're hiding something.

For Gittes everything now rests on forcing a confession from Evelyn and from the water authorities, bringing their secrets into the open. He hasn't been hired by anyone to do this, and if we trust what he says to Evelyn the fact is that he doesn't like being threatened by those in power. He returns to the room just outside the head of the water department's office—now Russ Yelburton—and is forced to wait again in the secretary's vestibule. All of the detectives we have met so far—Marlowe, Markham, Devlin/Alicia, Scottie and now Gittes too—seem to be in a state of existential expectation, as if awaiting something more momentous to happen to them. Their initial reluctance is as much a function of an intuition that the moment is upon them, the thing that always had to happen to them is now about to happen, and the momentousness of the imminence of that occasion gives them brief pause. Gittes is the most dogged of all of them, pushed forward by personal and physical slights until he is so far into a web of mystery that his commitment to it takes on its own momentum. Here boredom provides him with the opportunity to absorb (as he irritates the secretary by hanging around) the black-and-white photographs that decorate the walls, and in doing so he discovers the hidden psychohistory that involves the breakdown of a friendship between the two patriarchs that associated with Evelyn. The photographs show Hollis Mulwray and Noah Cross as partners over a decade before. They are the men who owned the water that feeds and irrigates the city of Los Angeles, that brought it into bloom; here in the photograph standing together proudly inside a massive pipe, posing like Victorian explorers on the cusp of discovery on the land that their partnership will transform. But, as the secretary informs Gittes, Mulwray believed the public should own the water, and so it was presumably taken into public hands, with Mulwray a public official where he could control it in the public interest. Hence his refusal to build a dangerous dam.

There is a lot in this film that remains unsaid, undefined. What was the moment of breakdown between the partners, when did a shading of different opinion crystallize into such deadly antagonism, and what role did Evelyn and her trauma, or her sister-daughter Katherine, play in that drama? To figure the world and its power as akin to the patterning of drama and conflict in a family is the stuff of great theater, and in the Hollywood cinema of the 1970s the family is typically a site of horror, repression, and disfiguring enmities. Gittes acts and talks like an orphan, a man without mother or father, floating much like Marlowe (although to a different tune) just above, at just enough distance, from ordinary things to notice when they are askew and avoid the polite turning away from normal frictions that most of us know to let pass by.

When Yelburton finally meets with Gittes, he tells him that he will go to the press to reveal the city's dumping of water during a drought. He accuses Yelburton of hiring him to ruin Mulwray's reputation, hence deleting the objection to building the dam; he also says that Mulwray was drowned. Yelburton spins a tale that they have been helping orange farmers in the northwest valley by diverting some water for irrigation which results in a "little runoff." Now, Gittes and the viewers have seen much more than a little runoff, so he threatens to expose Yelburton's infidelity (which is more or less assumed). "Who knows?" the detective concludes as he leaves, "Maybe we can lay the whole thing off on a few big shots and you can stay head of department for the next twenty years." The final shot of Yelburton's face shows us the kind of ordinary wisdom he shares with Walsh, that the "big shots" are not abstract entities to be swept away by exposure and fair dealing, but the true and effective powers behind the world whose visibility is obscured until their interests are threatened in the slightest.

Gittes bounds into his offices, sweeping off his hat to be told (silently) by Sophie that "Mrs. Mulwray" is already waiting for him. Something has happened after their last meeting that has convinced her to return to him, but what? She wonders why the people behind her husband's death have gone to all that trouble. "Money," says Gittes simplistically, but we all know money is hardly the driver of anything. It is what it can get you—freedom, power, and, critically, the time to think about what you might do with all that freedom and power (and just thinking about it is enough to occupy a lifetime). So now she hires him to find out who was behind the murder, but that doesn't satisfy Gittes in any way. It looks to him like a cover for something else, and it is something far closer to the relationship between family and municipal political shenanigans: "Tell me something, did you get married before or after Mulwray and your father sold the Water Department? Noah Cross is your father isn't he?' Mention of her father dismantles her in front of him, she fumbles for another cigarette, and reveals it was "after" the sale, when she was "just out of grade school." Her father and her husband fell out, over the sale of the water to the public and over the Van der Lip dam disaster. This implies that private interests involved in large-scale civil constructions pose mortal risks to the public since profit rather than community safety has authority over decision making:

EVELYN: Hollis never forgave him for it.

GITTES: For what?

EVELYN: For talking him into building it. They never spoke from that time on.

GITTES: You sure about that?

EVELYN: Of course I'm sure.

We know with Gittes, and thanks to Walsh, that Mulwray and Cross have indeed spoken very recently (about something to do with "apple core") outside the Pig 'n' Whistle, but Gittes does not tell her what he knows. Gould's Marlowe lived and worked in the 1970s, Gittes lives and works in 1937, but they share a similar sensibility, a distance from what they follow and observe. It is true that often we are positioned in the composition of a shot behind Nicholson, but just as often we are in front of him, watching him watch, and yet at the same time we feel, with him, a separation from the world as if, no matter how well we dress, how well we mirror the habitus of those around us, we cannot fit in and do not want to. For our position of distance was baked into us at birth, we are outsiders, like writers and screenwriters, observers rather than participants in the building of the world. That can lead to resentments, feelings of being shut out, excluded from its creativity however repulsive we discover it to be. Part of Marlowe's hurt at the end of *The Long Goodbye* is that what he took to be ordinary friendship was vouchsafed, a mere cover for raw brutality, greed, a kind of animalistic force that can never be "OK by me." Gittes who is a character from the 1930s but seen through the lens of the 1970s carries that trouble too, a romantic yearning for a world without the impersonal, bullying forces that made it the corrupt thing that it is. And yet, sometimes this feels all too easy politically: a moralistic, almost puritanical hostility to profit, to enterprise bringing water to the thirsty. Is Gittes's social conscience also a romantic one, revulsed at the weakening of the world under the shredding forces of modernity?

Chinatown radically shifts its mood over the next scenes that introduce us to Noah Cross. We move beyond the hot city to a seascape that carries a blue flag with a white fish depicted on it, flapping in the wind. The fish is an albacore and this is the Albacore Club that our detective has had to cross water to visit. When we first see Cross as Gittes arrives at his ranch, it is through the frame of a car windscreen, and he is backed by nearly a dozen men. "Mr. Gitts?" he says; "Gittes," says Gittes; Cross already smells the truth about Jake, his background in the dirt, as if this Old Testament hierophant can divine the truth of someone from the name they are given, not the one they wish the world to acknowledge. "Gitts" is awfully close to "shits," a pointing to the dirty underpinning of Jake's trade, something he cannot wash clean for public perception however finessed he appears.

We see Cross and Gittes sitting next to each other (not across from one another as we might expect) as lunch is served; it is a fish and Cross picks up his bifocal glasses to observe it. As he does, Polanski cuts to a close up of the fish, grilled with new potatoes and parsley and lemon, its eye dead center of the frame looking right back at us. "I hope you don't mind. I believe they should be served with the head," says Cross, with a wicked smile. Serving this way might put off some diners, but it also speaks to a man unaccustomed to letting a creature remain oblivious to its fate. As they eat, Cross questions Gittes about the case; the latter is upfront, telling Cross that he and Evelyn believe Mulwray was murdered; that Lou Escobar is capable although, as Gittes notes, "he has to swim in the same water we all do." Cross directly implies that Gittes is "taking [Evelyn] for a ride—financially speaking," and when he further questions the already ruffled detective if he is sleeping with her, Gittes gets up to leave. Not for the first or last time Gittes finds the notion that he is, like a kind of Jack Fisher, always ready to exploit the vulnerability of his clients for his own ends, offensive. But things are more complicated: "You may think you know what you're dealing with," Cross advises, "but believe me you don't."

CROSS: Why is that funny?

GITTES: It's what the district attorney used to tell me in Chinatown.

CROSS: Yeah? Was he right?

In *Chinatown* the secret is not even a secret, not even that Cross murdered Mulwray in the rock pool at his house, or that Evelyn gave birth to her father's daughter and now wants to protect her from him. The secret is the thing everybody knows from an early age: that power, real power—not the abstract, mystical force—is grounded and present before our eyes in the shape of powerful people who are powerful because they exercise their power successfully, in materially evident ways that shape the world. And, while this can be a positive thing—imagine a collective power transforming the world such that material prosperity is available to all plentifully—in Western fiction it almost always connotes corrupt evil. Cross embodies that in a way that is strangely charismatic and repugnant at the same time. Part of that quality comes from John Huston's elastic, tanned jowls and hokey farmer's costume (recreated in expensive silks) that is redolent of an aging bull grouper—slow-moving, ugly, but *dominant* and lethal. He now hires Gittes—much to the latter's surprise—to find Mulwray's girlfriend (in fact Cross's daughter); "just find the girl" is his repeated instruction. But why? What will he do with her, to her? To raise his daughter so that his other daughter cannot raise their daughter? Once we start to examine the film's strange doubling it begins to feel as if the world is folded over and over itself, with Gittes orbiting on the outside, trying to peek inside its layers.

In the next scene Gittes is flicking through the pages at the Hall of Records, examining the land sales in the northwest valley. By moving his finger over the record, he discovers the fact that most of the land in the valley has been sold over the last few months, that is, during the period when the dam construction was under debate including the past five days when Mulwray was murdered. He tears out the relevant piece of a page of the records and heads out to the valley itself, our next shot of him standing in front of a giant "For Sale" sign with the word "Sold" plastered diagonally across it. Hence, the records on paper accord perfectly with the facts as they are signed on the earth's crust, that featureless dry expanse where Gittes finds himself. Eventually he drives to some orange groves and is shot at by the farmers guarding it who sweep at him on horseback as he tries to outmaneuver them in his little convertible; a bullet hits the car's radiator, and as it skids to a halt in the dust, the hot water and steam blasts out of the front in a perfect picture of heat and dust and water and violence compressed into a single shot. Gittes is pulled out of the car by a couple of the farmers, one of whom has a crutch for his injured leg which he then deploys as a club, beating Gittes across the head and back as he struggles to get free. "Who are you with," asks the chief farmer, "the Water Department or the Real Estate Office?" In the struggle Gittes has lost the left lens in his sunglasses and now appears abjectly ruffled, the wound on his nose bleeding through the bandage across it. According to the farmer, the Water Department has been blowing up water tanks, poisoning wells, not irrigating the land as Yelburton claimed earlier.

After Gittes is beaten unconscious, Evelyn is the first face we see when he wakes, and she drives him back through the valley in the twilight. He tells her the dam is a "con job," that the water it contains will be sent not to Los Angeles but to the valley itself where the land has been bought up cheap by "those people"—the names in the obituaries, the aging residents of the Mar Vista retirement home that they visit next. "They're blowing these farmers out of their land and then picking it up for peanuts. You have any idea what this land would be worth with a steady water supply?" he tells her. Now in order to snoop around the Mar Vista Rest Home both Evelyn and Gittes play make-believe together, posing as a couple with an elderly parent they need to offload. At first Evelyn seems to marvel at the ease with which Gittes gulls Mr. Palmer (John Rogers), the director of the home. They wander around the facility, a bright pleasant place of music and relaxation for the elderly, with many activities listed on a board for each of them to lead on rotation, and all the names correspond to those who have bought land in the valley. When Gittes questions a lady in a group—Emma Dill (Cecil Elliott)—who is working on what looks like a blanket that carries the colors and the fish symbol of the Albacore Club, it is she who finally clarifies the aural mistake Walsh made when he overhead the argument between Mulwray and Cross: the word is not "apple core" but "albacore," she says, "it's a fish." Her grandson is a member, and the club takes very good care of them all.

Palmer has discovered who Gittes is and takes him out to meet Mulvihill, who has a concealed weapon in his jacket. Evelyn goes to their car while Gittes attacks Claude, pulling his jacket over his head and kneeing him, then punching him in the face until he is unconscious. Gittes exits the home, elegantly picking up his fedora slowly before he leaves, but the "midget" and an associate are closing on him; Evelyn, to the rescue, clears them out of the way with her car, and Jake jumps on to safety. The playacting and teamwork seal them as a couple; her loyalty to him in danger and his dependence on her. As they drive away Gittes seems to realize something has shifted between them, and for the first time he looks at her as something more than a client. Back at her house, she brings them drinks, and she marvels at how he survives such dangerous work, "If this is how you go about your work I'd say you'd be lucky to get through a whole day":

GITTES: Actually this hasn't happened to me for a long time.

EVELYN: When was the last time?

GITTES: Why?

EVELYN: It's an innocent question.

GITTES: In Chinatown.

EVELYN: What were you doing there?

GITTES: Working for the district attorney.

EVELYN: Doing what?

GITTES: As little as possible.

What is work for a detective? It is tracking: hunting down and following signs, each one folding into the previous sign, arrows pointing at arrows; interpreting the false and the real among them. In the police force, in Chinatown, the advice is not to get involved, to do "as little as possible," and thereby avoid misinterpretation and the consequences of action that might lead to injustice or worse. A job, then, that requires not so much tact as a kind of studied indifference to the signs, the sights and sounds, the pointedness of the world. It is a recipe for making vivid one's already uncomfortable estrangement from society as a cop, mocking the uniform and its pretense to serve and protect. "I help desperate people," Gittes tells the banker in the barber shop, because there was nothing he could do to help them in Chinatown. It is a place where the desire for just action meets the reality of one's impotence in the face of inscrutable forces. And just as he tells Evelyn this, we are moments away from their own coupling, one that has evolved through rapid stages by her rescue of him (twice) and now her care for the wound on his nose, which she treats with peroxide. This means their faces come close, and Gittes, hostage to his perception, gets to notice the mark in the iris of her left eye: "There's something black in the green of your eye." Evelyn calls it a "flaw," "a sort of birthmark." They kiss after she says this, and then the film cuts to a postcoital scene, Gittes smoking on the left side of the bed and looking toward the ceiling, Evelyn turned toward him, looking vaguely Asian in appearance, and stroking him with her left hand, her curiosity about him now amplified: "I don't know you. I want to know more about you." This is certainly not the Evelyn who claimed she did not see people for very long because "it's difficult for me." She appears to be falling in love with him; he has a mysterious past, something has happened to him not like the formation of a birthmark over which one has no control, but something where one, as an agent with will and authority over one's actions, became a victim of circumstances one did not understand:

GITTES: It bothers everybody that works there.

EVELYN: Where?

GITTES: Chinatown. Everybody. To me it was just bad luck.

EVELYN: Why?

GITTES: You can't always tell what's going on. Like with you. (*He turns to her and she now assumes the position he was in, looking up at the ceiling.*)

EVELYN: Why was . . . why was it bad luck?

GITTES: I was trying to keep someone from being hurt. I ended up making sure that she was hurt.

This is the center of the movie's mystery: what happened to Gittes was a result of him acting in a place where he was warned not to do anything; the warning turned out to be a prophecy. When Evelyn asks if the woman involved is dead, a solitary piano note sounds like a toll, and he doesn't get a chance to answer. Gittes will try to prevent Evelyn from harm and in doing so effectively ensure that she is harmed, killed. At a moment of maximum intimacy this couple somehow feel out their own tragic future as if it was a memory of the past rather than a presaging. Looking back at the signs from our past that we take to make up our identity can be a form of divination. The telephone rings as a kind of warning seal on this conversation, and in an odd gesture, before she gets up to answer it, Evelyn touches Gittes's lips with her fingers as if to stop him saying more.

As we find out later, the call is from one of Evelyn's servants to tell her Katherine has discovered her stepfather, Hollis Mulwray, is dead and is distraught. As Evelyn hurries to leave, Gittes is back on the job, "Where are you going?" From her point of view, the fact of Katherine cannot be confused with what she has found, just now, with Gittes—a kind of peace, a kind of fellow traveler who also is haunted by the pain of the past. She makes the mistake of asking him to "trust her this much," but he responds by surprising her in revealing he met her father that morning. Evelyn seems to draw back physically, as if the touch of her father lingers on Gittes's flesh too. She tells him she suspects her father may have been responsible for Hollis's murder. Her nervousness when her father is mentioned (and so proximately to her postcoital nakedness, she covers her naked breasts with her arms) misdirects Gittes, such that he doesn't heed her warning that Cross is "a very dangerous man, you don't know how dangerous, you don't know how crazy." "I need you here," she says, but he doesn't wait for her. He follows her car to her maid's house where Katherine is being hidden.

Here Gittes literally becomes a window snooper, watching as Evelyn tries to comfort Katherine in her bedroom and finally waiting in her car as she hurries to return. Once again Gittes mistakes what he has seen through the "lens" of the window, claiming that Evelyn has detained Katherine against her will. Evelyn tells him that the girl is her sister, and in an extraordinary lie, attempts to convince him she has allowed Hollis to sleep with her sister out of a kind of marital generosity.

Unconvinced, Gittes goes home. He has been working all day, a day which began—we assume—with his visit to Cross's ranch, then the Hall of Records, then the orange groves, then the Mar Vista Rest Home. We now see Gittes showering and then in his pajamas closing his bedroom curtains, throwing back the covers of his bed and collapsing inert on it, spent. The work of a detective requires not only finesse but travel, patience, bravado, deceit, and a capacity to defend oneself in moments of violence and intimidation. Gittes has demonstrated this full spectrum of resourcefulness: his identity is what he does, and what he does is follow and observe and question and observe and infiltrate and observe. Ending the day by lovemaking with Evelyn turned out to be another step in the investigation, and now, alone in his bed, he gets to rest.

Who we are is not what we want but what we have done, the outcome of our actions in the world. "Hollis Mulwray made this city," Cross tells Gittes at the ranch: imagine being the person who "made" a city. When we see Gittes look at the black-and-white photographs of Cross and Mulwray in the secretary's office at the Department of Water, they stand near the organs of their achievement rightly proud of the enormity of what they are doing. Power and wealth are not inert forces but creative ones—although their creativity often falls far below the moral standards we might wish for them—and Gittes's mistake is to assume Cross as an old man might be content to eke out his retirement at a ranch hosting fancy parades for local politicians. The restlessness of power, its wanting to expand, create, grow, and dominate sharpens with age, with proximity to eternity.

    The shot of Nicholson tired on the bed is wonderful because it underlines the sheer physical *effort* of the detective, *his* restlessness not to create but to *know*. And knowledge is impotent in the face of power because it simply clarifies how and why the knower has failed to obtain sufficient amounts of it to turn that knowledge into effective action. Jeff Markham wants to settle down in Bridgeport but he can hardly catch a fish, and he does what many of us are tempted to do—go back to what we are already good at. Alicia and Devlin discover a way of working together that forces them apart catastrophically, but they keep on at the job in the face of mortal danger. Scottie quits his job and becomes vulnerable because of this to exploitation, to being set up in work that was never real in itself but a theater that would capture and doom him to repeat the past. Gittes too, is so committed to his work, to the identity that his job provides, that he is vulnerable to the error of focusing on what he is good at: details, lies, deception. His insight never acquires the sufficient scale needed to appreciate the cosmic magnitude of ambition and evil he is dealing with.

    Gittes's rest has hardly begun before it is interrupted, in another rhyme, by his phone ringing. A male voice tells him Ida Sessions wants to see him and gives him an address. It is like hanging bait for a fish, and Gittes—eventually, he avoids the trap of the first call, but the caller is insistent—can't resist however tired he is. It is now early morning as he drives to Sessions' place in Echo Park. The front door shows signs of a break in, and as Gittes enters the little dark apartment it is clear something terrible has happened. Its darkness contains the emptiness of the dead at home; a lettuce lies grotesque on the floor near Sessions' murdered body, amidst the rude contents of her spilled shopping. She must have just returned from the shops and was followed, was unpacking it in her kitchen when she was strangled to death. Gittes checks her wallet where we notice a Screen Actors Guild membership card. A "working girl," actress for hire and a prostitute, a small victim that has to be tidied up. Escobar and Loach are hiding among the hanging laundry in her bathroom, waiting for Gittes. Loach—a lower version of "cockroach" surely?—called Gittes using the phone number scrawled in pencil above Sessions's telephone:

> LOACH: What happened to your nose, Gittes? Somebody slam a bedroom window on it?
>
> (*Uniformed cop guarding the exit sniggers. Gittes looks at him coolly then responds.*)
>
> GITTES: Nope. Your wife got excited. She crossed her legs a little too quick. You understand what I mean pal?

The currency of insult is cuckoldry, and Gittes's power is his professional command over the reality of weak men betrayed by wives who are restless or whose appetites they cannot satisfy. Escobar reveals he knows Mulwray was murdered because "he had salt water in his lungs" (this is news to Gittes—perhaps his talk with Morty the mortician prompted a more careful autopsy?) and that he suspects Gittes is being paid off by the murderer Evelyn Mulwray to keep quiet. But he doesn't know Gittes like we do, the Gittes who only helps "desperate people" who doesn't want their "last dime" and would never, as part of some code of honor, rip off his clients: "I wouldn't extort a nickel from my worst enemy Escobar, that's where I draw the line." Then we hear what Gittes thinks, and it is still far from the truth: "Mulwray was murdered and moved because somebody didn't want his body found in the ocean . . . He found out they were dumping water there, that's what they were trying to cover up." But when Gittes takes them to the outflow pipe, dry as a bone in blazing mid-morning sunshine, the cops have no evidence they can see for his claims, and Yelburton's irrigation story holds up. Gittes here and before keeps pecking at Escobar's inexperience, taunting him to "make a decision" and commenting on his hesitancy to arrest Evelyn as fear that he will lose his lieutenant's "gold bar." Gittes's observation has a deeper resonance for it means that at the crucial moment Escobar has neither the political nor professional foundation to do anything when the catastrophe at the end of the film occurs—he simply lets everyone go. As the cops leave the cliff tops, Gittes turns toward the deep blue sea, wet and delicious in the background, and runs both hands through his hair. We are behind him now, but what do we see? Is this gesture a sign that a decision is being made, or of puzzlement, confoundedness?

He arrives at Evelyn's house for the third time but finds it abandoned, the Asian maid covering the furniture and, outside on the veranda, the gardener who is now returfing the grass near the rock pool pond; Gittes remembers something, "bad for glass" he says to the gardener. "Bad for glass," the man replies more clearly just as we cut to a shot of Gittes's back as he goes to walk back inside: "Salt water very bad for grass." Gittes halts immediately, a pause as the line sinks in, and then he turns to us and walks to the pool. He tastes the water and then notices the glinting gold object he saw in the pool the first time he was there. The gardener retrieves it for him and we find out it is a pair of spectacles, objects that enhance sight, that clarify our perception; themselves partially hidden under the "glass" of the water. There are only four characters that we have seen wearing glasses—Walsh, Mulwray, Cross, and Gittes himself (sunglasses).

Gittes drives fast to Evelyn's maid's home and pushes his way past Kahn the butler. Evelyn is happy to see him, as if they can now go away together, have a life. Gittes is fathoms distant from this kind of thinking. What Gittes thinks at this point is that Evelyn has been lying to him all along, that she murdered her husband in the rock pool and that Katherine was a witness to that. Evelyn up to this point is simply nice to him, asking whether he slept, offering him lunch in the kind of welcome, embarrassed way lovers do the morning after their first time. But Gittes calls Escobar and, in a flourish that might remind us of his admonition to Walsh that the business requires "finesse" (the word spoken as he dries his hands on his handkerchief and replaces it in his top jacket pocket) produces a silk handkerchief from his pocket and gently unfolds it to reveal the spectacles the gardener took out of the Mulwray pond. According to him, Evelyn drowned her husband in it.

> GITTES: I'm gonna make it easy for you. You had a fight. He fell he hit his head. It was an accident. But his girl

is a witness. So you had to shut her up. You don't have the guts to harm her but you got the money to keep her mouth shut. Yes or no?

EVELYN: No!

Gittes has a lot to be upset about: if Evelyn killed her husband, she slept with him knowing that she did that, and that him losing his license is only part of the humiliation he will suffer when the truth comes out in court. But on a second viewing it is quite remarkable that he thinks any of this, since nothing we have seen of Evelyn even remotely makes her capable of such violent deception. She is no Kathie Moffat. And now we reach one of the most famous moments in the film, where Gittes literally slaps the truth out of Evelyn as he tries to find out who the girl really is. But her name is her identity, not what she does but only what she *is*, condemned by the act of her conception to be an *is*, not a thing that can define itself. As Gittes beats the truth out of her, she takes it as if in welcome punishment, its ferocity barely matching the obscenity of the event:

GITTES: What's her name?

EVELYN: Katherine.

GITTES: Katherine who?

EVELYN: She's my daughter.

GITTES: (*vicious slap*) I said I want the truth!

EVELYN: (*facing him evenly*) She's my sister. (*slap*) She's my daughter. (*slap*) My sister my daughter. (*two slaps*)

GITTES: I said I want the truth! (*he grabs her violently by the shoulders and throws her onto the sofa*)

EVELYN: All of it! She's my sister and my daughter. . . . My father and I. . . . Understand? Or is it too tough for you?

GITTES: He raped you?

(*Evelyn shakes her head emphatically.*)

What Evelyn means is that she was a willing participant as far as that goes. The script elaborates, but this is wisely avoided in the final cut since it would merely offer reasons where no clarity is needed for the drama. She was fifteen when it happened, and after she ran away to Mexico, Hollis came to take care of her; a further part of her shame was her unwillingness to see her child, the evidence of the incestuous act, the kind of marked creation that has little chance to thrive in the modern world. "Now I want to be with her, I want to take care of her," she says. It must take considerable powers of forgiveness to reach back into the past, to change what has happened to wipe away the wounds and scars, or at least try to make of that trauma something better, something productive, positive, something unchoked. Forgiveness, once again, is an immense achievement: we never imagine that Cross himself, who also wants to participate in Katherine's life, feels the same way.

A revelation of this magnitude finally explains Evelyn's behavior for Gittes. He is struck, transformed, and now resolute, decisive. Like Chandler's Marlowe, like Gould's Marlowe, his sense of right is activated in the face of terrible injustice, suffering, and her genuine desire to make amends. He tells her to leave, to go to Kahn's place as a start, and as she leaves the room she notes that the spectacles did not belong to her husband, and Gittes finally realizes what has happened, as he takes them from the handkerchief, the left lens cracked, and puts them in his jacket.

Evelyn then does something extraordinary. She introduces her daughter to Gittes, and I take this as one last shred of her hope they might have a life together, perhaps in Mexico where Gittes's finesse might have to dance to a different tune. And Gittes for the first time sees this woman not as a player in an adulterous affair but someone entirely innocent, good natured, more than a role of murderer or victim. She looks at him from midway down the stairs, and we cut to see him looking back up at her hands in pockets. Evelyn tells him that Kahn lives at "1712 Alameda—do you know where that is?" and—in one of the saddest camera movements exquisitely anchored to a painful chord on the soundtrack—we glide close to Gittes's knowing face: "Sure"—where else could it be?

Barney the Barber, Morty the Mortician, Duffy and Walsh—Gittes doesn't really have friends except the kind you might find in comics, and it is the isolation of the detective, his lone "white knighting" that condemns him to be a *knower* and not a *man of action*. For the world depends on dependencies, the necessity, if we are to thrive, to exist within webs of solidarity or pseudo-solidarity with other members of our society. Either we can compel them to serve us, or we can lead or be led by groups that share a common interest, a common direction and vision of the future that is inspiring enough to enlarge through the persuasive force of rational argument. None of this seems available to Gittes in the final scenes of the movie: he has not availed himself of allies sufficient to defeat the forces his quest for knowledge has uncovered in front of his eyes. All this time it has been going on, we are positioned as viewers, behind his back. For we know—don't we?—that the world depends not on what we think we know about it, but on what we can *do* about what we think we know about it, and we can do "as little as possible" by ourselves.

Gittes is fundamentally committed now to help Evelyn escape to Mexico, but first he must evade Escobar and the authorities. He calls Walsh and tells him to meet him at 1712 Alameda, and we hear Walsh on the phone say, "Jesus. That's in Chinatown, ain't it?" There is a lining of fearful concern in his voice, and for the first time we realize why the little conversation with Gittes about the inadequacy of his photography had such a strange dynamic. Walsh may lack "finesse," but he is older and wiser than Gittes, perhaps can see in Gittes what Escobar does when he says he will make sure he doesn't burn himself with the matches, or later when he says to Gittes, "You never learn do you Jake?" Perhaps they both can see that Gittes's isolation is self-sought and leaves him vulnerable to danger, from himself and from others.

Then we get a brilliant series of scenes that recoup the beginning of the film. When Escobar and Loach arrive at the maid's house, Gittes lies to them that Evelyn has already left and that he knows where she has gone, her maid's house in San Pedro. But when they get there, and Gittes is allowed to go inside the house alone, we discover it is Curly's place. His wife, whom we last saw in the photographs that Gittes showed to her husband, is now sporting a black eye (right side) as she answers the door already eating something—this is a woman of some appetite, and Curly looks as if he is wary to take his eyes off her lest she start doing it with another man whilst he's out of the room. Gittes convinces Curly to sneak him out back in his car and arranges for him to take Evelyn and Katherine to Mexico in his fishing boat.

What happens next is puzzling. For some reason Gittes calls Cross and arranges to meet him at Evelyn's empty house. Why does he do this? He already suspects Cross murdered Mulwray and telling him that he knows that is hardly likely to produce a penitent man ready to hand himself over to the cops. It is the most beguiling, haunting scene of the film and takes place at twilight, near the veranda where the rock pool is located. In a lovely call back, Cross arrives dressed in the same kind of clothing we saw him wear in the photographs where he posed with Mulwray in front of their water engineering projects; he even carries a walking stick like some explorer or pioneer; supremely confident, unfazed by what Gittes reveals he knows. Gittes hands him the obituaries column he tore from the newspaper he was reading before he met Evelyn at the expensive restaurant. When Cross takes out his bifocals (the ones he used to look at the grilled fish on Gittes's lunch plate) Gittes sees that they match the broken ones the gardener pulled from the pool in the garden:

CROSS: (*reading*) What does it mean?

GITTES: That you killed Hollis Mulwray. Right here in that pond. You drowned him. And you left these.

Gittes takes out the incriminating spectacles from his jacket. A means to perceive the signs of the world is a sign, evidence. Cross's response is poetic and points to the cosmic stakes in the murder drama that Gittes has missed: he is full of praise and admiration for the man he murdered:

CROSS: Hollis was always fascinated by tide pools. You know what he used to say?

GITTES: I haven't the faintest idea.

Cross: "That's where life begins!" Sloughs, tide pools. When we first come out here he figured if you dumped water into the desert sand and left it to percolate down to the bedrock it would stay there instead of evaporate the way it does most reservoirs. You'd only lose twenty per cent instead of seventy or eighty. He *made* this city.

As Cross says this he moves past Gittes and into the garden, and the camera pans with him so that when he says the final lines he stands facing us, the night crouching toward the city, and the white Doric columns and white rocks near the pool all form a pretty backdrop behind him, while in front of us are Nicholson's back and shoulders as Gittes listens to this speech. It is as if the pond becomes a stage for his speech. Cross tells him that he is doing just the same now, using the bond issue to dump water into the valley and hence expanding the city by dragging it and its citizens to where the water will be. That such a brilliant idea has to be achieved via murder and deception is at the core of a film that rightly takes its place among other paranoid cinema of the 1970s that exhibited a fundamental distrust of patriarchal authority. C. L. R. James saw in detective movies a mass appetite for violence, revenge, and justice, with the detective a shape-shifter who incorporated both gangster and cop, villain and knight; in *Out of the Past* there is just enough of domestic settled order for it to be a dream for Jeff to live in Bridgeport and escape the rough world of finance and criminality. In *Notorious* it is as if good works, holding back the expression of love, is the price a couple needs to pay for their precarious security, and in *Vertigo* we see the perilous nature of love detached from any societal commitment or responsibility beyond itself. In *Chinatown* the critique of corrupt municipal power, and its projection mainly in this tide pool scene, at a cosmic, eternalized scale, suggests there is no credible redemption or healing for the dedicated knower in the face of corporate expansion. There is nothing to be done, because it is never a question of money itself; what propels men is the quest to make an imprint on the world that is lasting, for immortality:

GITTES: How much are you worth?

CROSS: I have no idea. How much do you want?

GITTES: No, I just want to know what you're worth. Over ten million?

CROSS: Oh my, yes.

GITTES: Why are you doing it? How much better can you eat, what can you buy that you can't already afford?

CROSS: The future Mr. Gittes, the future! Now, where's the girl?

Of course it is not enough that Cross is a visionary, murdering and conniving his way around legal restraints in order to get his way; he is also a father who slept with his daughter and, shockingly, has no room to blame himself for the fact of doing it—it is as if the act provided yet another discovery about the truth of human life that he is proud, somehow, to know, to be able to bear the burden of it: "See Mr. Gittes most people never have to face the fact that at the right time and the right place, they're capable of *anything*." Huston plays the final word for its full melodramatic effect in a kind of rasping whisper: he is a pantomime Saturn in chthonic revelry over his dangerous, unspeakable acts that renew the world.

During their conversation Gittes joins Cross in the garden and they talk face to face. Now Cross turns to where Gittes was, to a place behind his back and says, "Claude take those glasses from him will you." The use of off-screen space stands in for Gittes's blind spot, what was at his back all along: the sheer muscle of agents ranged against the truth, against the constraint of evil. Gittes is now trapped and has to take Cross to Chinatown, to Evelyn and Katherine.

Famously Robert Towne's script originally had Evelyn survive with Cross dead, all evil vanquished. Polanski objected to this and wrote the ending we have, one which charges all that went before with a terrible, brutal, and ugly note. A Chinatown is an ethnically marked enclave in an urban center, culturally quarantined as if the Chinese people can only survive an encounter with the West by avoiding it as far as possible while living within it. Those that are supposed to represent the Chinese in this film are largely background figures, and since the ending is set there, we finally see a place where all rules, all law and order have disintegrated, and only raw power, raw courage, and brutal firepower prevails. When Gittes drives to the address and parks, we see Evelyn's white Packard parked outside; as Gittes, Cross, and Mulvihill approach it, we see Walsh and Duffy waiting. But they are handcuffed, and Escobar and Loach glide into the frame: "You're under arrest, Jake." "Good news," he responds as Loach handcuffs him:

> ESCOBAR: Withholding evidence, extortion, accessory after the fact.
>
> GITTES: I didn't extort nothing from nobody, Lou. This is Noah Cross if you don't know, Evelyn's father if you don't know. He's the bird you're after, Lou. I can explain everything! Just give me five minutes that's all I need! He's rich! Do you understand? He thinks he can get away with anything!

It is a rush of information far too late to be heard: as at the end of *Vertigo* there is just not enough time for the players in the drama to absorb the magnitude of the situation they are in, or to communicate its importance to others who might do something helpful about it. Then the action pivots again, as Kahn and Curly escort Katherine to the Packard: Cross approaches her and claims to be her "grandfather"; Evelyn grabs him and tells him to get away from her and once again, Huston produces a villain worthy of a horrible fairy tale, leaning his big shovel-like face into hers:

> CROSS: Evelyn, Evelyn, please, please be reasonable. (*He reaches into the car at Katherine.*) Come to my...
>
> EVELYN: Get away from her!
>
> CROSS: Evelyn! (*He grabs her and holds her tightly to him.*) How many years have I got? She's mine too!
>
> EVELYN: She's never going to know that!

Evelyn pulls a twenty-five auto pistol and warns him away, while Gittes—impotently, uselessly—advises her to let the police handle the matter ("He owns the police!" she responds, as if Gittes ought to have figured that out before he allowed himself to be handcuffed by them). Cross, in an extraordinary moment, does not give up, moving to the passenger side of the Packard to get at Katherine, and Evelyn shoots him in the arm and Cross merely takes it, acknowledging the pain stoically as if it were an insect bite (a few seconds later he appears to have forgotten all about the wound). Mother and daughter drive away, and Escobar fires his gun twice (the exact same sound effect used to signal the water outflow from the pipe that drenched Gittes a few days earlier). Gittes heroically prevents Escobar from shooting directly at the car by throwing himself on the cop's arm, but this frees Loach to take three shots at the car, and it stops in the distance, its horn blaring.

The spectators left behind slowly at first begin to approach it and then with more urgency. Polanski leaves us in long shot as Katherine begins to scream hysterically, and then suddenly cuts to a far closer position that allows him to whip the camera right to left to offer a close view of the driver's side of the convertible. Evelyn's head is slumped on the car horn, and Escobar opens her door allowing her body to fall into view, showing the exit wound that has replaced her left eye socket. Now we see the price Gittes pays for knowledge, as Escobar releases all of them: he stares down at Evelyn's ruined corpse and then looks up to see Cross, in another extraordinary gesture, cover Katherine's eyes with his big hand: "Don't look, don't look, don't look." He takes her away.

The camera pivots again, this time to a close shot of Gittes looking at Evelyn:

GITTES: As little as possible.

ESCOBAR: What's that? (*moves very close to Gittes*) What's that? (*pause; then to Walsh and Duffy*) You want to do your partner a big favor? Take him home. (*shouting*) Take him home! Just get him the hell out of here!

DUFFY: Come on.

ESCOBAR: Go home Jake. I'm doing you a favor.

DUFFY: Come on, Jake.

So finally there is community in the acknowledgment of hurt, the men now realizing that Gittes needs protection far away from this place, from this view of the world. And Walsh offers an impossible kind of wisdom often taken, at least, to mean accomplishing the impossible since the line comes as Gittes has his back to us and, impulsively, seeming without control, turns around as if he needs to keep seeing what he could not prevent, what he may have enabled: "Forget it Jake, it's Chinatown." Like Scottie at the end of *Vertigo*, we have a picture of a man facing the body of a woman, unseen to us, but there as a ruin. The detective is faced with the spectacle of death and cannot help but read it as a sign. As his operatives take Gittes away, backs to us, the screen is swamped, in a wonderful moment, with many Asian faces who also want to see. They are bullied away by the cops and the arriving ambulances. Jake's final line has a bleaker meaning, that there is nothing to be done about the world as it is and, more, that there is no region—nothing beyond Chinatown—where one might accomplish such a momentous thing as the restoration of justice. The vitality of the promise that C. L. R. James saw in the detective is utterly crushed at this moment, fine drama that it is, a moment of defeat and withdrawal into the darkness.

Conclusion

True Detectives

> [We have to] live in a world where evil and death are lurking, where uncertainty impertinently provokes reason, and where war is always waiting in the wings of peace ... [the son of Icarus] will stop cursing this incertitude when he has finally understood that the tragic is the bearer of meaning. Life has value in the antinomies among which it struggles.
>
> —Chantal Delsol, *Icarus Fallen: The Search for Meaning in an Uncertain World*[1]

THE FIRST EPISODE OF *True Detective* opens with an apocalyptic image of a field at night being set alight, the line of its orange flame seen in the distance beyond a lonely river and a few isolated trees somewhere in the backwaters of Louisiana.[2] The fire is part of the theater created by a serial killer who has left another of his victims, her broken and bruised corpse decorated with antlers and odd symbolism drawn on her naked body which is perched against a tree. The act is so oversignified it is effectively a parody of the search for meaning, a hodgepodge of found and borrowed thinking assembled by an uneducated, psychopathic school gardener—Errol Childress (Glenn Fleshler). In the final episode of the season we see Childress in his home, which is packed with the detritus of popular culture—books, magazines, toys, heaps of stuff—and in the middle of this cultural dump, the King of Death watches on television a scene from Hitchcock's *North by Northwest* where Roger Thornhill (Cary Grant), having been kidnapped and taken to Vandamm's (James Mason) house in the country, tries to find out why he has been abducted. We know that it is a case of mistaken identity (he has been mistaken for a man who does not exist), but it is too late and Vandamm is incredulous at Thornhill's insistence that he is an innocent and has no idea what is going on:

> THORNHILL: What the devil is all this about? Why was I brought here?
>
> VANDAMM: Games? Must we?
>
> THORNHILL: Not that I mind a slight case of abduction now and then, but I have tickets for the theater this evening. To a show I was looking forward to. And I get, well, kind of unreasonable about things like that.
>
> VANDAMM: With such expert play acting you make this very room a theater.

In George Wilson's superb analysis of the film he points out that this scene places Thornhill, as he talks, in front of drawn curtains so that Vandamm's comment that the room becomes a theater because of Thornhill's performance is given an extra frisson. The room turns out to be *false* in any case because Vandamm does not live there, and when we return to it the next day it has been altered and Thornhill's protestations to the cops he brings with him are met with a similar incredulity to Vandamm's. The film is about how the apparent correspondence between the reality of our perception—the people, spaces, and objects we see and hear—and the fact of matter is deeply uncertain because it rests fundamentally on shared social agreements about those facts, and Hitchcock uses his glorious art to demonstrate how fragile and vulnerable to deception that agreement is. When we see Childress watch the scene, what he takes from it is simply Mason's British accent (which carries the faint lining of a Yorkshire accent), mimicking it inexpertly. The writer of the show, Nic Pizzolatto, seems to want us to see how almost all culture, even something as self-reflexive, popular, and intelligent as the work of Hitchcock, can be degenerated on reception, lost in translation to an age where such matters as the correspondence theory of perception have ceased to register as problems at all. *True Detective*'s deep interest in the waning of meaning and its attempt to recuperate something out of a world that has lost the authority of normative meaning represents the end point of the detective identity that has been tracked in this book. Signs are abundant but their meaning has dissolved amidst disordered morality and the collapse of authority. Matters such as reluctance and commitment have been utterly shattered by the time we crest beyond mid-1970s Hollywood movies to be replaced by a kind of postmodern assemblage of referencing, compulsive homage, and playful but empty generic mixing. To try to rescue something from this artistically, to present a credible detective committed to a job once again, is the purpose of the show across its three seasons.

Chantal Delsol's *Icarus Fallen: The Search for Meaning in an Uncertain World* and Frank Furedi's *First World War: Still No End In Sight* in different ways evolve the claim that the fundamental antinomies that emerged in the late nineteenth century, as industrial capitalism made good on its promises to provide material prosperity, have not been resolved and that the elites of mass democratic nations (and supranational offshoots) have not risen to the occasion. From the early 1970s to the present, Western capitalism has not increased its rate of productivity, and the degenerate ways in which that economic order has maintained itself have failed, too, to establish a strong normative cultural or political meaning that would maintain social solidarity among its citizens. Instead, as commentators of all political shades have it, mass alienated atomization appears to be accelerating. What this means for the cultural imagination, for the art produced by Hollywood and elsewhere, is a far keener sense of apocalyptic possibility and one that finds it far easier to imagine the end of the world than the end of capitalism.[3]

C. L. R. James saw in the popular detective a vital fusion of the gangster and the cop, a lone but resonant figure who operated beyond the rules of the system and yet held onto a code of honor that was decent and not degenerate. In film we get concentrated stories about these figures but serial, episodic television with several hours to play with can expand and deepen our experience of them. Television drama has the possibility for *dilation*, the expansion of the imaginative canvas on which characters travel and evolve (which carries the risk of aesthetic *dilution*, where events and moments become a kind of padding, filling in time). *True Detective* ingeniously splits the fusion of detective and gangster, in several ways. Its central detectives are Rust Cohle (Matthew McConaughey) and Marty Hart (Woody Harrelson); the former was an undercover cop running dangerous narcotics missions after the breakup of his marriage occurred because of the accidental death of his only child. He is bookish and edgy, with an internal code whose misanthropy is driven by a belief in the fundamental darkness of human nature. Hart by contrast seems like a regular cop, a family man married to the local ER doctor, with two young girls, and is a well-liked colleague at the South Louisiana station where they work. But he is morally degenerate: a company man, cowardly, risk-averse, and an adulterer. The show takes advantage of its duration: in its first few episodes, a time in the past—the events of 1995 where Hart and Cohle investigate the serial killer—are framed via interviews of Hart and Cohle that take place in 2012, conducted by another team, both black detectives, Gilbough (Michael Potts) and Papania (Tory Kittles). In the 2012 timeline Hart and Cohle are no longer a team and no longer cops, and it becomes clear they have been called back for the interview because the case has been reopened. That means when we see events in 1995 they happen under a canopy of uncertainty as if everything we witness has a provisional stamp.

 Early on Cohle is established as a *knower*, a detective whose appetite for details, for the harvesting of deeper meaning, is voracious. In one episode it is revealed he was taught by his father how to hunt game with a bow: the elemental ancient sense of the detective as hunter is fused with the depiction of his hallucinogenic symptoms left over from his days as undercover narcotics cop. He sees visions. The detective is hunter and diviner, a knower and a mystic prophet. Somehow this aptitude for knowledge, this affinity for tracking signs and wonders, makes him unsuitable for domestic settlement, and our first glimpse of him is drunk, staggering outside of Hart's house on his way to join a family meal. In 2012, Hart tells his interviewers that Cohle was known as "The Taxman" because he carried a large A4 ledger-like notebook around with him, transcribing details of the crime scene, of interviews, of the symbols and theatrical designs the killer left for him to interpret. In this way Cohle functions rather like a surrogate for the audience that watched the show, some of whom, after an episode was aired, went online to drill into the mise-en-scène in painful detail.

True Detective uses the familiar genre of the "buddy cop" and combines it with what Stanley Cavell calls the "remarriage comedy," in which couples in a film break up and the rest of the story concerns how they will get back together.[4] Along with many male-centered popular genres, the show poses the paradox, in the case of Hart, of the dissatisfactions of settled domesticity. Hart has everything—a beautiful, intelligent, professional wife, Maggie (Michelle Monaghan), two lively daughters, and a job in which he is admired and finds reward. And yet he seeks further distraction in an affair, and there is a sense that his own failure to uphold a steady, honest moral stance in his personal life begins to degrade all of those around him. Calling his daughters away from their play in the bedroom in order to attend a family dinner, Hart looks back at their toys and notices the dolls they are playing with are arranged in what appears to be a gang rape. His wife knows that he is somehow being dishonest not only with her but himself, noting that he was "far smarter" when she first met him. Cohle's domestic life was shattered because of an accident, but he gradually finds solace in his interactions with Hart's family. At first he arrives to dinner drunk, afraid of the emotional upheaval a family event will prompt, but he quickly settles in and finds a kind of vitality and liveliness. Later, he mows Hart's lawn to thank him for lending the mower, and we see Cohle and Maggie all friendly in the kitchen chatting about her plans to fix him up with a work colleague. But when Hart returns home and finds them there he is incensed, taking Cohle's generosity as an intrusion on his domestic and sexual realm; his hostile reaction ("*I* mow *my* lawn") effectively ends the prospect of their friendship developing.

When Hart's marriage evaporates Cohle is unsympathetic, insisting they concentrate on their work finding the serial killer, and once Hart moves in with him they begin to form a closer relationship, culminating in the tracking down of two degenerate drug manufacturers hiding in the woods. On discovering two children imprisoned there, Hart summarily executes one of the men, and they then confect a cover story which they maintain even during the 2012 interviews. The show then gives us a brief montage of a happy friendship together, Cohle finally finding a partner and the buddy team successful breaking a number of cases. But when Hart once again falls into adultery, Maggie takes revenge by seducing Cohle and then confessing the act to her husband, effectively ending the marriage for good as well as destroying Cohle and Hart's partnership on the force. Both leave their work, Hart to become a private detective, Cohle disappearing for several years before resurfacing as a bartender.

The show then becomes about getting their team back together, effectively compelling Hart to become the "true detective" he failed at years before. Being a true detective means genuinely finding the commitment to life not as an obsessive tracker or hunter, but as a moral entity, vulnerable to the sights and pointedness of the world, not going along to get along, or avoiding it through sex, drink, or drugs. It transpires that Cohle has been monitoring other murder cases and that he believes they executed the wrong suspects in 1995. He convinces Hart to work with him on the case—now both of them as amateur sleuths—by showing him a video recording of ritualized child abuse; there is, he believes a conspiracy by wealthy and powerful people to abduct and rape children. However, their investigations eventually lead them to Childress whom they hunt down and corner in his gothic, oversymbolized lair, and together they kill him, although Cohle is seriously wounded in the final confrontation.

The show ends with the two of them outside the hospital where Cohle is being treated; Hart hands Cohle a little present (a packet of Blue Camel cigarettes, wrapped), and the team is finally restored. Somehow the comforts of solidarity with a friend become the fitting reward of "true" detective work, and unlike the extended ending of *Vertigo* with Midge and Scottie silently drinking in her apartment, this scene gives us a hopeful sense that the apocalyptic world and the evil within it can be at least ameliorated by the good intentions of moral agents.

Indeed, for all the outward despair that all seasons of *True Detective* manifest, Pizzolatto's mastery of the genre, his internalization of its key existential elements, produce an uncharacteristic optimism in the genre. The second season explicitly connects with the Los Angeles noir of *The Long Goodbye* and *Chinatown*—in fact the plot concerns a corrupt land deal very similar to that depicted in the latter film. Here the cop and gangster exist as two characters, Ray Velcoro (Colin Farrell) and Frank Semyon (Vince Vaughan). Ray is a corrupt cop, forever marked by his revenge killing of a man who raped his wife the identity of whom was given to him by Frank, a casino-owning gangster who wants to go "clean" through handling real estate. The two are uneasy friends, and when Ray eventually discovers the man he killed was not the rapist, he confronts Frank over morning coffee in his home, ready to kill him. Once again, at this moment of ultimate breakdown, the friendship eventually is restored at the end and the two work together. Both of them struggle with paternity: Ray is never sure that his son who does not at all resemble him is in fact his or the issue of the rape; nonetheless even in his final moments, hunted down in a forest setting that resembles the redwood one Scottie and Madeleine visit, he records a message of fatherly hope and advice to him. Frank and his wife cannot have children, and their efforts at fertility treatment and thoughts of adoption threaten to destroy an otherwise loving marriage. What is "true" in this season seems to be the act of faith in one's treatment of others, a feeling that only the vanishing values of loyalty, friendship, and parental responsibility can survive the dreadful, alienating shredding of the world by capitalist modernity. As in *Chinatown*, the alienating system is embodied by evil individuals rather than an attempt to depict the precise ways in which structural conditions give rise to interpersonal estrangement, but it is nonetheless effective drama.

In the third season of the show, like the first, spread across multiple timelines, we again have the examination of a partnership of two cops, Wayne Hays (Mahershala Ali) and Roland West (Stephen Dorff). Once again the abduction and murder of children initiates the plot, but its key concern seems to be the maintenance of ever fragile social bonds. Such bonds can only be maintained if we can agree on a shared history, if our memories coincide sufficiently such that we can agree on the satisfactions of our relationship in the past such that they are a reliable guide to its continuance into the future. But in the scenes set in the present the now elderly Wayne suffers from dementia and can no longer reliably remember the events that shaped his life. Before becoming a cop he served in the Vietnam war as a long-range scout, another kind of tracker, a hunter in the jungle. In one scene the elderly man, haunted by visions of his late wife, and struggling to piece together reality in the present, visits Roland who now lives alone with a number of dogs he cares for. They sit on his back deck, two old, retired detectives excellent at their jobs, worrying about the past. Roland, in a moving statement of wounded regret, details his life after their partnership dissolved now that they are being interviewed by a production company making a documentary about the case, where they—like Cohle and Hart—executed a suspect and covered it up:

> ROLAND: How are you gonna talk to these people, we done what we done? You don't know what you might say. Or might remember.
>
> WAYNE: If I remember what we done I'll remember not to say. [. . .] I can't. I really can't remember.
>
> ROLAND: You walked away.
>
> WAYNE: Not this time.
>
> ROLAND: This what you come to see me about? Twenty-five years. What, you doin' old man fantasy camp? You think you . . . think you can just roll up here and I'll be all, "Golly gee partner! Let's grab our junior detective clue-finders and have an adventure!" (*Stands up throws a ball to his dogs down below. Turns to Wayne.*) You. You know '80? We stopped being partners. You get married. It's natural for people to drift apart. This right now? This ain't that. All this time. You never picked up the phone. Never dropped by for a beer. Never said you're fuckin' sorry, once.
>
> WAYNE: Roland. . .
>
> ROLAND: And I was gonna put that shit aside. Have a drink with you. Reminisce. Maybe just watch the dogs play and the sun go fuckin' down. But look what you're doin'.
>
> WAYNE: (*Points to the half-drunk bottle of whiskey on the table.*) How many of those you go through a week?
>
> ROLAND: Hey fuck you man! I'm fine! Alone out here. (*Tears in eyes.*) No woman. No kids. And no old friends. So that means I get to drink exactly as much as I want to. You don't

judge me motherfucker. I know you. I know what you did. What I did. You talkin' about my drinking? I'd whip your ass if it wouldn't kill you. And you still ain't apologized.

WAYNE: Roland. I don't remember. I'm sorry but I just can't remember. I don't . . . I can't . . . I can't remember my life man. I can't remember my wife. I don't know. If you tell me I did something wrong well, okay, I'm sorry.

WAYNE: It's all right.

ROLAND: I'm sorry.

We see in this devastating, poignant scene the fact that our resentments and our regrets have no grip on the world without the company to whom we can express them. The "signs of life" that Stanley Cavell claims television as a medium monitors include those everyday civilities and moments of mutual company that are the adhesive lining that holds us, bonds us, to one another, to an imagination of the world, however spectacular and convoluted the evil is within it.[5] What sets detectives apart is their capacity to see all signs; but they see too much, too well. When their capacity to order and know the sights of the world is undermined by a failure of memory, how can they function anymore? There is a strong sense here that actions and events that happened only continue to have a meaningful grip on the world if their significance can be mutually acknowledged, but if the memories are inaccessible, the acts of forgiveness and apology lose their force, their capacity to undo the scars of the past. The fact of Wayne and Roland's presence to one another on the deck at this moment, however, means that if the past cannot be recovered, or forgiven, the present retains the potential to go on, to heal through the solidarity of common purpose. Both men continue to investigate the case, and even though they never realize the truth—as the audience does—the show asks us to weigh the benefits of that lack of knowledge, that failure of detection, against what we might want more dearly, the comfort of family and friends nearby. One of the final scenes also takes place on the deck of a house, a kind of perch for seeing; but this one is amidst family, children, young and old; it brims with the everyday comfort of family life free from evil and despair. *True Detec-*

tive as a television show found the means to escape the darkness of other detective fictions by growing the space in which the alienated restlessness of the sleuth might find peace and settlement.

The fact that memory supplies the foundation of, and motivation for, action means that detectives who are in the job of finding out how the architectures of the past imprint themselves on nefarious activities in the present are always monitoring and assessing the emergence of the past in the present. But if our memories are, like Wayne's, in the process of biological disintegration, how can a detective function properly? For nothing that might count as evidence to support our actions counts anymore: there is no memory of Kathie that would make Bridgeport an attractive settlement for Jeff, no John Huberman that Alicia could lay to rest and become free, no Madeleine (and no Carlotta) for Scottie; no incestuous rape that Cross and Evelyn contend with. Knowledge only counts as knowledge if it carries meaning—otherwise it is just data, information: and meaning is only meaning if we can act on knowing about it, take a stance in relation to it, make a judgment.

This is why two detective films, in a science fiction mode, seem to me to carry such a strange force in our sense of why we pursue meaning. *Blade Runner* (1982) and its sequel *Blade Runner 2049* (2017) are science fiction noirs that privilege the significance of memory in their plots. Set in Los Angeles in 2019, *Blade Runner* begins with its protagonist, Rick Deckard (Harrison Ford), called out of retirement to hunt down six rogue replicants, artificial humans created for the purposes of military, recreation, and commercial purposes. Blade runners are detective-hunters who track such creatures and execute them, as Deckard puts it in his voice-over: "That was my profession. Ex-cop. Ex-blade runner. Ex-killer." When we first see Deckard he is simply killing time in the dystopian, rain-swept city streets, reading his newspaper, eating street food. His former boss, Lieutenant Bryant, calls him back to the LAPD station: "I've got four skinjobs walking the street" he tells Deckard, whose voice-over (as if he too was watching the film) clarifies: "Skinjobs. That's what Bryant called replicants. In history books, he's the kind of cop who used to call black men 'niggers.'" This is the not-so-subtle indication that the film's moral interest in the distinction between replicants and humans has a real-life parallel in the way race has been used to differentiate members of the human race, often to catastrophic ends. In the film the replicants are not black (indeed the primary racial distinction is the preponderance of "Asian" faces in the crowds and advertising) but all white and, in the case of their leader Roy Batty (Rutger Hauer), distinctly Teutonic in appearance.[6] But Deckard is reluctant to re-enroll in his former job as their executor:

> DECKARD: I was quit when I come in here Bryant. I'm twice as quit now.
>
> BRYANT: Stop right where you are. You know the score pal? If you're not cop, you're little people.
>
> DECKARD: No choice, huh?
>
> BRYANT: No choice, pal.

This dialogue takes place in Bryant's office, like most of the interiors in the film a dark, shadowy place, with shaped lighting. Bryant's desk lamp has a rhomboid shade whose panes are translucent black and white photographs; one appears to be of a man sitting near a dead animal he has presumably killed on a hunting trip, another shows a landscape; Bryant's desk also has a number of framed photographs. As we find out photographs offer a kind of fossilized stand-in for memories, both a prompt to view into the past and an emblem of yearning for it, as if the intensity of the present threatens to erase all memories not sufficiently tethered to representational forms. Bryant sends Deckard to the Tyrell Corporation who design and build replicants, including the new Nexus-6 advanced models that have a four-year lifespan as a kind of inbuilt safety feature. The replicants' mission seems to be to avoid detection and find some way of disabling this safety feature; they work together and demonstrate solidarity, cunning, and guile. Deckard by contrast remains mostly isolated. At the Tyrell Corporation he discovers another replicant model, Rachael, who has no idea that she *is* a replicant: "How can it not know what it is?" Deckard asks her creator, Eldon Tyrell (Joe Turkel):

> TYRELL: Rachael is an experiment nothing more. We began to recognize in them a strange obsession, after all they are emotionally inexperienced with only a few years in which

to store up the experiences you and I take for granted. If we gift them with a past, we create a cushion or a pillow for their emotions, and consequently we can control them better.

DECKARD: Memories. You're talking about memories.

As with *The Long Goodbye*, *Blade Runner* is a disconcerting film to watch because it operates in two registers, the overt plot, and another kind of feeling in parallel to that, shadowing it like a spiritual lining. Rachael appears almost as a parody of noir's femme fatale, but that is just her appearance: her secret is not like Kathie Moffat's or Judy Barton's or Evelyn Mulwray's—it is the fact that she does not know *what she is*, and when she is later told by Deckard (who has access to the memories implanted in her), she becomes distraught. As Deckard says, "memories" to Tyrell we hear a strange Asian female voice singing on the soundtrack (diegetically it could plausibly be one of the large advertising ships that float across the cityscape) and a cut to Tyrell's face shows it lit by the rippling reflections of nearby water. The film marks the word aurally and visually. Deckard seems staggered by the notion that such things can happen at all, but his encounter with Rachael later in his apartment seems to humanize her for him—her upset, her pain, finally makes an impact on him. In other words the implantation of memories does its job ("More human than human," as Tyrell puts it), but *not* by providing a "cushion" rather the grounds for an existential crisis. This is what seems to attract Deckard to Rachael, her capacity to suffer like that. As he looks at one of her photographs, putatively of her and her mother, his voice-over once again clarifies for us what is at stake: "Tyrell really did a job on Rachael. Right down to a snapshot of a mother she never had. A daughter she never was. Replicants weren't supposed to have feelings. Neither were blade runners. What the hell was happening to me?" And this leads him to think about why it is that the other replicants, the Nexus-6 escapees, collected photographs, that "maybe they needed memories"; except of course their memories are only of the past—at most—four years; further memorializing that experience in photographs offers a strange contemporary sense that those with a vastly diminished sense of individuality compensate for it by accumulating echoes of every experience they have, such that the experience itself gets swamped in the very process of its memorialization which in itself becomes the primary memory. And since photography can only memorialize *exterior* forms, the body itself rather than the soul becomes the locus of meaning and action. Both Rachael and Deckard are strikingly attractive, yet both of them operate on a very crude understanding of human motivation (Deckard's voice-over is far less eloquent than Jeff Markham's for example, or the narrator of Judy's aborted letter to Scottie); in Deckard's case it takes his final deadly encounter with Roy Batty, seconds before he expires, until he hears true eloquence.[7] Indeed, the entire movie is striking for its emphasis on the density of surface details which it fetishizes at an incredible depth of attention.

Deckard finally vanquishes the rogue replicants and escapes with Rachael from the city, but it is very hard to see what kind of a life these impoverished human souls might assemble with one another. Our only promising hint is the beautiful sequence where they play piano together, shortly before their romance begins. *Blade Runner* is interesting for its borrowing of many of the tropes of film noir and the detective genre, and its partial sense of the moral issues that the manipulation of memory might imply. However, its sequel *Blade Runner 2049* (henceforth *2049*) is more eloquent in its understanding of the genre and the implications for it of the misallocation of memory.

Outwardly the plot is straightforward: we are told that the Tyrell Corporation and its production of replicants was swept away and replaced by yet another corporation (Wallace Industries) who simply created a new line of replicants who "obey." Older models—called Nexus-8s, who have unlimited lifespans—are hunted down by blade runners. The film opens with an astonishing extreme close up of an eye opening, redolent of the opening titles of *Vertigo*—and then a cut to vast long shots from above of similarly circular districts in California 2049. We get the sense that this eye, shot so close it becomes almost an alien thing, is both the perceiving "eye" of the camera, now authoritative above the strange overly ordered gray cityscape. It is *not* K's eye, the letter that names the film's leading character (played by Ryan Gosling), a blade runner who is a replicant himself and whom we see glide in his "spinner" (a kind of flying car) toward the first target of the film, some kind of remote farmstead or production facility just outside the city. "K" is a famous literary reference, of course, but the Josef K of Kafka's *The Trial* is not a policeman, instead the victim of a mysterious authoritarian system in which he finds himself helplessly trapped. The law and its agents in that novel appear merely as devastating frustrations to any legible meaning, and ultimately their deadliness is more decisive than any process K gets entwined in. *2049* does not make much of this association except to leave in the air the implication that K, as a detective and a replicant, is so thoroughly isolated from the world he is supposed to help make safe that he occupies another kind of trap which only a human, moral action can overcome. Indeed for a long time K believes himself to be partly human, a product of Deckard and Rachael's union which has been hidden by from the authorities by Deckard himself.

2049 updates the earlier film's interest in memory by having replicants like K implanted with artificial memories made by a company outsourced to Wallace Industries. During the first mission we see at the remote farm, and after killing his target, K notices something buried beneath a denuded tree. This turns out to be Rachael's bones; K finds a date carved into the wood of the tree that corresponds to one of his implanted memories of a childhood event. In that memory, a child at an orphanage tries to prevent his toy (a wooden horse) from being stolen by a gang of boys; they pursue him but he manages to hide the toy before the gang round on him. When he tells this story to his boss at the LAPD, Lieutenant Joshi (Robin Wright), she takes it as an emblem of his resilience, a memory that ensures he will diligently pursue his mission whatever the danger. This is a view of memory that suggests replicants, and by implication all humans, are bound to the authority of their past and that actions in the present flow from very early childhood experiences.

In many ways K represents the ultimate version of the screen detective that we have been watching in this book. He lives in a world already devastated by the kind of socio-environmental catastrophe that *True Detective* represents (especially in its first two seasons), and the ascension of the kind of corporate corruption of civic life we saw emergent in *Chinatown*. He is described by one of the film's writers as a "handbook" cop, one who works as if the authority of "process" subsumes all judgment; but because he is a replicant he is subject to the ongoing racism against "skinjobs" the first film introduced.

These elements combine to present a world that is confined, in the way a prison confines, to the twin authorities of technocratic process and corporate consumption.

When K returns from his mission to execute the protein farmer, Sapper Morton (Dave Bautista), a Nexus-8 model, he is subject to what we discover is a regular test to ensure his emotional stability; it is called a posttraumatic baseline test and consists of him answering questions alone in a white room racing some kind of camera-cum-measuring instrument. The questions are bizarre in that they repetitively compel him to repeat words associated with notions of organic fusion, as if his place in society seen as a functional organism demands that he repeat without emotional stress words that both confirm his status as a mere tiny component of that society, and his submission to the idea of an organic society itself:

Voice: Cells.

K: Cells.

Voice: Have you ever been in an institution? Cells.

K: Cells.

Voice: Do they keep you in a cell? Cells.

K: Cells.

Voice: When you're not performing your duties do they keep you in a little box? Cells.

K: Cells.

Voice: Interlinked.

K: Interlinked.

Voice: What's it like to hold the hand of someone you love? Interlinked.

K: Interlinked.

And so on, culminating in his repeating three times, "within cells interlinked"; in *Blade Runner* the test to identify replicants (Voight-Kampf) involved questions that implied some kind of cruelty to animals, the idea being that replicants—presumably because of how they were created, as well, perhaps due to their status as utilities for humans—were emotionally sensitive to such things.[8] But K's test seems more about confronting him with the awfulness of his situation and having him maintain an emotional resilience in the face of it. Half-assed psychological tests are, of course, the mainstay of many human resource and recruitment procedures, not to mention the underpinning of many digital algorithms that seek to track and organize our lives. In this depiction we see its oppressive form, but K passes with flying colors ("constant K, you can pick up your bonus," says the voice).

The scene that follows this has us watch K travel back to his apartment through a noisy, dirty, crowded, and seemingly quite dangerous urban environment, blanketed in dirty snow and illuminated by the persistence of commercial advertisements. His front door carries the scrawled message "fuck off skinner," and it does indeed appear as if he lives in a kind of prison. Once inside we see he has quite a pleasant apartment, compact but protected against the hate and dangers without. The film gives us a picture of a working man, forced to submit as part of his "performance review" to a humiliating test alone, and then allowed to have a bonus which he can enjoy at home where his "privacy" is mediated through the consumption of refined corporate products. And central to these is Joi (Ana de Armas), a holographic woman with advanced artificial intelligence—another kind of slave—who has clearly adjusted "herself" to him, as a kind of therapeutic companion. K has spent his bonus on a device that allows Joi to travel free from the apartment; their relationship, although brokered by this corporate technology, seems both touching and genuine, an outgrowth of the way some people find companionship in, say, games or pets, or films or television shows. But because Joi is played by a human being it is very hard to see how this is less than what we might ordinarily take as true human mutual affection, even though neither of the parties is in fact human.

It is Joi who convinces K that he is "special" (although that is precisely what the holographic product is supposed to do), and she helps him see how there is credible evidence for this once K discovers the date on the tree matches the date he remembers carved on the wooden horse in his memory. The film then shifts and K stops being a loyal cop and becomes a rogue detective, hunting down his own origins, his own identity. What he wants at this point is nothing less than the truth of his own origins, his own feelings. The Wallace Corporation cannot design replicants who can reproduce, and they pursue K's pursuit in order to find the child who will allow them to use this secret in their industrial expansion across the galaxy. When K finally tracks Deckard down to his hiding place in Las Vegas, he has every reason to believe he is his father, but the enforcer of the corporation, another replicant called Luv (in a classic femme fatale mode), has followed them. Deckard is captured and K left for dead; Luv also "kills" Joi in front of him by destroying the unique device that carries her data.

There is no world in which slavery does not produce a resistance, but the form this takes varies across history; here it is imagined, fairly crudely, as a "replicant freedom" movement, who rescue the injured K and inform him that Deckard and Rachael's child was in fact a girl. They tell him he must kill Deckard before he can reveal the location of the girl to the Wallace Corporation.

All of this plotting in a very long and very beautiful film takes us to a point of decision and judgment. In the end, that is what the detectives in this book are all faced with. None of them are special except for the judgment that circumstances make available to them. Their capacity to track, absorb, and contend with the sights and signs of the world is nothing without a concomitant ability to leverage a moral judgment on them. Marlowe kills Lennox because a society that allows anything to happen with impunity (the murder and brutalization of women, the suicide of lonely men) is intolerable for someone for whom up to that point everything is "OK by me"; Jeff would rather risk death at Kathie's hands than let a woman capable of that evil live free with him; Devlin risks everything for a woman who risked everything for him at a time he was too paralyzed by love to acknowledge it; Scottie and Judy annihilate one another for a fantasy of love they both know is psychologically perilous; and Gittes ends up seeing his past repeated in front of his face despite doing everything he thought was right to stop it.

In pursuit of his identity, K visits a facility where artificial memories are confected (real memories are not allowed to be implanted in replicants); he asks the artist who creates them, Dr. Ana Stelline (Carla Juri) if his memory of hiding the horse is real. If it is, that means he is not a replicant but a human being. What does that mean? Why would it mean anything? Because having a baseline memory as a kind of bureaucratic safety device robs him of autonomy, it prevents him from doing anything except reacting to the feelings the memory passively supplies. To have moral autonomy one must see oneself as more than a "handbook," a tool. One must have the authority over oneself, and one's past, to act, to judge, to decide in a way that changes the future that would have been had one not made that decision. Without that authority, or even a notion that it could be mustered as an internal force, we are hostage to our animal selves, and therefore responsible for nothing. Stelline tells him that the memory is real, and when he hears this K becomes emotional, tears in his eyes: "I know it's real," he says, "I know it's real." But then he suddenly becomes enraged, kicking his chair away and shouting, "God damn it!" Why? To recognize the responsibility of one's own autonomy, the necessity for courage in the face of it, is easily mistaken for a burden. Perhaps most of us might rather avoid it or outsource it somewhere else; the livelihoods of thousands of counselors, HR consultants, therapists, and psychologists depend on such avoidance. It is hard to be brave enough, to have the courage, to live. That is why bad faith is so prevalent. K walks outside the facility and we see it is snowing, and as he walks toward his spinner, he opens his hand to the air and a snowflake lands on his palm. He looks up to the heavens from whence it came and back down at his hand, and then beyond it as if thinking. What does it mean to discover something so monumental about one's past and then to carry on, in the same body, under the same skies? The uniqueness of the snowflake, its fragility, ephemerality, might be thoughts in mind.

But, as we have seen, K is not human, not the child of Deckard and Rachael, but a replicant. And being that he *still* has to decide what to do: it is as if in thinking he was human, and what that meant, he was able to occupy the space of moral decision making that is—or seemed to be until now—uniquely human in character. The wooden horse memory was real but it was Stelline's memory, and she is the "special" child that must be protected. So K decides to do just that, vanquishing the enemies of the Wallace Corporation, faking Deckard's death, and reuniting him with his daughter at the memory facility. By this point K has been mortally wounded; he hands Deckard the wooden horse that he had retrieved, now knowing it was Stelline who bravely hid it, and *her* memory that gave him some sustenance during the awful job he felt he was forced to do:

DECKARD: Why? Who am I to you?

K: Go meet your daughter.

K has no reason to help either of them except that he decided it was the right thing to do. It was. The snow falls gently on both men, and then, as Deckard goes inside, we are left with K alone. He notes the large amount of blood from his wound soaking his clothes and, sitting on the steps, opens his hand once again, catching the snow and once again looking heavenwards in an eloquent movement that is also the beginning of him leaning back to die as the soundtrack evokes a similar moment at the end of *Blade Runner* when Roy Batty also acknowledges the moment of his death. It is a very literary moment, evoking the democracy of snowfall that finishes what is perhaps the greatest story ever written, James Joyce's "The Dead," a story about memory and forgiveness and the joy that comes in seeing the universalism in one's particular heart in front of one's eyes, in one's imagination, as aesthetic spectacle. To be a true detective then is to discover in oneself the capacity to make a substantial moral judgment and to follow it through, watching as the world absorbs it.

Notes

Introduction

1. *The Long Goodbye*, directed by Robert Altman (Lion's Gate Films/United Artists, 1973).

2. I am aware that this is vulnerable to the riposte that these are just features of any kind of framed composition, any depicted instancing of things that are viewed or put on view; so obvious as to be faintly ridiculous in the way, for example, that David Bordwell writes about assertions of cinematic reflexivity in critical writing in his book *Making Meaning* (Cambridge, MA: Harvard University Press, 1991), 112–114. And it is true that what I am describing is virtually unavoidable in any film, viz any film or television show is necessarily going to show or represent objects that are seen and beings or devices that see/perceive/record since such things are simply part of the world that most narratives would include as part of their claim to realism and plausibility. Of course, it is the job of criticism to make the case whether or not these are significant features and how they are significant: "if criticism can't explain, can't peg things out in words, it can . . . show us what there is to be looked at, prove there is a crossroads where we so far have seen only a single, well-trodden track." Michael Wood, *On Empson* (Princeton, NJ: Princeton University Press, 2017), 107.

3. Late in the revision of this I read George Toles's remarkable book *Curtains of Light: Theatrical Space in Film* (Albany: State University of New York Press, 2021) which explores the nature of cinema's entanglement with theater; see especially the discussion on p. 45. Toles's formidable and enchanting critical prose eloquently provides a rich sense of this and other scenes from *Vertigo*. I take the cinematic to be a more primal aspect of vision perhaps derived from our evolutionary past, one that includes the theatrical potential of anything that is in view or framed. Michael Fried claims that "any composition, by being placed in certain contexts or framed in certain ways, can

be made to serve theatrical ends." *Absorption and Theatricality: Painting and Beholder in the Age of Diderot* (Chicago: University of Chicago Press, 1980), 173. My claim is that anything selected for view, or passing into it that is noticed (rather than merely registered), is in the realm of the cinematic.

4. Robert Pippin, *Fatalism in American Film Noir* (Charlottesville: University of Virginia Press, 2012), 11.

5. Harry G. Frankfurt, *The Importance of What We Care About* (New York: Cambridge University Press, 1988), 175–176.

6. Frankfurt, *The Importance of What We Care About*, 163.

7. Robert Pippin, *The Philosophical Hitchcock* (Chicago: University of Chicago Press, 2017), 5.

8. Pippin, *The Philosophical Hitchcock*, 6.

9. Murray Pomerance, "High Hollywood in *The Long Goodbye*," in *A Companion to Robert Altman*, ed. Adrian Danks (Chichester, UK: John Wiley and Sons, 2015), 249.

10. Pomerance, *High Hollywood*, 237.

11. Kevin Thomas, "'The Long Goodbye' Sacrilege," *Los Angeles Times*, December 16, 1973, 548.

12. David Thomson, *The New Biographical Dictionary of Film*, 5th ed. (New York: Alfred A. Knopf, 2010), 390–391.

13. Stanley Cavell, *The World Viewed* (Cambridge, MA: Harvard University Press, 1979), 56.

Chapter 1

1. *Out of the Past*, directed by Jacques Tourneur (RKO Radio Pictures, 1947).

2. Michael Eaton, *Based on a True Story: Real Made-Up Men* (Nottingham: Shoestring Press, 2020), 67.

3. Paul Auster, *The New York Trilogy: City of Glass / Ghosts / The Locked Room* (London: Faber & Faber, 1987), 162.

4. See Robert Pippin, *Fatalism in American Film Noir* (Charlottesville: University of Virginia Press, 2012), 29. In Marny's Café, after Joe tells Marny about how he realized that Jeff was in Bridgeport because he saw the sign above the garage, she replies, "It's a small world." "Yeah," he says, "or a big sign." What he doesn't tell her is that he recognized Jeff himself—as Jeff Markham—and the sign told him Jeff was pretending to be someone he wasn't. But none of that means he was hiding out: it is almost as if the emphatic two-sign signal to the world is a stake or claim that asserts his identity as this person, here and now, that he is willing to defend publicly. He certainly is not reluctant to tell Ann the truth, even though he does not have to; she seems to want him to be mysterious, but he's done with all that.

5. James Heartfield, *An Unpatriotic History of the Second World War* (Winchester, UK: Zero Books, 2012), 124.

6. David Thomson, *The New Biographical Dictionary of Film*, 5th ed. (New York: Alfred A. Knopf, 2010), 671.

7. Martin Jay, "Trump, Scorsese, and the Frankfurt School's Theory of Racket Society," *Los Angeles Review of Books*, April 5, 2020.

8. C. L. R James, *American Civilization* (Cambridge: Blackwell, 1993), 118–119.

9. James, *American Civilization*, 126.

10. James, 127.

11. See for example Dennis Broe, *Class, Crime and International Film Noir* (London: Palgrave Macmillan, 2014).

12. James, *American Civilization*, 127.

13. James, 128.

14. James, 130.

15. James, 157.

16. James is scathing about the theory of mass distraction: "If even for the sake of argument, it is agreed the publishers, the movie magnates, the newspaper proprietors and the banks which directly or indirectly control them, are interested in distracting the masses of the people from serious problems or elevated art, then the question still remains, why, at this particular time, this particular method of distraction should have arisen and met with such continuous success. To believe that the great masses of the people are merely passive recipients of what the purveyors of popular art give to them is in reality to see people as dumb slaves. It is a conception totally unhistorical" (*American Civilization*, 122).

17. Lee Server, *Robert Mitchum: "Baby, I Don't Care"* (New York: Faber and Faber, 2001), 126–127.

18. According to Tourneur: "There are a large number of players who don't know how to listen . . . While one of their partners speaks to them, they simply think, I don't have anything to do during this; let's try not to let the scene get stolen from me. Mitchum can be silent and listen to a five-minute speech. You'll never lose sight of him and you'll understand that he takes in what is said to him, even if he doesn't do anything. That's how one judges good actors." Quoted in Server, *Robert Mitchum*, 126.

19. Pippin, *Fatalism in American Film Noir*, 29–30.

20. George Toles rightly notes that this is a moment of theater as well. *Curtains of Light: Theatrical Space in Film* (Albany: State University of New York Press, 2021), 3.

21. Although I imagine most of the film's audience would agree with George Orwell's sentiment that "no-one is patriotic about paying taxes": "Towards the government I feel no scruples and would dodge paying the tax if I could." George Orwell, *Diaries* (New York: W. W. Norton, 2009), 305.

22. Although as usual the production of the script during the studio era was a complex affair: Mainwaring's first draft was given to James M. Cain to rewrite, then to Frank Fenton, and eventually back to Mainwaring for the final rewrite (which is much closer to his novel).

23. Pippin, *Fatalism in American Film Noir*, 33.

24. Pippin, 113.

25. Andrew Klevan provides a thorough account of the various ways Stanwyck's Dietrichson has been variously evaluated over the years by critics, noting that her performance is far more nuanced than she has been given credit for. *Barbara Stanwyck* (London: Palgrave Macmillan, 2013), 88–94. And while this is true of the other performances and characters I've mentioned, it is a stretch to absolve any of them from complicity in the ultimately murderous crimes the films hinge around.

26. In another mirroring touch, a decoration on the wall opposite Whit is a framed horsehead, a reminder of his little story about losing money on a horse and subsequently buying it and taking good care of it that he tells Jeff when they first meet in New York. If Kathie is the horse who let him down once, and he took her back too, it is a mistake he knows only too well.

27. Greer has remarked that Douglas was far less gentle in these physical scenes than Mitchum.

28. James, *American Civilization*, 127.

29. Pippin, *Fatalism in American Film Noir*, 46.

30. Pippin, 49.

Chapter 2

1. From a document of notes on the film given by Perkins to the author in 1998.

2. *Notorious*, directed by Alfred Hitchcock (RKO Radio Pictures, 1946).

3. Murray Pomerance, "Boy Meets Girl: The Architectonics of a Hitchcockian Shot," *Senses of Cinema*, posted April 18, 2012, accessed October 8, 2019, http://sensesofcinema.com/2012/feature-articles/boy-meets-girl-architectonics-of-a-hitchcockian-shot/.

4. Miami, Florida, 3:23 p.m., April 24, 1946, a Wednesday.

5. John Gibbs, *Mise-en-scène: Film Style and Interpretation* (New York: Wallflower Press, 2002), 6.

6. The rearview mirror is a kind of close-up in this allegory. And it is always shown as a close-up containing a long shot.

7. Pomerance, "Boy Meets Girl."

8. Pomerance.

9. Pomerance.

10. Michel Houellebecq, *Serotonin* (London: William Heinemann, 2019).

11. See Murray Pomerance, "Close to You: Notorious Proximity in Cinema," *Movie: A Journal of Film Criticism* no. 9 (2020).

12. One example of eloquence: in the apartment when Alicia pours her drink, we see her from the other side of a window frame with net curtains and a single tassel hanging from the blind; the view compresses a sense of the "honeymooner" stage of marriage where the blind remains pulled down (à la *Rear Window*), and this moment is redolent of the catastrophe when a marriage disintegrates and one's only companion resides in a bottle. That Alicia mentions marriage only a few moments before might alert our "registering systems" to this.

13. Alicia's rough handling of the chicken carcass and her stated aversion to cooking adds an eloquent touch to the notion of her having to take command of appetite.

14. von Ledebur was from an Austro-Hungarian aristocratic background who went on to make a good living in the US as an actor among other things. There is a certain lining of joyful sleaze carried in his angular looks.

15. The prop that opens that lock has an interesting history worth looking up.

16. As Elliott Logan pointed out to me: "Perhaps, as is so often the case, it is the effect of an ambient suggestion that is the sum of many details, in this case especially in the performances and staging. For example, the way her leg is sufficiently close to brush the draped fabric of his trouser, their bodies not touching, but close enough to feel physical contact they could easily withdraw from but do not. The compliments delivered with a lining of sadness, or the way a darkly wry humour has crept into their observations of the bind they are in."

17. V. F. Perkins, "Film Authorship: The Premature Burial," in *V. F. Perkins on Movies: Collected Shorter Film Criticism*, ed. Douglas Pye (Detroit, MI: Wayne State University Press, 2020), 229.

18. James Chapman, *Hitchcock and the Spy Film* (London and New York: I. B. Tauris, 2018).

19. Michael Wood thinks so, see his *Alfred Hitchcock: The Man Who Knew Too Much* (Boston: New Harvest: 2015).

Chapter 3

1. *Vertigo*, directed by Alfred Hitchcock (Paramount Pictures, 1958).

2. Obviously the scene is constructed such to confirm that Elster is unlikely to get away with his crime; but whatever the reason for its shooting,

it offers a marvelous reminder that even at the end of *this* film, it is possible to imagine life going on and not in suspension.

3. The shapes are, 1. Pink, rotating counterclockwise; 2. Pale blue, counterclockwise; 3. Pink (counterclockwise) evolving into; 4. Pale blue (clockwise); 5. Green, counterclockwise; 6. Pale blue, not rotating and the most eye-like of all of them, behind which emerges; 7. Lime green, counterclockwise, behind which; 8. Orange which changes to red, behind which; 9. Yellow appears and then spirals backward into the anonymous woman's eye as Hitchcock's credit pushes forward toward us, the eye almost appearing to read (presumably in reverse) the credit. None of this captures the extraordinary beauty of the sequence; it feels graphically eloquent in odd, obscure ways.

4. This is the useful phrase Robert Pippin uses in "Le Grand Imagier of George Wilson, *Seeing Fictions in Film: The Epistemology of Movies*, by Wilson, George," *European Journal of Philosophy* 21, no. 2 (June 2013).

5. Just below the stick's resting on the wall is a pencil sketch with the word "RIO"; I take it to be a gesture toward *Notorious*'s happy moment of landing in that city so that we might measure the distance from that couple—in the first flush of formation—and this one, already blocked, stuck with each other.

6. Elliott Logan has a useful reading of this moment: "Does this distance from the role of a house guest suggest that Scottie instead occupies a role closer to that of the now-thoughtless and unloving husband, one who nags at and has become annoyed by his wife's habits and pleasures?"

7. Michael Wood, *Alfred Hitchcock: The Man Who Knew Too Much* (Boston: New Harvest, 2015), 88.

8. The music resembles the score of *Tristan and Isolde* in particular the Liebestod; its relentlessly sad, yearning movement connotes a terrible kind of emotional pain born of the entanglement of death, loss, and love.

9. Murray Pomerance, *Cinema If You Please: The Memory of Taste, the Taste of Memory* (Edinburgh: Edinburgh University Press, 2019), 86–87.

10. G. E. M. Anscome, *Intention*, 2nd ed. (Cambridge, MA: Harvard University Press, 2000), 56.

11. Carlo Ginzburg, "Clues: Morelli, Freud, and Sherlock Holmes," in *The Sign of Three: Dupin, Holmes, Peirce*, ed. Umberto Eco and Thomas Sebeok (Bloomington: Indiana University Press, 1988), 88. A film that shares with *Vertigo* this primal quality of detection fused with a fascination with the mysteries of an image is *Blow-Up* (Antonioni, 1966); the photographer at the center of the film inadvertently photographs a murder and becomes steadily obsessed with the image and the place the image was taken; as one

character remarks early in the film (regarding an abstract painting), "It sorts itself out like finding a clue in a detective story."

12. Pomerance, *Cinema If You Please*, 89.

13. Wood, *Alfred Hitchcock*, 90–91

14. See Murray Pomerance's discussion of vortexes of seeing and pointing and looking in this scene in "Visit to a Gallery," *Film International* 16, no. 4 (December 2018).

15. This depiction of *subjective orientation* is discussed by Michael Fried in his essay, "Orientation in Painting: Caspar David Friedrich," in *Another Light: Jacques-Louis David to Thomas Demand* (New Haven, CT: Yale University Press, 2014).

16. Pomerance, "Visit to a Gallery," 51.

17. In response to Scottie's request that she sit by the fire, her lips slowly open again signaling her artful responsiveness to the request. Such unconscious gestures are easily learned and faked.

18. As Elliott Logan reminds me, Midge's hatred is also directed outwardly: "She violently slashes the paintbrush against the canvas (we don't see the reverse but it looks like where her face would be), and then turns and throws the brush at the window in which she is reflected—throws it outward, but at herself."

19. Elliott Logan reminds me that the same truth might apply to our first encounters with films like this one (and the others in the book).

20. One might add the interior of the Argosy Book Store also contributes to this sense of graphical design by including things like the lettering on the exterior of hardback books.

21. See excellent account by Robert Pippin, *The Philosophical Hitchcock: Vertigo and the Anxieties of Unknowingness* (Chicago: University of Chicago Press, 2017), 89–95.

22. Pippin, *The Philosophical Hitchcock*, 32.

23. "White I must say has always affected me strongly, all white things, sheets, walls and so on, even flowers, and then just white, the thought of white, without more." Samuel Beckett, *From an Abandoned Work* (London: Faber & Faber, 1958), 12.

24. Edward Gallafent, *Adultery and the Female Star* (London: Palgrave Macmillan, 2018), 133.

25. The relevant sentence in that novel occurs just before Gatsby kisses Daisy as they walk in the autumnal moonlight on the rich streets near her house, and it is, fittingly, one concerned with ascension: "Out of the corner of his eye Gatsby saw that the block of the sidewalks really formed a ladder and mounted to a secret place above the trees—he could climb to it, if he climbed alone, and once there he could suck on the pap of life, gulp down

the incomparable milk of wonder." F. Scott Fitzgerald, *The Great Gatsby*, (New York: Bantam Books, 1974), 113.

26. Of course class-crossing romances are a generic staple in both literary and popular forms. There we often discover that working-class men often get sick of the bourgeois vapidity of their conquests.

27. Elliott Logan raises a pertinent question in this respect: "How is it that she has fallen in love with him? Because of the tenderness and love he displayed to Madeleine? So she is in love with a man on the basis of his being in love with someone she pretended to be? So there is again the question of what it means about her that she wants him, or maybe it isn't much of a question, and just a doubling of the warning about romantic fantasy that issues from Scottie."

28. Alejandro Jodorowsky and Marianne Costa, *The Way of Tarot: The Spiritual Teacher in the Cards*, trans. Jon E. Graham (Rochester, VT: Destiny Books, 2009), 121.

29. Julian Jaynes, *The Origin of Consciousness in the Breakdown of the Bicameral Mind* (Boston: Mariner Books, 2000), 236–246.

Chapter 4

1. *Chinatown*, directed by Roman Polanski (Paramount Pictures, 1974).

2. The final paragraphs of Robert Pippin, *The Philosophical Hitchcock:* Vertigo *and the Anxieties of Unknowingness* (Chicago: University of Chicago Press, 2017), 127–128, deal with this matter.

3. Hannah Arendt, *The Human Condition* (Chicago: University of Chicago Press, 2018), 237.

4. See Michael Eaton's excellent book *Chinatown* (London: British Film Institute, 1997).

5. Most obviously this begins with Gittes's name itself: J. J. Gittes is both doubly repetitive (two Js and two Ts), false and pretentious (only John Huston correctly pronounces it in the movie; Curly says, "Geetees" picking up on its Frenchified pretension). Or consider the sinuously watery and undulating sound of the name Evelyn Mulwray.

6. See David Thomson, *Suspects* (New York: Knopf, 1985) for a fantasy reading of Gittes's life before the film begins.

7. Murray Pomerance, *The Horse Who Drank the Sky: Film Experience beyond Narrative and Theory* (New Brunswick, NJ: Rutgers University Press, 2008), 147.

8. The wound on his right cheek has the shape of a sea creature, maybe a starfish.

Conclusion

1. Chantal Delsol, *Icarus Fallen: The Search for Meaning in an Uncertain World* quoted in Angus Kennedy, "Conclusion: The Self and Its Prospects," in *From Self to Selfie: A Critique of Contemporary Forms of Alienation*, ed. Angus Kennedy and James Panton (Palgrave Macmillan, 2019), 221–222.

2. *True Detective*, season 1, written by Nic Pizzolatto, featuring Matthew McConaughey and Woody Harrelson (HBO, 2014).

3. Mark Fisher, *Capitalist Realism* (London: Zero Books, 2009), 8.

4. Stanley Cavell, *The Pursuits of Happiness: The Hollywood Comedy of Remarriage* (Cambridge, MA: Harvard University Press, 1984), 2.

5. Stanley Cavell, "The Fact of Television," *Daedalus* 111, no. 4 (1982): 89–90.

6. The implication, made explicit in the opening of the sequel, is that replicants are slave labor. In the final confrontation with Deckard, Batty makes it clear what that means: "Quite an experience to live in fear isn't it? That's what it is to be a slave."

7. This is the famous "tears in rain" speech that Hauer reportedly scripted himself.

8. Some of the dialogue during the test is taken from Vladimir Nabokov's novel *Pale Fire*, a copy of which we see in K's apartment, although we never see him reading it.

Bibliography

Anscome, G. E. M. *Intention*, 2nd ed. Cambridge, MA: Harvard University Press, 2000.

Arendt, Hannah. *The Human Condition*. Chicago: University of Chicago Press, 2018.

Auster, Paul. *The New York Trilogy: City of Glass / Ghosts / The Locked Room*. London: Faber & Faber, 1987.

Beckett, Samuel. *From an Abandoned Work*. London: Faber & Faber, 1958.

Bordwell, David. *Making Meaning*. Cambridge, MA: Harvard University Press, 1991.

Broe, Dennis. *Class, Crime and International Film Noir: Globalizing America's Dark Art*. London: Palgrave Macmillan, 2014.

Cavell, Stanley. "The Fact of Television." *Daedalus* 111, no. 4 (1982): 75–96.

Cavell, Stanley. *The Pursuits of Happiness: The Hollywood Comedy of Remarriage*. Cambridge, MA: Harvard University Press, 1984.

Cavell, Stanley. *The World Viewed: Reflections on the Ontology of Film*. Enl. ed. Cambridge, MA: Harvard University Press, 1979.

Chapman, James. *Hitchcock and the Spy Film*. London and New York: I. B. Tauris, 2018.

Delsol, Chantal. *Icarus Fallen: The Search for Meaning in an Uncertain World*. Wilmington, DE: ISI Books, 2003.

Eaton, Michael. *Based on a True Story: Real Made-Up Men*. Nottingham: Shoestring Press, 2020.

Eaton, Michael. *Chinatown*. London: British Film Institute, 1997.

Fisher, Mark. *Capitalist Realism*. London: Zero Books, 2009.

Fitzgerald, F. Scott. *The Great Gatsby*. New York: Bantam Books, 1974.

Frankfurt, Harry G. *The Importance of What We Care About*. New York: Cambridge University Press, 1988.

Fried, Michael. *Absorption and Theatricality: Painting and Beholder in the Age of Diderot*. Chicago: University of Chicago Press, 1980.

Fried, Michael. *Another Light: Jacques-Louis David to Thomas Demand*. New Haven, CT: Yale University Press, 2014.
Gallafent, Edward. *Adultery and the Female Star*. London: Palgrave Macmillan, 2018.
Gibbs, John. *Mise-en-scène: Film Style and Interpretation*. New York: Wallflower Press, 2002.
Ginzburg, Carlo. "Clues: Morelli, Freud, and Sherlock Holmes." In *The Sign of Three: Dupin, Holmes, Peirce*, edited by Umberto Eco and Thomas Sebeok, 81–118. Bloomington: Indiana University Press, 1988.
Heartfield, James. *An Unpatriotic History of the Second World War*. Winchester, UK: Zero Books, 2012.
Houellebecq, Michel. "Michel Houellebecq: Q&A with His Readers." Uploaded November 29, 2019. https://www.youtube.com/watch?v=8IyJEFbBhXo.
Houellebecq, Michel. *Serotonin*. London: William Heinemann, 2019.
IMDb. "Chinatown (1978)—Trivia." https://www.imdb.com/title/tt0071315/trivia?ref_=ttfc_ql_trv_1.
Jacobs, Steven. *The Wrong House: The Architecture of Alfred Hitchcock*. 2nd ed. Rotterdam: 010 Publishers, 2014.
James, C. L. R. *American Civilization*. Cambridge: Blackwell, 1993.
Jay, Martin. "Trump, Scorsese, and the Frankfurt School's Theory of Racket Society." *Los Angeles Review of Books*, April 5, 2020. https://lareviewofbooks.org/article/trump-scorsese-and-the-frankfurt-schools-theory-of-racket-society/.
Jaynes, Julian. *The Origin of Consciousness in the Breakdown of the Bicameral Mind*. Boston: Mariner Books, 2000.
Jodorowsky, Alejandro, and Marianne Costa. *The Way of Tarot: The Spiritual Teacher in the Cards*. Translated by Jon E. Graham. Rochester, VT: Destiny Books, 2009.
Kennedy, Angus. "Conclusion: The Self and Its Prospects." In *From Self to Selfie: A Critique of Contemporary Forms of Alienation*, edited by Angus Kennedy and James Panton, 207–223. Palgrave Macmillan, 2019.
Klevan, Andrew. *Barbara Stanwyck*. London: Palgrave Macmillan, 2013.
Orwell, George. *Diaries*. New York: W. W. Norton, 2009.
Perkins, V. F. *Film as Film: Understanding and Judging Movies*. London: Penguin, 1972.
Perkins, V. F. "Film Authorship: The Premature Burial." In *V. F. Perkins on Movies: Collected Shorter Film Criticism*, edited by Douglas Pye. Detroit, MI: Wayne State University Press, 2020.
Perkins, V. F. "Ophuls contra Wagner and Others." *Movie*, no. 36, (2000): 73–79.
Pippin, Robert. *Fatalism in American Film Noir*. Charlottesville: University of Virginia Press, 2012.

Pippin, Robert. "Le Grand Imagier of George Wilson, Seeing Fictions in Film: the Epistemology of Movies, by Wilson, George." *European Journal of Philosophy* 21, no. 2 (June 2013): 334–341.

Pippin, Robert. *The Philosophical Hitchcock: Vertigo and the Anxieties of Unknowingness*. Chicago: University of Chicago Press, 2017.

Pomerance, Murray. "Boy Meets Girl: The Architectonics of a Hitchcockian Shot." *Senses of Cinema*. Posted April 18, 2012. Accessed October 8, 2019. http://sensesofcinema.com/2012/feature-articles/boy-meets-girl-architectonics-of-a-hitchcockian-shot/.

Pomerance, Murray. *Cinema If You Please: The Memory of Taste, the Taste of Memory*. Edinburgh: Edinburgh University Press, 2019.

Pomerance, Murray. "Close to You: Notorious Proximity in Cinema." *Movie: A Journal of Film Criticism*, no. 9 (2010): 3–10.

Pomerance, Murray, *An Eye for Hitchcock*, New Brunswick, NJ: Rutgers University Press, 2004.

Pomerance, Murray. "High Hollywood in *The Long Goodbye*." In *A Companion to Robert Altman*, edited by Adrian Danks, 231–253. Chichester, UK: John Wiley & Sons, 2015.

Pomerance, Murray. *The Horse Who Drank the Sky: Film Experience beyond Narrative and Theory*. New Brunswick, NJ: Rutgers University Press, 2008.

Pomerance, Murray. "Visit to a Gallery." *Film International* 16, no. 4 (December 2018): 51–58.

Server, Lee. *Robert Mitchum: "Baby, I Don't Care."* New York: Faber and Faber, 2001.

Thomas, Deborah. *Beyond Genre: Melodrama, Comedy and Romance in Hollywood Films*. Moffat: Cameron and Hollis, 2009.

Thomas, Kevin. "'The Long Goodbye' Sacrilege." *Los Angeles Times*, December 16, 1973.

Thomson, David. *The New Biographical Dictionary of Film*, 5th ed. New York: Alfred A. Knopf, 2010.

Thomson, David. *Suspects*. New York: Knopf, 1985.

Toles, George. *Curtains of Light: Theatrical Space in Film*. Albany: State University of New York Press, 2021.

Towne, Robert. *Chinatown, The Last Detail*. New York: Grove Press, 1994.

Wood, Michael. *Alfred Hitchcock: The Man Who Knew Too Much*. Boston: New Harvest, 2015.

Wood, Michael. *On Empson*. Princeton, NJ: Princeton University Press, 2017.

Index

abandonment: in *Out of the Past*, 45–46; in *Notorious*, 84; in *Vertigo*, 139–140, 144
acrophobia, 119–120
action vs. words in *Notorious*, 92–93, 101, 104, 109
aesthetic experience of cinema, 4, 52, 62–63, 105–106, 131
Altman, Robert, 1, 12, 14, 17–19, 20
apocalyptic imagination, 215, 218
appetite, 7–8, 13, 14; in *Notorious*, 84, 89–91, 92, 96–97, 106, 108–109. *See also* desire

Bel Geddes, Barbara, 148
Bergman, Ingrid, 83–84, 88, 90, 93, 106
Bernard Herrmann, 116, 126, 128, 129
Bigger Than Life (1956 film), 54
Blade Runner (1982), 222–225, 227–228, 231
Blade Runner 2049 (2017), 222, 225–231
Blow-Up (1966 film), 238n11
Bogart, Humphrey, 18–19, 33

Chandler, Raymond, 13, 14, 17, 33, 182, 205

Chinatown (1974 film), 7, 8–9, 10, 11, 146, 171–212 passim, 218, 219, 226, 229
cinema apparatus as detection, 2, 4–5, 9, 25, 132–133
cinematic dandy, 18
comedy of remarriage, 86, 217
commitment, 2–5, 6, 7–9, 10, 11, 82, 215, 218; in *The Long Goodbye*, 15, 16, 17; in *Out of the Past*, 25, 46, 51, 53; in *Notorious*, 90, 92–93, 104, 113; in *Vertigo*, 155, 169, 208; in *Chinatown*, 191, 201, 206
communication, 81; in *Out of the Past*, 27, 38; in *Notorious*, 92, 104
constructed film world, 1–2, 4, 5, 214; in *The Long Goodbye*, 12–14, 19; in *Out of the Past*, 23, 39, 42–43, 45, 52, 58, 60; in *Notorious*, 82–83, 85; in *Vertigo*, 124, 125–127, 129, 158
costume: in *Out of the Past*, 37, in *Vertigo*, 152; in *Chinatown*, 165–196
credits sequence: in *The Long Goodbye*, 19–20; in *Out of the Past*, 23; in *Vertigo*, 116–119

247

desire: ours, 2, 9; detective's, 6–10, 20–21, 26–27, 31, 36, 38, 58, 97, 113, 116, 154, 163–164, 198
detective figure, origins, 129–131
detective identity, 26, 64, 200–201, 215, 228–229
detective work, 7, 20–21, 25, 131–132, 177, 198–199, 218. *See also* tracking
Dietrichson, Phyllis, 62–63, 236n25
Dishonored (1931 film), 113–114
domestic life, 27, 30, 192; in *Out of the Past*, 36, 46, 48, 66, 77, 208; in *True Detective*, 216–217
Double Indemnity (1944 film), 62–63
Douglas, Kirk, 38–39, 47–48, 68, 236n27
dyads in *Out of the Past*, 24, 27, 28

facial communication, 81–82; in *Chinatown*, 10, in *Out of the Past*, 28–29, 32, 43, 58–60, 61, 63, 66, 68, 70, 72, 75, 77; in *Notorious*, 83–84, 88–89, 95, 97, 100–101, 108, 111; in *Vertigo*, 117–118, 120, 121, 123, 126, 128, 137, 150, 152, 154, 156, 164, 165, 167, 172; in *Chinatown*, 181, 186
Family Plot (1976 film), 85, 146
Farewell, My Lovely (1975 film), 18
fate in film noir, 24, 27, 35, 40, 41, 54, 72, 75
Female spy characters, 113–114
Femme fatale, 6–7, 41–42, 62–63, 78–79
film noir, 5–7, 8–10, 17, 20, 24, 25, 31, 37, 41–42, 53, 63, 66
Five Easy Pieces (1970 film), 188
flaneur, wanderer, 132, 136
flashbacks, 38, 41

Fleming, Rhonda, 54, 56
forgiveness, 173; in *Out of the Past*, 49, 68, 72; in *Vertigo*, 167, 173; in *Chinatown*, 174, 205; in *True Detective*, 221
fourth wall in *Vertigo*, 152, 154, 158, 159

gangster films, 32–34
gangster-detective amalgam, 33, 35; in *Out of the Past*, 51, 66, 208, 215; in *True Detective*, 216, 218
gender roles: in *Out of the Past*, 43; in *Notorious*, 104, 114
generic modes, 53–54
Gould, Elliott, 1–2, 15, 17–18, 78, 194, 205
Grant, Cary, 6–7, 83–84, 91, 95, 101
Greer, Jane, 42, 53, 54, 59, 63, 68, 70, 71

habitus, 142, 157, 160–161
Hammett, Dashiell, 33
haptic evocation: in *Notorious*, 86; in *Vertigo*, 118; in *Chinatown*, 177, 178
High Sierra (1941 film), 33
Hitchcock, Alfred, 85, 82, 95, 119, 157, 214; direction of *Notorious*, 82–83, 84, 88–89, 92, 95–96, 103, 104–108, 110, 113–114; maternal figures, 97; in the spy genre, 105; authority figures, 110; direction of *Vertigo*, 120, 122, 125–126, 131, 135, 138, 141, 147, 153, 163; direction of *North by Northwest*, 214
Hollywood Hotel (1937 film), 19–20
Homes, Geoffrey, 55
Huston, John, 195–196, 209, 210

isolation of the detective, 2, 5, 21, 37–38, 192, 194, 198, 206, 221–222, 226
It's a Wonderful Life (1946 film), 26–27, 30, 50, 122

knowledge, 3–4, 30, 97, 126, 169, 201, 216, 222

Le Carré, John, 105
Leopoldine Konstantin, 97, 112
Lissajous curves, 118–119
Los Angeles, 1, 3, 19, 23, 176; Los Angeles *noir*, 218

Mad Men (2007 television show), 83
Mainwaring, Daniel, *see* Homes, Geoffrey
Marlowe, Philip, 33, 205; in *The Long Goodbye*, 1–22 passim, 78, 191, 192, 194, 205, 229
mass culture, 31, 32–35, 66, 71, 215, 235n16
Mata Hari (1931 film), 113–114
memory, 219, 221–222; in *Out of the Past*, 58, 64, 74, 78; in *Notorious*, 82; in *Blade Runner*, 223–225; in *Blade Runner 2049*, 225–226, 228, 229
mimesis, 136, 152
Mitchum, Robert, 25, 30, 31–32, 38, 39, 43, 53, 57, 59, 71, 235n18
modernity, 78, 113, 130–131, 133, 149, 194, 219
morality: in *Out of the Past*, 46, 75, 78; of *femme fatale* characters and film noir, 62–63; in *Notorious*, 91, 115; in *Vertigo*, 143–144, 146, 150–151, 157, 166, 168–169; in *Chinatown*, 172, 174, 180; in *True Detective*, 215, 216, 217, 218;
in *Blade Runner*, 222, 225; in *Blade Runner 2049*, 226; of the detective, 229–231

Nicholson, Jack, 10, 172, 178, 180, 188, 201
Night Moves (1975 film), 12
North by Northwest (1949 film), 85, 97, 214; Clara Thornhill, 97
Notorious (1946 film), 6–7, 9, 11, 81–114 passim, 115, 132, 133, 137, 157, 165, 191, 201, 208, 229; Madame Sebastian, 97, 98, 102, 108
Novak, Kim, 142–143, 148, 157–158, 159–160, 163

obsession, 1, 3, 5, 10–11, 116, 218
Out of the Past (1947 film), 6, 8–9, 23–79 passim, 81, 89, 113, 116, 133, 145, 165, 201, 208, 229

patriotism, 87, 114
performativity: in *The Long Goodbye*, 12, 13, 14, 16, 19, 20; in *Out of the Past*, 43, 60, 63, 64, 71, 74, 76; in *Notorious*, 107, 113; in *Vertigo*, 128–129, 132, 139, 144, 146, 158, 168
point of view, communicated via camera: in *Out of the Past*, 43, 60, 61, 81–82; in *Notorious*, 82–84, 95; in *Vertigo*, 119–120, 123, 124, 126–129, 134–136, 137, 140, 141, 149, 151–153, 158–159, 164, 167; in *Chinatown*, 179, 181, 182–183, 194, 209
Polanski, Roman, 171, 178, 183, 184, 186, 194–195, 209, 211
postwar culture, United States, 30–31, 50

promotion of *The Long Goodbye*, 17
Psycho (1960 film), 85, 97, 103; Marion Crane, 85, 103; Norma Bates, 97, 103
psychology, 118–119

racial and cultural stereotyping, 180–181, 185
Rains, Claude, 95, 96, 102–103, 112
rebirth in *Notorious*, 88–89
reception: of *The Long Goodbye*, 17–18; of *Vertigo*, 164
recruitment, 40, 228; in *Notorious*, 85–86, 87
reluctance, 2, 5–6, 191, 215; in *Notorious*, 9; in *The Long Goodbye*, 12–13, 17, 19; in *Out of the Past*, 51; in *Vertigo*, 125, 128
repetition and mirroring, 128: in *Out of the Past*, 42, 44, 45, 50, 54, 67, 69, 72; in *Notorious*, 86, 95, 103, 110; in *Vertigo*, 118–119, 125, 127, 128, 136–137, 141, 142, 149, 150–151, 153, 158, 161, 162, 164; in *Chinatown*, 177, 179
Romantic movement, 149, 194
Rope (1948 film), 122

Scarlet Street (1945 film), 62–63
seeing, clarity of sight, 136–137, 214; in *Out of the Past*, 62, 72; in *Vertigo*, 115, 116, 120, 133, 149–150, 153, 166; in *Chinatown*, 181, 205, 221
signs and symbols, 11, 25, 34, 81, 116, 131–132, 215, 198–199, 207, 221, 229; in *Out of the Past*, 23–24, 25, 26, 27–28, 67; in *Notorious*, 91; in *Vertigo*, 117–118, 120, 121, 134, 147, 152–153, 166, 212; in *True Detective*, 213–215

social bonds, 214, 219
social class: influence on the detective figure, 129–131; in detective movies, 34–35; in *Out of the Past*, 27–28, 29–32, 50; in *Vertigo*, 157, 160–161, 163, 167, 172; in *Chinatown*, 174, 181, 189; class mobility, 32; meritocracy, 31, 35; cross-class relationships, 161, 181, 240n26
social power, 140, 163, 174, 192–193, 195, 201, 202, 209
soundtrack: in *The Long Goodbye*, 1, 19–20; in *Out of the Past*, 46, 72; in *Vertigo*, 116–117, 119, 128, 134–135, 162; in *Blade Runner*, 224; in *Blade Runner 2049*, 231
Spade, Sam, 33
spectacle, 2, 13, 19; in *Vertigo*, 212
spectatorship, 60; in *Notorious*, 91, 114; in *Vertigo*, 124–125, 128–129, 132, 133, 135, 137, 169; in *Chinatown*, 177, 181, 212
spycraft, 105
Stewart, James, 115, 120, 122, 126, 163–164, 166–167, 168

television medium, 215–216, 221
The Dead (Joyce short story), 231
The Great Gatsby (Fitzgerald novel), 142, 161, 165, 239n25
The Last Detail (1973 film), 188
The Long Goodbye (1973 film), 1–22 passim, 191, 192, 194, 205, 218, 224, 229
The Man of the Crowd (Poe short story), 130
The Singing Detective (1986 television show), 138–139
The Thin Red Line (1998 film), 81, 82

The Trial (Kafka novel), 226
theatricality in cinema, 233n3; in
  Out of the Past, 55–56, 58, 61;
  in *Notorious*, 91, 107; in *Vertigo*,
  129, 145–146, 152; in *North by
  Northwest*, 214
Three Faces East (1930 film), 113–114
Tourneur, Jacques, 24–25, 29, 37,
  56, 235n18
tracking, 9, 25, 131–132, 133,
  137–138, 139, 169, 198–199, 216,
  218, 229. *See also* detective work
transactional relationships: in *Out
  of the Past*, 28, 49–51, 56, 65; in
  Notorious, 91, 94, 99, 105, 109
transformation, detective's, from
  reluctance to commitment, 2–7,
  9–10, 25, 82, 191, 215; in *Out
  of the Past*, 40, 45–46; in *Vertigo*,
  128, 145; in *Chinatown*, 191, 205

True Detective (2014 television
  show), 10, 11, 213–222 passim,
  226

Valentine, Paul, 61
Vertigo (1959 film), 5, 6, 8–9, 11,
  62, 115–170 passim, 171–172,
  173, 187, 208, 210, 212, 218,
  225, 229, 233n3, 238n6, 238n11,
  239n17, 240n27
viewing choices, 52
violence: in detective movies, 34,
  208, in *The Long Goodbye*, 17, 20;
  in *Out of the Past*, 29, 31, 70; in
  Chinatown, 196, 200

wholeheartedness, 7–8, 25, 82; in
  The Long Goodbye, 11, 13, 17, 19.
  See also commitment
World War II, 27, 31

www.ingramcontent.com/pod-product-compliance
Lightning Source LLC
Chambersburg PA
CBHW030536230426
43665CB00010B/912